Life With The Boro
The Ayresome Years

First published in Great Britain in 2008 by Linthorpe Publishing, Multi Media Exchange,
72-80 Corporation Road, Middlesbrough TS1 2RF

ISBN 10 0-9553363-7-6

ISBN 13 978-0-9553363-7-9

Designed by Kallkwik, Middlesbrough

Cover design by Ross Marshall

Printed by Tien Wah Press, Singapore

Photographs courtesy of the Middlesbrough Evening Gazette
Ayresome Park gates at the Riverside photo by Sam Loughran

Proofreaders Alastair Brownlee, Gordon Cox, Andrew Haslam and Sam Loughran

Life With The Boro
The Ayresome Years

By Eric Paylor

DEDICATION

To all the doctors and nurses on Ward 32 at James Cook University Hospital whose enthusiasm and dedication is second to none.

Acknowledgements

I WILL always owe a major debt to the hundreds of employees at Middlesbrough Football Club over the years, players and officials alike, who made it possible for me to fulfil my duties in reporting the club's activities for the *Evening Gazette*.

I am fortunate to be able to regard many of them as close friends, all of us having come through the same experiences over the years.

I particularly want to thank Boro chairman Steve Gibson for his unstinting support and availability since our very first meeting and also chief executive Keith Lamb and his staff for their help in providing me with vital information overt many seasons.

The Boro managers I worked with throughout the history of this book, Willie Maddren, Bruce Rioch, Colin Todd, Lennie Lawrence and Bryan Robson, could hardly have been more helpful. Their willingness to be interviewed at all times of day and night made my job a lot easier.

Naturally nothing could have been achieved without the backing of the various editors and sports editors at the Middlesbrough *Evening Gazette*, who have supported me throughout the past 23 years and given me a free role to carry out the job as I saw fit. In recent years sports editors Allan Boughey and Philip Tallentire have been my strongest supporters.

I must also thank Gordon Cox for his much valued companionship and driving duties on our long trips all over the country spanning many years and also my fellow *Gazette* sports writers who have accompanied me.

I also have to give my thanks to my wife Brenda, who eventually decided that if you can't beat them then you must join them and became a loyal and regular Boro supporter herself.

Finally, I must thank Alastair Brownlee, Gordon Cox and everybody at Linthorpe Publishing for making this book possible.

ERIC PAYLOR

Contents

INTRODUCTION

BORO fans occasionally tell me that I am the luckiest guy in the world with the most romantic job possible. I have the enviable opportunity to travel throughout Britain and occasionally Europe watching the Boro, all for nothing. I understand their feelings. I never tire of going into work. I've not been attracted by the thoughts of taking any other job since accepting the role of chief sports writer with the Middlesbrough *Evening Gazette* in 1985.

However, while thoroughly enjoying every working day, I've never considered that reporting on the fortunes of the Boro was in any way romantic. In fact there have been many occasions when I have struggled to cope with the pressures.

I've been fortunate that the vast majority of the officials and players that I have dealt with over the years have been both good guys and very understanding people. It has made my job a lot easier. As a local football writer, you have to be everybody's best friend, even when you have just slagged off players in print for performing badly, or managers for having made tactical mistakes, and it helps if they like you.

So romantic, certainly not. Fulfilling and satisfying, definitely. Hard work and time consuming, you're not kidding.

When I took over the coverage of the Boro for the *Gazette* in the summer of 1985, I had no illusions about the potential problems I would be facing. I had worked closely with former *Gazette* Boro writers Cliff Mitchell and Paul Daniel over the years and knew what was involved. Reporting on the Boro was tough and demanding and as a result I initially envisaged being in the role for no more than six years. The fact that I am not too far away from reaching a quarter of a century as the *Gazette*'s Boro man is more remarkable to me than it will be to anybody else.

Naturally I've enjoyed some great times, but also struggled through some troughs. It can be difficult to maintain a smile on your face when the team is suffering from a losing run. But it's part of the job.

There is not much Boro-wise I haven't experienced, and as a result I have long considered writing a book about my time as the *Gazette*'s chief sports writer. However, it was not until I was struck down by a major illness early in 2008 that I finally began putting pen to paper, so to speak. In two months, while I was awaiting an operation at James Cook Hospital, I typed up more than 60,000 words.

It quickly became obvious that I could not contain the full story of my Boro reporting career in one book. So it made sense to split it into two volumes. There was a natural division. Boro started a new era when moving from Ayresome Park to the Riverside Stadium in 1995, although the change of grounds was not my reason for ending the first volume in this particular year.

I have experienced two distinct working eras as a football reporter, the first of which ended around 1995. In the first ten years or so, I had the freedom to walk anywhere in Ayresome Park at any time, including the treatment room, and also to ring players at any time of night or day. I was, in fact, made to feel almost part of the team.

But football changed dramatically in the mid 1990s, nowhere more so than at Middlesbrough. The Premier League became big business virtually overnight, and Boro had to change accordingly. The club altered from a small time football-based organisation into a huge business machine within a couple of years and, as a result, it was no longer possible to afford the local reporter the opportunity to please himself.

Officials who always stopped for a chat no longer had the time, while players who came from the same background as me were suddenly thrust up the social ladder as they signed lucrative new contracts which made them millionaires overnight.

The need for the club to adopt a new approach in every aspect of its business was exacerbated by the increasing media interest in the Boro and the Premier League in general. When I first started reporting on the fortunes of the Boro, myself and erstwhile *The Northern Echo* reporter Ray Robertson were the only media people who visited Ayresome Park on a daily basis. We virtually had the field to ourselves, so picking up regular exclusives was a doddle.

After the mid 1990s, reporting the club's fortunes became more difficult and I had to change accordingly to match the new trends. I became increasingly more distant from certain people at the club, including most of the players, but maybe I developed into a better journalist as a result.

There have been many occasions when I have been accused of being in the club's pocket. I can certainly think of times when I have been given a good story off the record, which I have not been allowed to print. But off the record stories from the various managers were usually accompanied by one or two good tales which were very much on the record, and this ensured the back pages of the *Evening Gazette* were always filled with news. It was the way we worked, together, in the early days.

I believe that football is considerably worse off for the breakdown in personal relationships between club employees and media people, but that is something the game has created for itself.

Not that I have lost the trust and support which has been built up over the years. I like to think that, in the modern era, I maintain a working relationship with Boro manager Gareth Southgate and communications manager Dave Allan for example, and I still receive my fair share of tip-offs. Virtually every story which emerges from the club nowadays appears in the *Gazette*. Maybe the readers and the newspaper have benefited from this change of direction.

However, if there was any romance, maybe I took it from the Ayresome Park era of reporting the Boro. This book tries to tell the story of what it was like to be a football reporter in those days, before the game became really big business, and also highlights the many personalities and characters within the club. There are no untold exclusives, apart from the off the record information which I have long forgotten, the big stories were printed in the *Gazette* at the time of their breaking. I still think there's a tale to tell, and with luck the reader will get a surprising insight into the world of local newspaper football reporting. I hope fans will enjoy reading the book as much as I have enjoyed writing it. Here's to volume two.

ERIC PAYLOR,
Middlesbrough Evening Gazette
October 2008

Foreword

It is a privilege and a pleasure to be given the opportunity to write this Foreward for Eric.

Our paths first crossed towards the end of 1985 and the beginning '86 which was a very, very special time as it was the time Middlesbrough Football Club was going into provisional liquidation.

Eric was chief sports writer of the local paper, the Evening Gazette, and I became manager of the Boro.

Events through that period were very special for Eric and I.

The football club has a big part to play in the local community and Eric was so good, so kind and honest in his support for me and the staff. His loyalty and integrity were beyond reproach. It would be fitting to say we could give Eric some information and we knew it would be kept by him until the time was right to use it.

Eric Paylor is a fine, fantastic person, a really good friend and a very fine journalist who can be trusted explicitly in every way. It was wonderful to be able to work with such a fantastic human being.

I'm sure this book will reflect and remember some great memories.

Bruce Rioch, manager of Middlesbrough Football Club
February 1986 to March 1990

CHAPTER 1

MY Boro football reporting career got off to a very ignominious beginning. Boro banned me from the club before I had seen them even kick a ball.

I was not a happy bunny. I had been so excited to have been awarded the job as the *Evening Gazette*'s new 'Boro Man' in the summer of 1985. I was following in the footsteps of several top writers, including the legendary Cliff Mitchell, in bringing all the latest Boro news and gossip to the *Gazette* readers. It was a tremendous responsibility and one I could not wait to sink my teeth into but the club shunned me before I had the opportunity even to introduce myself. I could not talk to manager Willie Maddren and was refused access to the players.

To make matters worse, the ban was imposed as a result of something which was completely beyond my control. Personally, I hadn't done anything wrong. I couldn't have done. I hadn't yet written a single word about the club.

I returned sun-tanned from my annual fortnight's holiday and walked back into the *Gazette* office on a Tuesday morning just in time to hear our editor, David James, having the mother of all arguments over the phone. I quickly realised that the person on the other end of the line was somebody from the Boro. It transpired that it was chairman Alf Duffield. The editor was very angry, and was virtually shouting down the phone. I suspected that Duffield was doing exactly the same.

After the editor had finished making his point, the phone was slammed down and I was called into the editor's office.

"The club have banned us," he told me.

David then filled me in on all the details. Boro had played a friendly match at non-league Scarborough on the Saturday of the previous weekend. The *Gazette* had reported on the Monday that Boro fans had rioted during the interval and refused to leave the pitch when the players returned from the dressing rooms for the second half.

The *Gazette* had carried the story on its front page. When Duffield read it, he had taken exception to the tone of the report. He rang David on the Tuesday morning, claiming that the facts were wrong. The editor disagreed; hence the war of words.

Whatever the facts of the matter, it wasn't good news for me. The upshot was that Duffield told the editor that *Gazette* reporters were forthwith to be banned from talking to anybody at the club, or travelling to away games on the team coach. It meant, effectively, that I was denied access to all my potential contacts before I had written a word.

To say that it came as a body blow was an understatement. I had been thinking about almost nothing but my new job while I was away on holiday. I had big plans and ideas. I could hardly wait to get my teeth into the task of writing daily Boro news stories and match reports. I wanted to stamp my personality on the job and hopefully maintain a great tradition at the *Evening Gazette*.

Now I had my hands tied firmly behind my back. In fact I was in a virtual strait-jacket. I don't know the rights and wrongs of the *Gazette*'s front page story because I wasn't at Scarborough to witness the events for myself. Later, some Boro fans who were at Scarborough that day told me there was no riot from their point of view. They claimed that the incident was just a collection of boisterous lads carrying on, on the pitch, with a ball.

The *Gazette* had different information and I couldn't argue with that, but it did me no favours. I found myself beginning an important new job without the opportunity to build any contacts.

In addition, the loss of the privilege of travelling to away games with the team was a major setback. The *Gazette*'s previous Boro writers, Cliff and Paul Daniel, had always travelled on the official club coach. There was no other accepted method of transport to away games. Naturally, travelling with the first-team squad would have provided me with the opportunity to get close to Willie Maddren and his players pretty quickly, and now it was denied.

To make matters worse, coming just a few days before the start of the new season, the ban left me wondering how on earth I was to get to Boro's away games. I'd had no opportunity to check out train or bus timetables, while I didn't know how to get to the stadia and how much travelling time would be needed.

The *Gazette* sports desk did not even have its own car at that time, while the company would never have sanctioned me using my own car because my mileage expenses would have been astronomical, we didn't even have a budget for train tavel.

So it was a dilemma, especially as the Division Two campaign contained two early trips to South London to tackle Wimbledon and Charlton.

Gazette sports editor Alan Berry suggested I contacted Middlesbrough Supporters' Club, which organised transport to every Boro away game. The supporters club, which at the time was run separately from the football club, consisted of a small but passionate band of fans who did whatever they could to raise funds for the club. In addition they carried out vital part-time jobs at Ayresome Park such as repainting the stands in the summer.

The chairman of Middlesbrough supporters' club was Fred Appleton, a regular and popular figure around the club, who never missed a game. I gave him a bell.

"Of course we'll give you a lift to the game," Fred said. "You can come with us whenever you want, free of charge."

The *Gazette* could have afforded to pay for my trip, but Fred's excellent gesture was accepted. So, weighed down with sandwiches, flask, notebook and pens, I joined the supporters' coach outside Ayresome Park at 7.30am on the morning of Saturday August 17 1985 for Boro's first game of the season at Wimbledon.

We set off on a Cleveland Transit coach, which was more or less full, as might be expected for the first game of the new campaign. I found a seat in the middle of the bus, having been welcomed aboard by Fred occupying his regular seat at the front.

Most of the travelling Boro fans were young, being mainly teenagers. They were friendly and inquisitive, but I couldn't answer their questions when they asked me what Willie Maddren or Tony McAndrew or David Currie was like.

The long journey south started off well, but soon turned into a nightmare. Ten miles north of Trowell Services on the M1, the coach spluttered and eventually broke down. The driver pulled over on to the hard shoulder.

He turned to face the sea of worried faces on the bus and said: "It's knackered. You'll all have to get off. You can't stay on the bus while it's on the hard shoulder."

So we all piled on to the grass embankment and stood there bemused, in a large group, while the passengers in the southbound traffic waved and grinned at us sadistically as they whizzed past.

Negative thoughts were flooding through my head. This was a situation from hell. I was banned and now in grave danger of failing to get to my very first Boro match. In the days before mobile phones, I could not even contact the office to let them know what was happening. So I stood there contemplating my navel and inhaling exhaust fumes.

Eventually, after three quarters of an hour or so of combined stress and boredom, a local coach from the Nottinghamshire area arrived to take us away from the hard shoulder and on to Trowell Services. Once there, we were informed that we had to wait for a replacement Cleveland Transit coach to arrive from Middlesbrough to take us on the remainder of the journey to Wimbledon. Wonderful! It was not what I wanted to hear. If the local coach had been able to take us all the way to London then everything would have been ok, but that was too simple.

I rang Alan Berry from a public phone at Trowell to tell him what was going on. "We could be here for hours," I told him. "I don't think I'm going to get to the game in time."

Alan said: "You have to carry on. You've no choice. You might still get there in time."

However it was after one o'clock when the new Cleveland Transit coach arrived. They were not my favourite people at that moment in time. I felt like kicking the coach. I knew that I had absolutely no chance of reaching Plough Lane in time for the kick-off. So the final 100 miles or so of the journey to London was full of sheer frustration. The fans felt the same way. The coach was deathly quiet.

When we arrived in London we hit horrendous queues of traffic, as might be expected at that time of year. I don't know whether the driver took a back street route to Wimbledon or a busy one but we seemed to be gazing out at London's blank-faced inhabitants for ages.

When I finally alighted from the steps of the replacement coach at Plough Lane, I heard the shrill sound of the half-time whistle. My first match was half over and I still hadn't seen Boro kick a ball.

There was no *Sports Gazette* at the time. The weekly publication was put on the back burner temporarily because Boro's results had been so poor that 'Pink' sales had been dipping dramatically. The *Gazette* could not justify the printing and distribution costs at that time because the 'Pink' was losing money.

However, while I had not needed to submit a running match report for the *Gazette* during the first half of Boro's opening game, I was supposed to send a report to our sister paper, the *Newcastle Chronicle*, for inclusion in their 'Pink'. So I was grateful that Ray Robertson, *The Northern Echo*'s 'Boro Man' of many years standing, had noted my non-arrival and kindly sent a first-half report to the Chronicle in my absence.

It was a typical hot summer's day and I was sweating profusely as I tried to battle my way to my seat in the Plough Lane press box. This particular press box was health and safety free. It was long and thin, running on both sides of a central entrance, and you had to climb over your fellow reporters because there was no room to get past, either in front or behind them. I lost count of the number of times I had to say 'sorry', as notebooks received Dr Marten imprints and pens and pencils were scattered around.

"Where've you been?" asked Ray.

"It's a long story", I said, as the players ran out for the second half.

My day had been bad enough but the match had not been going well either. Boro were already trailing by two goals when I arrived. Ray filled me in with the details of the goals and the other major incidents and it appeared that Boro had made very little impression.

When the second half started, my first Boro experience was seeing young left-back Stephen Corden break his leg on his debut when making a tackle within three minutes of the restart. It was not a pleasant moment to witness, especially as Stephen never played for the first team again. Lawrie Sanchez scored the third goal for the Dons in the 64th minute and my first impression was that Boro looked a pretty poor side which wasn't good considering it was the very first match of the season. I didn't have anything to compare the performance with because I hadn't seen too much of the Boro in the preceding years, other than the odd night match. A lot of the players, such as Steve Pears, Gary Pallister and Don O'Riordan, were completely new to me. Others like Brian Laws and Archie Stephens I'd hardly seen.

In fact, having spent the previous four years reporting rugby union on Saturday afternoons, I knew very little about most of the Boro players. There was no opportunity to get quotes after the final whistle because I had to be back on the coach at 5pm for the return journey to Teesside. As nobody from the Boro was allowed to speak to me, as ordered by Alf Duffield, it hardly mattered.

So my initial match report in the *Evening Gazette* was based on 45 minutes of football, and pretty dismal stuff at that. I wrote up my reports on the Monday as if I had been there from the start and, as there were no complaints from readers, I think I got away with it.

My second trip to London ten days later was no more enjoyable. Boro were playing a night match against Charlton Athletic at The Valley. Once again the Supporters' Club kindly helped me out but there was no full-sized coach leaving Ayresome Park at midday. There was little demand from the fans for such a gruelling trip. This time we had a small collection of a press man and supporters in a mini-bus. It was a 19-seater and there were 12 hardy souls on board including myself and Fred. This time the Cleveland Transit mechanics had done their job and we had an incident-free trip to London and arrived at The Valley in good time for the kick-off.

My main memory of the game was in gazing across the pitch at the highest terracing in Britain as it climbed endlessly into the sky. Unless I crouched in the main stand I could not even see the top of the terracing. Most of the stand was roped off to supporters because it was considered unsafe but I was pleased to see it for myself before it was later demolished. I could hardly start to imagine what it must have been like for visiting teams at The Valley years earlier to play in front of such a massive, foreboding wall of Charlton fans.

Unfortunately Boro were no better at Charlton than they had been at Wimbledon. This time they lost 2-0. As a result there was not much to talk about as we dozen frustrated souls trudged back on to the mini-bus ready for the ponderous journey home.

It was almost impossible to sleep on the way back, propped up against the seats of the coach. Whenever I did nod off I was awoken by a thud as my head fell against the glass window.

The only positive moment in the journey came when we stopped off at a motorway service station in the early hours and I was introduced to a man who was to become an integral part of my football life. He was Gordon Cox, himself a relative newcomer on the Boro press scene who had been to Charlton to report on the game for BBC Radio Cleveland.

It was a chance meeting but an important one. Gordon went on to give me a lift to hundreds of away games over the next few years and we developed an enduring and close friendship.

Once back on the mini-bus, I dozed on and off throughout the remainder of the journey home as the bumps on my forehead grew increasingly larger. We finally arrived back at Ayresome Park at 3.45am and I had to drive home to enjoy a couple of hours of regular sleep in my welcome bed. I was back at the *Gazette* office at 8am to start writing up the reports.

Those early weeks were difficult times as I tried my best to circumvent the ban. I got through that period by living on my wits and drawing on my 15 years of vital experience as a reporter working in both Hartlepool and Middlesbrough.

Despite their apparent ambivalent attitude towards me, Boro were a homely club in those days. There were many fans who had close relationships with players and club employees and as a result there was always somebody who knew a juicy tale or two. In any case, a Boro player's groin strain would make a back page lead in the *Gazette* in 1985. That kind of news makes the last paragraph nowadays. However, I gradually became comfortable in dealing with the ban, despite nobody from the club officially helping me at all. Fortunately, the *Gazette* was rarely short of good stories.

The best story I picked up during the ban was a tasty exclusive. It concerned the signing of Bernie Slaven. I was working in the *Gazette* office one day when I received a phone call from a freelance journalist in Scotland. He told me that Bernie, who was the top goal scorer in the whole of Scotland 1984-85 having scored more than 30 goals for Albion Rovers, was coming to Teesside to sign for the Boro.

The journalist even told me the time of the train on which Bernie would be arriving at Middlesbrough railway station. As Bernie was not actually on the Boro payroll at that time, I could see no reason why I should not turn up to try to interview him.

I walked along Albert Road to the station and decided to go under the underpass to the southbound platform in order to try to get a quick word with Bernie as he stepped off the train before anybody from the Boro could whisk him away.

When I reached the stone steps leading down from the southbound platform, there was a guy wearing a suit leaning against the underpass wall reading a newspaper.

I'd never seen a photo of Bernie, nor did I have a description, so I had no idea what he looked like. But this guy looked the part even if his presence suggested he must have arrived on an earlier train than the one I had anticipated.

"Excuse me, are you Bernie Slaven?" I asked. "I am," he said, in a familiar Glaswegian brogue, putting his paper in his pocket ready to be taken to Ayresome Park.

"No, I'm not from the club, I'm from the local paper," I explained.

Bernie was simply pleased to hear a friendly voice, and certainly had no objections to giving me an informative interview. I was given full details of his career so far, and his hopes and aspirations.

It was a good interview and must have lasted 15 or 20 minutes. When we finished, we shook hands, but there was still no sign of anybody from the Boro arriving to collect him.

I needed to get back to the *Gazette* to write up the story but I didn't want to see Bernie left marooned. "I'll have a walk up top and see if I recognise anybody from the club, so they can come and get you," I said.

"Righto," said Bernie." If not, I'll just catch the next train back to Glasgow."

I didn't want that to happen. I told him not to move an inch and I would sort it out for him, even if I needed to ring the club for the first time.

I walked back through the underpass and up the stone steps into the main area of the station. There was a guy standing alone, looking rather impatient and with nothing to suggest that he came from the club but he was the only possibility.

"Are you from the football club?" I asked him. He was. "And are you looking for Bernie Slaven?" He was. "Well he's leaning on the wall in the underpass."

The relieved guy, who I later discovered was Boro chief scout Barry Geldart, went to collect Bernie and the rest is history. I later got to know Barry very well and maintained contact with him when he moved on to Blackburn Rovers as their chief scout. He knew the game inside out and I always felt he was a good judge of a player. When he eventually went part-time later in his scouting career, Barry was a regular visitor to Boro reserve matches so I was able to stay in touch.

However, I got to know Bernie even better. The Glaswegian needed a few months to get used to the higher standard of football in England and the training that was involved at professional level but it was obvious from day one that he knew how to put the ball in the net.

It was under Bruce Rioch's reign after liquidation that Bernie really blossomed. He was a confident player but he also responded to occasional kicks up the backside from Rioch. I've heard the theory expressed on many occasions that Bernie was only a six-yard box player but I can recall him scoring several spectacular goals from outside the area. In any case, being a six-yard box man is not a bad thing - in fact it can be the most difficult part of a striker's job. I've seen lots of strikers who don't know how to get into the right positions to score goals from close range. It seems so basic yet it's an uncanny talent and Bernie had it.

However, it wasn't the easiest of times for a new player to settle in. Boro were on a run of league games without a win. There were not enough committed players in the side and the promising batch of youngsters who were being nurtured by Willie Maddren and his assistant David Mills were not quite ready to push through.

Boro went to Hull City for a Full Members Cup tie on November 5 and Maddren took the opportunity to blood teenager Colin Cooper as a second-half substitute. We weren't to know it then but Coops would become something of a club legend in the modern era although his debut at Boothferry Park might not have happened but for other events.

Tony McAndrew was one of the few Boro players on whom you could put your shirt at that time. He was a strong and committed defender who knew only one way to play and that was wearing his heart on his sleeve.

Tony was battling his way through the game at Hull as usual when he suffered concussion following a clash of heads. A stretcher was called for and a combination of St John Ambulance men and home officials waddled on to the pitch and lifted him on to the stretcher before carrying it away.

The press box at Boothferry Park was situated just above the tunnel at the time and there was a loud thud shortly after the stretcher had disappeared from view.

I didn't think too much of it until after the game when one of the St John Ambulance guys said to me: "Is that lad of yours ok?"

"What do you mean?" I asked.

"The one who came off the stretcher. They dropped him in the tunnel and he landed on his head."

It transpired that the bearers had dropped McAndrew from the stretcher as they tried to manoeuvre him into the dressing room and he ended up with a double dose of concussion.

At that time I was getting to know the players as footballers. I still wasn't allowed to talk to them and I believed them to be a bit of a motley crew with differing levels of both ability and commitment.

You need eleven focused individuals to make a team and it did not take me long to realise that manager Willie Maddren did not have that luxury. The team was carrying too many passengers.

Things were going badly for the team even when Boro played to their maximum. They played reasonably well on Bernie Slaven's debut at Leeds United but still went down 1-0. Then they went to Roker Park for a midweek game and were quite clearly the better side but missed chances cost them dear and Boro went down 1-0 again.

I was not too critical of the team in the *Gazette* following the Sunderland defeat because Boro had shown plenty of commitment. A few days later I went to a fans' forum hosted by Alf Duffield and sat discreetly at the back while the chairman tried to adresss the fans' concerns. Alf said, during the course of the evening, that he thought my match report from the Sunderland game was one of the best he had ever read. I was chuffed, though there was still no sign of the ban being lifted.

With Boro struggling for results I began to feel increasingly sorry for Maddren. I could see that his heart and soul was in the club. Boro were his hometown team, the only club he had played for and bringing the good old days back to Ayresome Park meant so much to him. While Willie desperately wanted to turn things around, he was working on a shoestring and there was no cash available to improve the team. In addition I did not think that every player in the dressing room was giving him 100 per cent effort.

Boro were losing cash hand over fist and with attendances at Ayresome Park regularly dipping under 5,000, I couldn't sense any positive vibes on the terraces either.

Things were so bad financially that Boro director Dick Corden had volunteered to pay the wages of young defender Gary Pallister out of his own pocket. If not for Corden's financial contribution, Boro would have had to release Pallister on a free contract. Just think what the consequences would have been for the club in later years.

Pallister took some time to establish himself in the side that season and endured his difficult moments but Maddren always believed in him and it was Willie who paired Pally with Tony Mowbray. Players need time to develop successful partnerships, even good players, and with Boro struggling to control many of their games in midfield the young defenders regularly found themselves under pressure in a side which lacked confidence.

Maddren had done well to pick up experienced players such as Brian Laws and Archie Stephens for a song while Irving Nattrass, Don O'Riordan, Tony McAndrew, Gary Rowell, Pat Heard and Paul Ward were among the other senior players in the dressing room.

I thought there was a lack of pace in the side, except for the tricky home grown left winger Peter Beagrie, who rarely came up against a right-back he couldn't go past. But Peter was still learning the game, and this wasn't the best of sides in which a young player could make a big impact.

Maddren stuck with Beagrie, however, because he could see the winger's terrific potential and again proved that his judgement was spot on when giving Slaven his chance in England – and at a cut-price fee of only £25,000. But, Slaven was far from the finished product when he first signed a contract at Ayresome. It was the following season when he really blossomed into a striker who was a genuine threat in front of goal.

Overall the team had a lack of spark in 1985 which was reflected in results. When Slaven arrived on Teesside, Boro had scored only four goals in their first ten Division Two games. Three of those came from the boot of Gary Rowell, including a penalty.

Slaven scored for Boro in his second game, a 1-1 home draw against Bradford City but it was almost Christmas by the time he found the net. Slaven's goal opportunities were limited anyway because the team didn't create too many chances while defending badly too.

Going into the New Year, even on the back of three wins in four games in December, Boro had potential relegation fodder written all over them.

CHAPTER 2

BY the time 1986 dawned, I had come to know Willie Maddren quite well. In public he always declared that he was supportive of Alf Duffield's ongoing ban of the *Evening Gazette* but in private he had been feeding me useful stories for some time.

Maddren was everything that I had been led to believe he would be. Honest as the day, brimful of integrity, as nice a guy as you could ever wish to meet and above all possessing an over-riding passionate love for the club. Willie would have crawled over broken glass to bring success to the Boro.

Having watched him at work and had several ban-busting chats with him, I believed that Maddren was potentially a better manager than results indicated. He was a superb judge of a footballer. He had brought players of the calibre of Steve Pears, Brian Laws, Gary Pallister, Archie Stephens and Bernie Slaven to the Boro, all of who were to play a major role in the club's dramatic rebirth and resurgence after liquidation. There was deadwood in the team, however, and because of a lack of available funding, Willie still had his hands tied behind his back. This restricted his attempts to take the club forward because he was unable to overhaul the squad. At times he must have felt he was treading water – especially when attending board meetings and being informed that the club's finances were ever deteriorating.

Willie knew full well that he had a large clutch of talented kids coming through. He enthused about them on several occasions but stressed he did not think they were quite ready to be thrown into the fiery cauldron of second division football. Willie believed he just needed that extra bit of time before he could nurture the kids through the ranks and freshen up the side at the same time. Unfortunately Boro were struggling near the foot of Division Two with a pressing need for immediate results. Time was something which was not on Willie's side.

I was not privy to what had gone on at the Boro in recent seasons or why the club were apparently in such a huge mess financially. The much criticised sports hall seemed to bear the brunt of he blame for most of the finger pointers. I was already aware that the sports hall was under-used and not bringing in much in the way of income. However, as Boro did not appear to be spending any more on the sports hall then surely, I thought, it could no longer be regarded as the reason for Boro losing money hand over fist every week.

When I asked what the club might do to halt the weekly loss of valuable funds, I was told that the only hope was for Boro to start winning on a regular basis again and bring the fans back through the turnstiles. However, without a significant cash investment, hopes of this particular team winning on a regular basis were a pipe dream. It was a Catch 22 situation and I quickly began to appreciate why the team was struggling and in grave danger of ending up in the third division.

Maddren had some fine men around him but maybe lacked an experienced coach who might have come in from outside and made an impact on the squad. Willie was already an inspiration to the kids who were pushing through but I did not believe that all the senior pros were running themselves into the ground for him.

The view that a new coach could make a difference was shared by Alf Duffield. The chairman liked to be hands on at the Boro and was not slow to voice his opinions. I felt Alf did not always say the right things in public, even though his quotes made for good copy in the *Evening Gazette*. He was outspoken and this, at times, put extra pressure on the manager. But then Alf had a right to look for improvement in the team because he had put his money on the table to keep the club afloat. Alf was certainly not involved with the Boro to make money but success on the field was as important to Alf Duffield as it was to anybody else at Ayresome Park.

So it was Duffield who gambled on yet another expense for the club by encouraging Maddren to bring in another brain into the coaching team. This led to the arrival of Bruce Rioch.

Rioch, captain of Scotland during his illustrious playing days, had previously been manager of Torquay United but had left Plainmoor under a cloud following an unsavoury training ground incident. He worked with FC Seattle in the States for a while, but had been out of the English game for two years before he got the coaching job at Boro.

Rioch had a terrific background in football and despite being away from the game for what might have been regarded by some as a worryingly long period, he had the necessary experience which Boro needed in the backroom team – Alf certainly thought so. I was absolutely positive from the start that Rioch was Duffield's appointment, not Maddren's.

Once I got to know Rioch well, I could appreciate why he would have impressed Duffield at his interview. Bruce, too, loved the game with a passion and was an eloquent speaker. He would have spoken very well at his interview while his forthright style was to later play a key role in his dressing room team talks.

I don't know how many applicants were interviewed for the job of First Team coach but I can't imagine that any of the other candidates would have held a candle to Rioch. He would have impressed Duffield and any other chairman for that matter. Yet I'm utterly convinced Maddren would certainly not have appointed Rioch, given a free hand in the matter. As a manager you have to have your own men around you and I never felt that Willie and Bruce had much in common.

They had been opponents on many occasions as players and had come through similar football experiences together but they were personalities away from the pitch and this was not a marriage made in heaven.

Again, Rioch's appointment did mean that Duffield had brought in a man who was potentially a top-class coach. I was unsure about Rioch when I first met him because I wondered why he wanted to come to a struggling club like Boro but Bruce needed to have a job and a foothold back in the game. In any case there was no doubting Rioch's football knowledge and we were soon to discover that his ability to deal with players and his commitment to the job were top drawer.

As a player, Rioch was a strong-tackling, ball-playing midfielder who had a distinct physical edge to his play. He played in a period where players had to look after themselves because they did not get much protection from referees. Rioch's occasional rushes of blood on the pitch not only got him into trouble, but made opponents wary of him. It was this edge that I felt helped him to kick-start Boro after liquidation because the young players in the squad were never too keen to enter into an argument with him.

Rioch travelled to Teesside in the December and Maddren allowed me to circumvent the *Evening Gazette* ban and interview him on his arrival. As I have said, I thought a club like Boro was an unusual choice for any top coach wanting to make an impact in the game, but I could not help to be impressed by Rioch's passion. I could see he was excited by the prospect of getting to work on the training pitch again with a squad of players.

Within a few weeks of Rioch's arrival, the *Gazette* ban was finally lifted by Duffield. He told me that it had gone on for long enough but stressed that the club had been right to make its point in this manner.

I was welcomed fully into the fold by Willie Maddren with whom I had slowly been developing a strong bond and finally was offered a place on the team coach for Boro's long trip to Brighton on January 18.

By that time I had cemented my friendship with BBC Radio Cleveland reporter Gordon Cox who had offered me a regular place in his car for Boro away trips. He had taken me on long trips to Millwall, Fulham and Norwich, in addition to several games in the north and we were getting on like a house on fire. I even offered him a cup of coffee from my flask on occasions. However, I'm sure that Coxy appreciated why our blossoming friendship was temporarily put on hold while I took advantage of the privilege of travelling on the Boro team coach and getting close to the players for the first time.

Despite my doubts over the collective ability of the squad, I immediately found them to be a fine upstanding set of lads. They welcomed me into their midst with open arms. I was pleased to see that there was plenty of good-humoured banter within the squad, despite the lack of results.

I can recall Don O'Riordan offering me a cup of tea on the trip back from Brighton. What a pleasant gesture, I thought, as he hardly knows me. I gratefully accepted Don's offer but once passed the plastic cup of tea I realised that it was rather weightless in my hands. It turned out that Don had inverted a plastic lid upside down inside the top of the cup and it contained only half an inch of tea. How we laughed! Humour is crucial within any squad of players and I regarded that little jape as my immediate acceptance into the inner sanctum. Within a couple of weeks I began to feel more like one of the lads as opposed to a reporter from outside.

Boro always travelled to away games by coach on the Friday and stayed in a hotel overnight. It was a wonderful experience for a rookie reporter like me, enjoying a slap-up evening meal and then sitting down with a pint of Guinness with Maddren and his coaches to listen to football stories into the early hours.

When Rioch became caretaker manager I found myself staying up often until three o'clock in the morning, still drinking Guinness and being completely enthralled by his tales. Often there was just Rioch and I sitting in the bar after everybody else had gone to bed but I couldn't drag myself away until Bruce was ready to hit the sack. What a pity this experience lasted no longer than the end of that season.

Maddren's reign didn't last much longer than the Brighton game. Boro played well at the Goldstone Ground and drew 3-3 with Gary Rowell scoring twice and Bernie Slaven netting the other. On the way back, everybody was buoyant on the coach and there was a belief that better times lay ahead.

However, it was not to be. Boro played reasonably well at Portsmouth seven days later but went down 1-0. The crunch came on February 1, when Boro were beaten 3-1 at home by Charlton Athletic in front of less than 4,500 fans.

They were absolutely dismal on the day and were completely outplayed.

It seemed inevitable that Willie would be on his way after this abject performance. Journalists get an instinct for these things. Ray Robertson from *The Northern Echo* and I hung around in the tunnel after the game, anticipating the worst for Willie, and eventually Alf Duffield emerged to talk to us.

The chairman revealed immediately that Maddren had been dismissed. saying: "I thought that performance was one of the worst I have ever seen by a Middlesbrough side. It was totally unacceptable. I couldn't allow things to go on like this any longer."

Alf added that a new man was already temporarily in place at the helm. Bruce was caretaker manager.

While I was not shocked by the news, I felt bitterly sorry for Willie because I knew in different circumstances he had the qualities to make a good manager. The players had let him down very badly in that last match against Charlton, just as they had on several previous occasions. There were a lot of honest players in the team but when one or two were not doing it, it became impossible for the remainder.

In any case, this was a sacking waiting to happen. Willie had been working with very little cash at his disposal throughout his time in the hot seat and found it virtually impossible to take the club forward. He had worked diligently to bring in some bargain basement signings and had a handful of kids pushing through who would eventually make all the difference to the side. But, as I have said, time was something Willie didn't have and with the club's financial situation becoming increasingly grave, he was always treading water in his final season. He deserved better but good guys don't always get what they deserve.

I'd criticised the team's performances in the *Gazette*, but I don't believe I ever put the knife into Willie. I liked him a lot. In any case I was still a bit green behind the ears in dealing with football people who had been superstars in their own time. It would not have been easy for me to have publicly criticised Willie and then faced him in his office the following day. In any case Willie had been very good and given me plenty of exclusives which meant that I was providing the Boro news service which the *Gazette* readers were looking for.

While I was sorry to see Willie go, I was pretty confident that I would easily build up a working relationship with Bruce. It was handy that I had already come to know him reasonably well over the last couple of weeks. I did not have to start building a relationship from scratch, as I would have done if Duffield had brought in somebody from outside.

It was clear from day one that Bruce also realised the value of being pally with the local reporter. He took me under his wing immediately and began to feed me lots of tasty stories.

The bonus was that Bruce told me absolutely everything that went on at the club. For example, if two players had been fighting on the training ground, he would give me all the details even though I had known nothing about the fight in the first place. I would get the names of the players, who threw the best punches and even who pulled them apart. Then Bruce would add with a twinkle in his eye: "Of course that's all off the record."

As a sop, Bruce would then give me a half-decent exclusive on the record about another subject. In this way he kept the dodgy stories out of the *Gazette* while at the same time ensuring that the positive ones went into print. Bruce knew he could trust me implicitly to keep my mouth shut about the off the record negative stuff. It was very clever but I was the last one to argue because Bruce ensured that I was never short of a story.

Boro were a club which tended to attract negative stories by its very nature but Bruce was determined to put a positive slant on everything. It summed up his approach to the game in general.

Within 48 hours of his appointment, Rioch had put a notice on the wall of the home dressing room. It read: "The biggest crime in football is giving the ball away to the opposition."

The sign on the wall was a clear indication to the players that they were expected to pass the ball and keep possession accordingly. It was Rioch's personal ethic for the way the beautiful game should be played. Even though he probably knew he did not have the greatest band of footballers in the world at his disposal, Bruce was still determined that they would go out to play the game in the right manner.

Amazingly Rioch had more than a month on his hands before he was able to take charge of the team for the first time in a competitive match. The second division grounds were frozen solid throughout the February of 1986. As a result Boro did not play another match for several weeks following their defeat to Charlton.

I went to see Rioch every day during the freeze-out and he always had a story for me. There were no doubts that he was revelling in the role as caretaker boss. After two years out of the hot seat in the English game he was burning with ideas and plans for the future.

In many respects Rioch probably appreciated the month's break more than most, because it offered him the opportunity to try to stamp some of his character into the side. As the month unfolded, Rioch told me that he was planning to rejuvenate Maddren's side from within.

When Boro finally took to the field again for a home game against Grimsby Town on March 4, players who had not played for the team for some time like Gary Gill, Peter Beagrie, David Currie and Irving Nattrass, were back in the starting line-up. Within a few weeks Rioch had added the youthful zest of teenagers Colin Cooper and Stuart Ripley as regulars in his first choice line-up. Boro's immediate response to a month of Rioch's coaching was a convincing 3-1 victory against Grimsby, which was the team's first win of the year. Bernie Slaven, wearing the No.7 shirt for the first time instead of No.9, scored twice.

Unfortunately, even with the changes and bubbling adrenaline, Rioch wasn't able to make a silk purse out of a sow's ear. His young players were very inexperienced, which placed more responsibility on the older ones, and the new-look side struggled for consistency. However, Boro thrilled a Tuesday night crowd in mid March by leading Sheffield United a merry dance at Ayresome Park. Amazingly, despite almost completely dominating the match, Boro lost 2-1. They had plenty of chances but couldn't put the ball in the net, save for one goal from Don O'Riordan.

Chairman Alf clearly enjoyed the performance against the Blades as much as the fans had done. Rioch was made full-time manager of the club immediately following the final whistle.

The new boss was left with just ten games to try to save Boro from relegation. His team went on to win four of those games but blew hot and cold. Rioch remained positive throughout and talked a good talk both on and off the training ground. I was becoming hooked on his committed approach to everything he did. He would not entertain negative thoughts from me, never mind his players.

Rioch was clearly working his socks off to try to bring the best out of the players in his mixed side. But the consistency which the team desperately needed evaded them. Boro lacked mental strength under pressure and home defeats by Hull City and Carlisle United proved to be killers.

At the same time they were always in with a chance right until the end of the season and a goalless draw at Barnsley in late March kept the pot boiling. On the journey away from Oakwell we were looking for a fish and chip shop on the journey away from Oakwell when the coach was attacked by yobs. It happened so quickly. Stones thrown from a bridge shattered three or four windows of the coach simultaneously.

Half of a red brick ended up on my lap. At first I did not know what had happened before realising that my hands were covered in blood. They had been cut by tiny pieces of glass.

Boro physio Steve Smelt was quickly off the mark. "You all right?" he asked me. I didn't answer at first. I was still in a state of shock.

Steve began checking my hands, my face and my neck. The cuts were all on my hands, and he tended them, while helping the three or four players who were also bleeding.

Fortunately nobody was seriously hurt. In my case, the cuts on my hands were only superficial. Steve applied the same little strips to my hands that shavers attach to their face to stop cuts from bleeding.

I was able to write up the *Gazette*'s match reports the following day without any problems. But the incident brought home how vulnerable football team coaches can be when yobs are intent on causing damage.

We did stop further along the road in order for the driver to contact the police from a telephone box. But we were already on the outskirts of Barnsley by that time. The police suggested we went straight home to Middlesbrough, while they checked the bridge in case the yobs were still hanging around. It was a very cold journey back up the A1 and A19. The front windscreen had also been put through by one of the bricks and the cold March evening air turned the inside of the coach into a fridge over the next hour and a quarter.

Afterwards Boro enjoyed a little purple patch. Wins against Blackburn and Portsmouth in early April created the belief they could stay up. However, once again they struggled to cope with the pressure and lost consecutive away games to Oldham and Bradford. Goalkeeper Phil Kite played in both of those games because Steve Pears was injured.

The mood of the players was fairly good travelling to the away fixtures and I felt that Rioch's positive approach was having an effect. But the atmosphere on the coach on the way back was difficult. The writing was on the wall after these defeats, though Boro dug deep to win their penultimate game when crushing Millwall 3-0 at Ayresome Park.

It left Boro with a testing trip to Shrewsbury on May 3 to try to avoid the drop. Ironically this was a repeat of the same last-day fixture from the previous season, when Boro had saved their skins with a 2-0 win at Gay Meadow.

The fans were still hopeful and Boro took several thousand away supporters to Shrewsbury. They were packed into the away end behind a large metal fence. Boro needed these fans to act out the role of a 12th man, but it didn't happen. The general mood of the fans was ugly, rather than relaxed, and several of them climbed the fence before and during the game in an attempt to tear it down. As a result, the atmosphere was awful throughout, and the trouble did nothing to help the concentration of the players.

Boro's young starlets Colin Cooper and Stuart Ripley were both injured in the build-up to the match and another teenager, Lee Turnbull, started his very first game up front. Boro needed to win to have any chance of avoiding the drop but the game always had bad vibes and Boro's fate was virtually sealed when Gary Pallister was sent off. Boro went down by 2-1 and were back in Division Three for only the second time in their history.

The police and stewards were left to deal with the angry fans after the final whistle, while Rioch had to deal with the pointed questions of the press. He seemed relatively relaxed at first, but then lost his cool when asked a perfectly reasonable question by Ken Daley from BBC Radio Cleveland and jumped down poor Ken's throat. I was standing alongside Ken at the time and it could just as easily have been me who bore the weight of Rioch's outburst.

I felt sorry for Ken, but also for Bruce. All he was doing was expressing the feeling of utter frustration that we were all suffering from at the time. As good a manager as he turned out to be over the next two seasons, Rioch had no magic wand to wave.

From the fans' point of view, they had every right to feel let down. It was almost a disgrace for a club of Boro's standing to be facing a campaign in the third division and it hurt everybody. From Bruce's point of view, all his hard work on the training ground had just failed to produce the desired results, even though it had gone down to the wire.

However, while relegation was bad for the Boro, worse was to follow. Much, much worse.

CHAPTER 3

IN the difficult, dark, first half of 1986, nobody at Ayresome Park would ever hide from the fact that the Boro were in deep financial trouble. You could virtually smell the stench of decay around the place. A once great club was literally on its knees.

During my relatively brief relationship with Maddren, he had told me on several occasions how the club was hanging on by its fingertips. Willie was unable to strengthen areas where he felt the team was weak, because the club was not paying its way and there was no available money for new signings. It hurt Willie deeply to see the club he loved in such a state and he would have done anything humanly possibly to turn the tide.

Boro's debts were rising all the time and threatening to get out of hand. The club was hurtling towards disaster at a rapid rate of knots. Alf Duffield and some of his fellow directors had already dipped into their own pockets, but this merely ensured the club kept ticking over. They were incapable of producing the level of financial input which would have made a significant difference. It appeared there was no way of reversing the continual downward trend, with gates dropping alarmingly and no obvious major sellable assets within the squad.

Bruce Rioch, too, was under no illusions when he took over as manager early that year. There was not enough cash for him to go out and sign even one player to strengthen the team. Rioch was told quite clearly from the start that he had to work with what he had got.

So Rioch did his job within his remit. I thought he did his best to revitalise the side from within in his first few months in charge, mainly by bringing in some youthful vigour and getting other players to raise their game. It almost worked as Rioch nearly masterminded the great escape but Boro were relegated with a last-ditch defeat at Shrewsbury and with no obvious prospects of halting the slide in the immediate future.

They were bleak times, which became much bleaker when the club went into voluntary liquidation in the May of 1986. It was a deliberate move, designed to try to escape from a financial strait-jacket and resurrect a new club with a fresh beginning. Duffield had already stepped down as chairman having handed in his resignation in April. His place at the helm went to fellow director Steve Gibson.

I didn't know Gibson too well. All my interviews at board level had been with chairman Alf. The other directors had tended to maintain a low profile in public. What I did know about Steve was that he was 28, surely one of the youngest football directors in the country and one of his much publicised personal achievements was that he was Middlesbrough's youngest ever Labour councillor when elected in the Park End ward at the age of 21.

Gibson was also a self-made businessman, having formed his own company, Bulkhaul, in 1981. Clearly he had a unique business brain, especially as Bulkhaul was a progressive company which was already creating a niche for itself on the international market. The company dealt with the world-wide transportation of potentially hazardous products. I wondered whether Steve had accepted a poisoned chalice by taking over the reins at the Boro.

With stories of Boro's demise splattered all over the national media, I wanted to know Gibson's plans for the club. I did not have to wait for long. Steve rang me at the Evening *Gazette* and asked me to meet him. I drove down to the Bulkhaul offices at the Riverside Park industrial estate more in hope than expectation.

My first impression of the new chairman was that Steve did not look like a typical businessman, nor did he speak like a businessman. He came across very much as an average Teesside guy and looked a lot younger than his 28 years; but first impressions can be deceptive.

I was captivated by Steve's positive manner and his single-minded commitment to keep the Boro alive. He made it absolutely clear that the word 'failure' did not appear in his dictionary.

"I've got to save the club," he told me, with a steely determination in his voice.

"Middlesbrough Football Club belongs to the town. It's part of the town. It mustn't be allowed to die."

Steve admitted he had no guarantee of success, but stressed that he would leave no stone unturned in his attempts to keep football alive in Middlesbrough.

It was an enthralling chat. Steve made no attempt to keep anything secret from me and explained the full dilemma facing the club, warts and all. He delved into the background of the crisis, the causes of the financial slide and why the move into voluntary liquidation had been necessary.

Steve did not tell me how he would save the club, mainly because I don't believe he knew at that stage exactly what lay ahead. However, he was positive in his belief the club must be kept alive. The alternative, he told me, was seeing the Boro go to the wall. This would deprive the town of its football team, and potentially its very identity - unthinkable as far as Steve Gibson was concerned.

Steve had already taken legal advice to prepare for the twists and turns which might face the club in its survival bid, while he was talking to leading people in the town to try to garner more support.

Despite his positive manner, even at that early stage, Gibson could hardly have imagined the already developing pitfalls and setbacks which would bring Middlesbrough Football Club to within an inch of losing its life in that crazy summer. I wonder if he would have been prepared to take on the battle if he had known exactly what lay ahead.

Shortly after the club went into voluntary liquidation, I also had a visit from Councillor Edmund Pearson. He was a keen Boro fan who, alarmed by the doom and gloom stories in the media, had started the Save The Boro Fund. Councillor Pearson opened an account at the Yorkshire Bank and appealed for fans to pay in whatever they could afford, with a promise that the money would be exchanged for shares when, and if, the club was saved.

Like Gibson, Pearson also stressed that the Boro belonged to the town. He said: "The fans can save the club. We have an opportunity here for the community to save the club and then run it."

I could see that Pearson's heart was in the right place, and was happy to publicise details of the fund in the *Evening Gazette*. More than £20,000 was pledged by fans very quickly. But as it had been revealed that the club's debts were £1.8m - the immediate impact made by the Save The Boro Fund was just a drop in the ocean. I realised that the fund had no realistic chance of helping to save the club from liquidation.

So it was all down to Gibson. The new chairman was already getting stuck into the task. He rang me to say that he had devised a series of policies to try to save the club, and had outlined his plans to his fellow directors. Steve asked the other directors for full executive powers to run the club. When this was granted, he sacked them all.

As Gibson was the only credible force in the market place trying to save the club, and the only one with the clout to do anything about it, it quickly became clear that he was the only possible saviour. I decided to nail my colours to his mast, not that the picture looked bright as the rest of the media had already written off the club.

Bristol City had been wound up in similar fashion a few years earlier and then resurrected as a new company, effectively wiping out the old company's debts at a stroke. It was a method which Boro could potentially utilise to survive. In fact Duffield had already petitioned in the High Court to wind up the Boro.

The stumbling block was that the Football League was insisting that this resurrection route would no longer be open to those clubs who were in financial trouble. In Boro's case, the League stressed that all creditors would have to be paid in full if the club was to survive as a League member.

The chances of Gibson being able to generate £1.8m looked small, even with the support of the business people in the town. It seemed to be a massive amount of money at the time. I could see that the League ruling was a massive hurdle in Gibson's path, and so could the national media. As far as they were concerned the Boro were already a dead dinosaur. They did not have the benefit of Steve's confidentiality and all they could do was to print the regular doom and gloom prediction of the League's press spokesman. As a result, Boro's survival chances were nationally dismissed as negligible.

I was appalled at the attitude of the League because I believed the very foundation of their existence was to support all member clubs. What was the point of being part of an organisation which did not seem to be supporting its members? However, if I had been a major creditor of the Boro, I accept that I would probably have taken a completely different view

While the storms clouds were becoming ever blacker, I was adamant that the *Gazette* should support Gibson to the hilt and do whatever was necessary to support the push to save league football in Middlesbrough.

So I backed Gibson all the way in print through that summer and, professionally, it was one of the best things I ever did.

I was grateful for my bosses at the newspaper allowing me to remain so positive with my stories when everybody else was being negative. In any case the *Gazette* had nothing to gain from losing the very soul of its sports coverage. I'm sure that Gibson appreciated the support from his local newspaper and I, as our relationship developed, was able to open a telephone hotline to his office and pick up vital information which would hopefully give the fans hope.

Every time there was a negative story elsewhere in the media, I contacted Gibson for his comments and he relayed details of the latest development from his side of the fence. I don't think any other media organisation matched the balanced reporting of the *Gazette* that summer and I was delighted to be the man in the middle.

Even so, it did look bleak at times. There were many occasions when I felt that the scales had tipped in the wrong direction. Gibson was forced to switch tack early on, when his initial plans were thwarted, and survival attempt No.2 involved trying to put together a consortium which might be capable of raising the necessary funding.

At first Steve did not receive much in the way of response. Already he had found it difficult to generate interest from within the business community of Middlesbrough. The business people of the town either did not have any spare cash or were simply not interested in trying to help save the club. It didn't make sense to me. I couldn't understand their apathy. A football club is the greatest publicity any town can have and therefore it was in their interests to save it, but then I didn't have money to burn either.

A provisional liquidator was already in place at the Boro by this stage and was asking for offers. Tony Richmond was a chartered accountant from Leeds and I met him shortly after he was appointed; he seemed a pleasant enough guy. From a media point of view he was both amiable and available, though it was quite clear that he was on Teesside to do a job. I realised that he could not allow himself to show any sentiment over the future of the football club.

One of Richmond's first moves was to place an advert in the Financial Times looking for buyers for the club. He was ready to sell anything if he could attract the kind of price which would be acceptable to the creditors. He had listed the club's possessions and been through the books. In commenting on the financial plight which had led to the club going into voluntary liquidation, Richmond referred especially to the much criticised new sports hall adjoining Ayresome Park and questioned whether the club really could have afforded to build it.

Richmond soon discovered that the all round interest in the club was low. There was little response to his ad in the Financial Times. However, while the provisional liquidator was failing to attract any potential saviours, Gibson phoned me to reveal that he had finally made a breakthrough. After protracted negotiations, he had got Middlesbrough Council on board.

This was a catalyst, because the council alerted ICI, who also agreed to help. Then Newcastle and Scottish Breweries joined the consortium.

Suddenly it looked promising, though Gibson told me that the money which even these huge organisations had pledged was not going to be enough to save the club if the League continued to dig in their heels. The consortium were light years away from achieving a cash target which matched the £1.8m debts.

Gibson's next step was to place an advert in The Times. This brought Henry Moszkowicz on board. Henry was a Boro-supporting businessman from London, though I'm not sure whether he had been to Ayresome Park for a long time. Henry spotted the newspaper advert and replied.

Gibson told me that he flew to Heathrow to meet Moszkowicz as soon as he made contact. The meeting went well and Gibson was handed a cheque for £200,000 before they parted. It was a remarkable gesture by Moszkowicz. The consortium was up and running.

At this stage, Gibson believed there was enough financial clout within the consortium to open negotiations with Tony Richmond in an attempt to buy the club, though initial talks were doomed to failure. At a press conference which I attended, Richmond welcomed the consortium's interest but added: "We have had an interesting discussion but I have to say that the consortium are a long way from putting together a package which might be acceptable to the creditors."

I maintained regular contact with Steve Gibson over the next few weeks, but did not get to meet the consortium as a whole until around the middle of July. At that time they had £900,000 at their disposal, which consisted of £200,000 each from Middlesbrough Council, ICI, Scottish and Newcastle Breweries and Henry Moszkowicz, and £100,000 from Gibson.

The Council's representative on the consortium was chief executive John Foster, who I found to be a very pleasant man with the club's interest at heart. ICIs Colin Henderson initially gave the impression of being serious and austere, and a typical hard-headed businessman. But I soon got to know him well and found him highly likeable. He believed passionately that the club must be saved.

I already knew Graham Fordy from Scottish and Newcastle Breweries. He was an area rep for the company and was a regular visitor to Ayresome Park on business. He was also a Teessider and a strong Boro fan. It was that love for the club which had led to Graham going cap in hand to his employers to ask for the cash to inject into the consortium.

Henry Moszkowicz was difficult to work out at first. He was totally committed to the venture, but seemed to have no real Boro-supporting background, other than he had followed them from afar. Henry was one for me to work on and try to generate a relationship. I achieved that and got on reasonably well with him in time, though most of our chats were by telephone because he had ongoing business responsibilities in London.

It was shortly after the consortium went public that the Boro players returned for pre-season training. All the squad was still together, along with Bruce Rioch and his assistant Colin Todd, though physio Steve Smelt had accepted the offer of a contract at neighbours Sunderland. Three of the players, Peter Beagrie, Archie Stephens and Brian Laws, had taken the club to a Football League tribunal for alleged breach of contract, but the tribunal deferred making a decision and so the squad initially remained intact. The players' wages were being paid by the consortium, which I felt was a huge message of intent.

The very first day that I met up with Rioch again, following the close-season break, he took me to one side for a chat. Bruce revealed how determined he was to keep the squad together and how he believed the club would be saved. He said some very passionate things, but it was ra-ra stuff and, deep down, I don't think he knew much more than I did about the latest state of the survival battle.

I came away from our meeting thinking that it was a deliberately designed morale-boosting session to make sure that he kept me on board. The last thing Rioch wanted to read was the *Gazette* encouraging the players to leave because there was no hope for them at Middlesbrough. In this respect I think Rioch did everything right in his battle to maintain dressing room confidence. I have always believed that if Boro had a weaker man than Rioch in charge of the squad that summer, then the whole thing could easily have fragmented.

However, despite the players being back for pre-season training, it was becoming more difficult to obtain stories. Steve Gibson did feed me occasional pieces of news, but it was often off the record. The negotiations which were going on behind the scenes were becoming increasingly delicate and the consortium did not want them to become public. They did not want stories to appear in print which might prove prejudicial to their case. However, it was clear that conversations with Alf Duffield had gone well because the former chairman withdrew his winding up petition.

However, there was a body blow for the consortium when Middlesbrough Council withdrew, taking their £200,000 with them. They blamed rate capping for the decision. As a fan I was gutted because I felt it was a worthwhile cause for any council to try to save its football club.

The story of the Council's withdrawal was a front page lead in the *Gazette* and it did not convey good news to the fans. Gibson admitted to me that the Council's withdrawal was a huge setback for the consortium, but he stressed that it was not the end and the battle would go on.

Moszkowicz's reaction to the loss of the Council's cash was to make a magnanimous gesture. He produced another cheque for £100,000, making his overall contribution £300,000. Gibson, still building up his Bulkhaul business, found another £25,000, leaving the consortium just £75,000 short of its previous funding. It was a terrific reaction from both camps, probably a crucial one.

While the consortium members had temporarily steadied the ship, things were to get much worse soon afterwards. The Inland Revenue took over Alf's High Court petition and Boro were officially wound-up on July 30. Boro's players had been using the changing facilities at Ayresome Park during the past two weeks as they built up their fitness for the new campaign, and their training gear was stored in the dressing rooms.

The official receiver arrived on August 1 to padlock the gates with the gear inside and the bemused players outside. The club ceased to exist.

This was definitely the end as far as the national newspapers were concerned. I needed a Boro reaction so I phoned Steve Gibson for guidance. He revealed that the situation had become increasingly difficult and painted a black picture. My confidence was lowered, but Steve still refused to throw in the towel, despite all the hurdles which were being placed in his path. He indicated there were avenues which the consortium could explore which might yet give them ownership of the club and so the battle would go on.

Gibson stressed that it would make a big difference if the Football League were supportive of the consortium's attempts to keep football alive on Teesside. Instead the League continued to demand that any rescue package must involve paying the creditors in full. To make matters worse, they were also now insisting that if Boro were to start the season as a going concern then they must also have £350,000 of working capital with which to meet future financial commitments.

Still the players were training hard. I phoned Rioch every day and his stance remained the same; he was ultra positive in everything he did. He was working hard to keep the players thinking along the same lines. I went to watch Boro training at Longlands College on one occasion and it was pitiful - they had to put down jumpers for goalposts.

Rioch would not allow the players to give official press interviews throughout the whole of the battle to save the club. But I knew most of the lads well enough by this time and rang one or two on several occasions to maintain some level of contact.

I realised that, not surprisingly, every member of the squad was extremely worried about his future. The players had families to feed and mortgages to pay. There were no millionaires in the squad in those days. The players were paid a few hundred pounds a week and probably had little to fall back on.

In an ideal situation I believe that virtually all the players wanted to stay at the Boro, mainly because most were settled in the area and did not fancy the idea of trying to find new clubs just hours away from the start of the new campaign. That is a major reason why Rioch was able to keep them more or less together. They were clinging to the hope that the club would be saved, along with their futures.

Despite everything, the players knew no more than anybody else whether they would be turning out for Boro in the new season, or hurriedly trying to negotiate last-minute contracts elsewhere. It was a very uncertain time for all of them and that's why Rioch did a great job to maintain morale during the daily training sessions.

In the end, it was only natural that some players would be lost to the club. Winger Beagrie left in mid-August to join Sheffield United under freedom of contract, while Don O'Riordan followed him out of the club soon afterwards when obtaining special Football League dispensation from the Football League to sign for Grimsby Town.

Ten days before the new season was due to start, the Football League revealed they had turned down the consortium's salvage proposals. It was a bombshell and once again I was left wondering whether I had backed the wrong horse. Then the League gave permission for every one of Boro's players to talk to other clubs. I still don't believe most of the players fancied moving on, but they knew it was in their own interest to speak to any club which made an approach. Several talks took place yet, incredibly, not one further player jumped ship.

Soon after the League had made its announcement, Rioch called me in for another pep talk.

"I love this club," he told me, in total sincerity. "That's why I am going to see it through."

Rioch insisted he would stick with the club until the battle was over, one way or another and he believed that the players would stay, too, because they wanted to be part of Middlesbrough Football Club. I carried the story and in effect Rioch was publicly appealing to the players to stick with the club and, again, this helped to delay the possible departure of those members of the squad who might have been wavering.

The end of the struggle, whatever the outcome, was only nine days away. I had a heart to heart chat with my wife. If the club went to the wall, then the *Gazette* would have no need for a Boro reporter. I did not think I would be made redundant, even though it was a distinct and perfectly legal possibility. I felt that, at worst, I could be offered a job somewhere else in the editorial department but I might be offered a post that I would refuse for any number of reasons. This would lead to me looking for a new job, which could take the two of us and our young family anywhere in the country. I might even be out of work for some time before finding employment elsewhere. It was a difficult time for me personally, just as it was for the players and the coaches. I felt that I was on their side of the fence, rather than outside looking in, and it helped me to appreciate what they were going through.

I was lifted a few days before the start of the season when Colin Henderson called a press conference and revealed that he was hopeful that the consortium would save the club. It was common knowledge by this time that ICIs legal department had become involved and were helping to fight the battle. Even so, Henderson was able to publicly reveal only a small amount of information about the latest state of play because of the delicate nature of the negotiations.

Henderson revealed that Hartlepool had offered Boro the use of their Victoria Ground in order to fulfil their opening Division Three fixture which was at home to Port Vale. It was not possible to play the game at Ayresome Park because the gates were still padlocked.

At first Hartlepool had been ruled out because they were due to play a fourth division match at home to Cardiff City. But Boro were unable to play at Sunderland or Darlington because the police had said they did not have the resources to effectively man the game. The police also vetoed the possibility of playing at Billingham Synthonia.

So Boro kept on going back to Hartlepool. Following protracted talks with the Pool officials, the two clubs settled on a Boro v Port Vale kick-off time of 6.30pm, which was more than an hour and a half after Pool's own game was finished. This seemed to be the only viable option, especially as it did not attract police opposition.

Looking back, it's still remarkable to think that Boro were saved and were able to fulfil that opening fixture. The Football League continued to remain sceptical about Boro's chances of survival until the day before the season was due to kick off and, publicly at least, offered little encouragement.

As a fan, and not being privy to discussions between Boro and the League, it appeared that the League had deliberately put every possible obstacle in front of the club. I kept wondering whether the League really cared whether one of their member clubs lived or died.

I knew they had to protect the integrity of their clubs but this seemed to be a trifle intransigent to me.

All of these ongoing problems didn't make it any easier for the players as they built up towards their opening game. They were still banned from speaking to the media but Rioch continued to talk a good talk on their behalf.

The crunch arrived on the afternoon of Friday, August 22. Middlesbrough Council had continued as members of the consortium, despite their lack of financial commitment and they hosted a press conference in the Town Hall. I was told to turn up at 2.30pm when I could expect to hear the outcome of the consortium's battle to save the club in their showdown meeting with the Football League in London. At that stage there were only 28 hours to go before Boro were due to kick off against Port Vale.

This was reduced by a further four hours by the time the announcement was eventually made. When I first walked into the Stainsby Room at the Town Hall the mood was not good. I can't recall the name of our host but it was clear from initially meeting him that he was receiving negative vibes from the London meeting.

"No news yet?" I asked, perplexed.

"'Fraid not."

"How are things going?"

"Not very well from what I can gather. We'll just have to keep our fingers crossed."

It transpired that the consortium had been given a 5pm deadline by the League to produce an acceptable offer, but the indications were that they were struggling to reach an agreement.

There were very few of us in the Stainsby Room that afternoon. I can't recall any national newspapers reporters being present. Local radio was represented and also *The Northern Echo* but there didn't appear to be too much media interest which suggested that the general belief was that the battle was already lost.

It was the very first time that I had felt a genuine feeling of depression throughout the summer. I could not talk to anybody to find out exactly what was going on and as the clocked ticked away, it appeared the club's survival chances were receding rapidly. Even at this late stage, I felt that few people really cared whether the club lived or died. Our small group sat there, hardly talking and drinking endless cups of tea.

Five o'clock came and went. One of my media colleagues asked of our host: "Do you think there's any point in us remaining much longer?"

Our host, while putting the kettle on for the umpteenth time, assured us that negotiations were carrying on past the deadline, but we were becoming impatient. The silence was deafening. I was hungry, bored, and feared the worst.

Naturally the feeling of elation was wonderful when, at exactly 6.30pm, the news that the Boro had been saved came. There was much hugging and back-slapping in the Stainsby Room and we were able to smile for the first time that day.

The consortium had won the day. The news was delivered along with a statement from Colin Henderson in which he declared, quite rightly, that the club needed a new, solid foundation and must never again find itself in a similar situation.

I went back to the *Gazette* to write up my reports and eventually drove home for a very, very late tea. But it was one of the best meals I've ever eaten. Not only was the club safe, but so too was my job.

CHAPTER 4

BORO'S survival was complete in the chaotic summer of 1986 when their opening Division Three match against Port Vale went ahead at Hartlepool as planned. It was Saturday, August 23, my sister's birthday and a memorable day in the Boro's history.

I wanted to make the best of the occasion and enjoy the build-up to Boro's return from the dead. So I sat quietly at the back of the Mill House Stand at the Victoria Ground and watched Pool's game against Cardiff City, which kicked off at 3pm. There was no *Sports Gazette* being published at that time, and therefore no on-day match reports to write, so I simply soaked up the atmosphere.

I don't know if any Boro fans took in both games though, if they did, they probably had to pay twice. The Hartlepool stewards insisted on clearing the stadium completely after the first game, except for the press box. Football grounds always take on a different aura when they are empty. Suddenly I was aware of an eerie feeling, maybe the lull before the storm, as I sat gazing out over the bright blue North Sea munching tuna and cucumber sandwiches that I had taken with me for tea.

When the gates were re-opened at 5.45pm, I expected to witness a huge influx of red and white. But there was only a trickle of Boro fans in the opening 15 minutes or so and, for a while, the small contingent of Port Vale fans created the most noise.

The police had set a safety limit of 5,600, but the final attendance never looked like reaching that total. There are tens of thousands of Boro fans who will tell you they were at the first game against Port Vale, but they weren't. The Victoria Ground is situated less than 14 miles from where Ayresome Park used to stand, but the official attendance of 3,690 that night was the correct one.

Maybe it shouldn't have come as a surprise, neither to the media nor the consortium which now controlled the club. It was a Boro home game, but was also away from home. In any case, on several occasions in the previous campaign there had been fewer than 5,000 fans at Ayresome Park for games – though never less than 4,000.

Having been born in Hartlepool, I don't know anybody from my home town who hasn't been to Middlesbrough. But I know lots of people in

Middlesbrough who have never been to Hartlepool, save to pass through it on a train bound for Newcastle. To many Teessiders, Hartlepool is on a different planet.

Even so, those Boro fans who did turn up were making their presence felt in the few minutes before the kick-off. It helped create the right mood for Boro's re-awakening.

It was a warm, pleasant evening with a low sun illuminating both goalmouths as it shone through the gaps at either end of the Mill House Stand to create a weird combination of brightness and shade across the pitch.

Gary Pallister was suspended, following his sending-off at Shrewsbury in the last match of the 1985-86 season, so the team was:

Pears; Parkinson, Mowbray, Gill, Cooper; Ripley, Laws, Kernaghan, Hamilton; Slaven, Stephens. Sub: Turnbull.

In effect the team had picked itself. Rioch did not have any other players.

The sun shone brightly on Boro at the start. Twelve weeks of built-up adrenaline exploded forth and Boro led 2-0 thanks to an Archie Stephens double. But they were unable to maintain the tempo and gradually began to run out of steam, partially due to having experienced such an erratic and uncertain pre-season. The fitter Vale players hit back in the second half and forced a 2-2 draw.

I felt more relief than elation at the final whistle, just happy that everything was back to normal again. However, once I started carrying out interviews afterwards it was as if the liquidation saga had never happened. It was business as usual. It was easy to become blasé and forget that the dramatic events of the summer had almost ended everything.

Boro got the keys to Ayresome Park on September 1 and played their first proper home match against Hartlepool, of all teams, in the second leg of their first-round tie in the Littlewoods Cup. Boro had played the first leg at Hartlepool on August 26, meaning that they were both the home team and the away team at the Victoria Ground within a matter of four days. They drew 1-1 at Pool and won the home leg 2-0 in front of 7,735 fans. This was 1,500 up on the average crowd from the 1985/86 season. It was not exactly brilliant, it was a clear indication that the club still retained a fairly small fan base at that time.

While the fans were relatively slow on the take-up, the team was not. With Rioch masterminding things, Boro were unbeaten in their first 12 league and cup games, which took them into October. It was an incredible achievement. Yet you had to pinch yourself that it was happening, because Rioch's squad was half-full of untested kids who were still wet behind the ears.

Gary Parkinson had made his debut at Hartlepool, while fellow teenagers Colin Cooper, Alan Kernaghan, Stuart Ripley and Lee Turnbull had played only a few games between them. Even Gary Pallister had been playing league football for less than a season. The astonishing achievement by Bruce Rioch in getting this collection of rookie teenagers and journeymen pros to believe in themselves and blend into a competitive team should never be underestimated.

The Boro's success on the field made things a lot easier for the new board of directors, now chaired by Colin Henderson, to get their act together off it. I asked Rioch if the board would make any cash available for new signings.

"I've no idea," he said.

"Why's that?" I asked.

"Because we're banned by the Football League from buying players from other clubs."

It was the first time that anybody from the Boro had revealed details of such an embargo. It transpired Football League had imposed a buying ban because of money which was allegedly owed by the club to the PFA.

Still Rioch would not entertain any negativity, especially as the players were performing so well - and staying fit – that there was no desperate immediate need to bring in new blood immediately.

He said: "We've got a great set of lads in the dressing room. They love this club and they want the club to be successful. They love coming in every day for training. They could not be working any harder. What they are achieving here is just magnificent."

Just how Rioch got through those first few difficult months after liquidation with only 13 players was a minor miracle in itself. If the squad had picked up two injuries at any one time, they would have been unable to field a substitute – not unless Rioch or Colin Todd could be hurriedly registered as a player. I've cracked the joke a few times about being ready to bring my boots in an emergency, and in 1986 I was as close to realising that ambition as I could ever have imagined.

In the event, Rioch added another player to the squad in the November when he signed striker Paul Proudlock from non-league side South Bank. Proudlock was available as a free agent, a situation which was not affected by the League's buying ban.

Proudlock was a part-timer, working for his father's construction business in Hartlepool during the week and playing for the Bankers on a weekend. Not surprisingly, the opportunity to take a back seat from the business for a while and become a professional footballer was one he could not resist.

Rioch then brought in Scottish midfielder Ronnie Coyle, who was also a free agent though, despite the valuable increase in numbers, neither Proudlock nor Coyle went on to play ten games for the club.

Still Boro stayed at the forefront of the promotion chase. I can remember every goal and virtually every kick in that rollercoaster campaign, though the one game which stands out prominently in the first few months was the away game at Newport County in the November.

I had lost my coveted place on the club coach in the week leading up to the first official away game at Wigan Athletic on August 30.

Rioch rang me at the *Gazette* to say that he would no longer be taking pressmen on the coach. He said he wanted his young side to be allowed to concentrate on their football without other distractions. I couldn't understand his reasoning, because I felt that I was part of the set-up rather than an outsider, and I was hurt. But I had to go along with Rioch's decision.

So I renewed my travelling arrangements with Gordon Cox, who was then working for BBC Radio Cleveland. We quickly developed the strongest of bonds and Coxy went on to drive me all over the country to matches over many seasons. To this day he drives to every single Boro away game and back on the same day.

We arrived rather early at Newport following an uneventful journey to South Wales and parked up in front of a wire fence bordering railway lines, close to the stadium.

Trains were travelling in front of us from both directions. As we sat eating our sandwiches, Coxy said: "Will the next train come from the right or the left?"

I quickly took up the bait, and we devised a betting game in forecasting the direction of each ensuing train. There were lots of trains, and we took turns to guess. I can't remember the stakes. They weren't very high. But as I regularly forecast wrongly, Coxy made a tidy sum to add to the petrol money I owed him.

When we walked into Somerton Park, the weather had taken a distinct turn for the worse. It was bitterly cold and raining heavily. Blown by a strong wind, the rain was teeming into the ground-level press box which was situated just under the lip of the main stand. My notebook was saturated instantly. As the kick-off approached, the weather became worse, as rain was replaced by hailstones. As the teams took to the field, the hail was so heavy that you could hardly see more than a few feet in front of you.

The players seemed confused by the biting hail as they took to the field and, in an unprecedented situation that I have never witnessed either before or since, they turned around and started to walk back off the pitch in the direction of the dressing rooms. It was at this point that Rioch and Todd appeared from the players' tunnel. Immediately sensing what was happening, Rioch waved to the players to get back on the pitch.

Then Rioch and Todd sat down on the away team's small wooden bench, which was situated close to the pitch and exposed to the elements. Neither Rioch nor Todd was wearing a hat. The cold, slushy water was running off their heads and must have been pouring down their necks. But they never moved nor flinched from the bench and carried on as if it was a sunny day.

The hail and rain continued for much of the game, which was also memorable for the activities of the fans in the open end to my right. They were neither Newport fans nor Boro fans. They were Exeter City supporters who had been on their way to Northampton when they discovered their match was off. So, keen to watch some football, they took a detour to Newport. There were only around 40 of them but the police had apparently insisted they were housed in the open end at Somerton Park, which would have otherwise remained closed. The Exeter fans had no shelter, and probably no refreshment facilities. But I will never forget them gleefully doing the conga virtually non-stop throughout the game in the most severe of weather conditions.

In those days, I also wrote the Boro match report for one of the *Gazette*'s sister papers, the *Sunday Sun*. I was so cold at Somerton Park and keen to get away from the press box that I phoned the *Sunday Sun* copytaker, Sandy, and started submitting my report before the final whistle. It was 0-0 and neither side had created much in the way of chances.

Sod's law usually intervenes in these situations, and did. In injury time, Tony Mowbray headed the winning goal for Boro. I was delighted but a little embarrassed at the same time.

"I'm sorry Sandy," I said. "I'll have to start again."

"What?" he demanded.

"Tony Mowbray's just scored for Boro."

"Well why didn't you wait until the game had finished?"

I could only apologise profusely and start all over again. Sandy was not a happy man and it was understandable. I learned a harsh lesson from that mistake and now always wait until the final whistle before starting to submit match reports. Since then I have developed a strong friendship with Sandy, despite him being a Newcastle United fan, which endures to this day even though I have never met him face to face.

A month after visiting Newport, Boro were away to Brentford. The match was switched to the Sunday, for whatever reason, and was played just four days before Christmas. To make matters worse, it kicked off at 11am. That was fine for the manager and team, who had travelled down to London the previous day. But for us pressmen and supporters, who were travelling on the day, it was a nightmare. Maybe that's an understatement. You can go back to sleep after a nightmare. This trip opened my eyes wide open to what football journalism is all about.

For starters, I had to set the clock alarm for 4am. That was a rude awakening in itself. When I looked out of the bedroom window the whole street was covered in a layer of thick snow, and it was still snowing. Fortunately the main roads were relatively clear and I was able to drive through to Gordon Cox's house without any problems. After cleaning the frozen snow from the windscreens of his car, we set off shortly before five o'clock. Coxy managed to make good progress all the way to Wetherby without encountering any problems.

That's when it began to get difficult. The snow on the A1 between Wetherby and Doncaster was deep and virgin. And it was coming down thick and fast. There was hardly any other traffic at that time of the morning and we faced trying to drive through long stretches of the A1 without being able to work out exactly where the road was. There was a foot of snow lying in all directions and the road was completely hidden under the white blanket. There were no car tracks to follow ahead of us. It was like driving wearing a blindfold.

There were several scary moments when Coxy came off the road. It was unavoidable, because he couldn't tell where the road was. It was even worse on the couple of occasions when we got stuck fast.

"You'll have to get out and try to push us backwards," said Coxy with a straight face.

"There's two feet of snow out there," I replied.

"Yeah."

So I forced open the door and got out. The snow soaked into both my trousers and my thermals. I had long lost the feeling in my toes and my fingers went white as the blood stopped circulating. I knew my hands were on the car's bonnet, but I couldn't feel my hands were on the car bonnet. Every time I got back into the car, after between us we had managed to manoeuvre the car into a position in the snow which probably had tarmac beneath it, I resembled the Abominable Snowman.

I don't know how Coxy managed to drive us through that white hell and on to Doncaster, but he did. After that, the snow became thinner and it was completely clear by the time we reached London. The heater in the car dried me out and warmed me up again.

We still faced a panic to get to the game in time because we had to drive through London to reach Brentford. As I recall, there was little traffic on such a cold morning, but we encountered further problems parking and finally waltzed into Griffin Park at five to eleven.

My major memory of the game was of Brentford's on-loan striker David Geddis, who was later to join the Boro coaching staff and become a good friend. He embarrassed Boro's defenders in the first half and had four gilt-edged chances to score, but fluffed all of them. As Geddis was a recognised finisher, it seemed certain he would finally kill off Boro in the second half. But the Brentford manager took him off at half-time. I couldn't believe it, and I bet Boro couldn't either. As a result Rioch's men cruised through the second half and won 1-0 courtesy of a goal from Bernie Slaven.

The return fixture at home to Brentford was also not without incident. I've received many threatening letters over the years, most of which were safe to ignore. But one death threat that I received out of the blue one morning was particularly nasty. The writer, who omitted to give his or her name, said that I would be 'bumped off' during Saturday's match against Brentford. It was a little bit unnerving to receive a murder threat and I showed it to the editor at the time. He didn't like the tone of the letter either and passed it on to the police.

Cleveland Constabulary took the letter very seriously and told me that I would be allocated a personal bodyguard on the afternoon of the match.

I can't recall the officer's name, but he was a detective and he carried out his job to the letter. It was like something off a TV drama, as we walked into Ayresome Park together amid the stares from my media colleagues. They were wondering what on earth was going on. But I was grateful to have such committed support. The detective arrived at the *Evening Gazette* offices at around 1.30pm and accompanied me in my car, which I parked up in the schoolyard next to Ayresome Park. He shadowed me everywhere, sat next to me throughout the game, and stood alongside me when I carried out my post-match interviews.

Afterwards I dropped him off at the police headquarters. He had been constantly alert all afternoon and I suspect that if anything had happened, he would have been ready for it. Fortunately nothing did happen, but it was a case of better safe than sorry. The detective also got to watch the match for free and Boro won 2-0 with goals from Slaven and Lee Turnbull.

The team had continued their winning ways despite having to operate with a wafer-thin squad. With the buying ban lifted, Rioch brought in his first cash signing early in the New Year. The board stumped up £45,000 for the manager to sign Aston Villa reserve striker Paul Kerr. This was a new name to me and a transfer signing was a relatively new occurrence, because I hadn't experienced many incoming players since I started reporting on the team.

The first thing I noted about Paul, who was born in Portsmouth, was that he had a strong southern accent. This was quickly picked up on by the Boro lads and Paul was handed the rather-cleverly devised name of Nookie, which has stuck to this day.

I can remember interviewing Paul soon after his arrival on Teesside. He was very outgoing.

"I've come to Middlesbrough to score goals," he said.

He did just that, though Nookie was never prolific and clearly would have scored a lot more if he had been employed as an orthodox striker. He was given a different role by Rioch and quickly carved out a new niche for himself as an effective attacking midfielder. He was a bubbly character, highly likeable, and always popular in the dressing room.

I was delighted to see him stay on Teesside at the end of his career and carry out an important role for the Professional Footballers Association, in addition to looking after the financial affairs of a whole host of players throughout the country.

Unfortunately, Kerr's arrival at the Boro virtually coincided with a major injury setback for Rioch to deal with. Brian Laws, who was also a makeshift midfielder, having been converted from right-back, suffered a cruciate knee ligament injury in a home game against Bristol Rovers. He was sidelined for eight months.

At that time a cruciate injury was a major worry. In previous years it had prematurely ended the playing career of Brian Clough, not to mention many other top professionals. Fortunately, surgery techniques had improved dramatically and a method of rebuilding the knee had been developed shortly before Laws was injured. As a result he had an operation on his knee which proved to be successful and saved his career.

The signing of Paul Kerr virtually gave Rioch a direct replacement for Lawsy and left the squad no bigger than it had been previously. Still, though, they kept winning.

What Bruce Rioch and his team achieved in that remarkable first season following liquidation was incomparable. While promotion came at the end of it, maybe the manager's biggest contribution was to give several young hopefuls the belief in themselves to develop careers as professionals when they might not have been offered the same opportunities elsewhere. Colin Cooper, Gary Pallister and Stuart Ripley never looked back and went on to become full England internationals.

Skipper Tony Mowbray played for England B and also was regarded as the player who epitomised most what Boro fans felt their team was all about. He was born locally, he led by example and he would run through a brick wall for the club.

I was the fortunate journalist to be given, exclusively, the now legendary quote from Rioch, when I asked him about his captain. Rioch said: "If I was on a rocket ship heading for the moon, the one man I would want to have sitting alongside me is Tony Mowbray."

Mogga might have been embarrassed by such ebullient comments, but the tag stuck and eventually this was the name chosen by the producers of the club's first, and only surviving, fanzine 'Fly Me To The Moon'.

This initial season following relegation was a great time to be involved with the Boro. It was as if the whole club had been reborn. There was a sense of pride in everything that was achieved and everybody, from the directors to the office staff, worked as a team. I drove to Ayresome Park every day and was part of the furniture, always to be found leaning against the cold, brick wall in the tunnel outside the dressing room door, waiting for interviews.

The vibes all around the club were all positive. The players were now full of self belief, always bubbly and chatty, and Rioch ensured they gave 110 per cent on the pitch, week in and week out. So there was rarely a reason for me to slag off the players in print. They trusted me and I was accepted into the clan. As a result I have strong friendships with most of the lads from the 1986/87 squad which extend to this day.

I was also friendly with the directors, who officially had a new chairman in Colin Henderson. A fifth director, Reg Corbidge from Scottish and Newcastle Breweries, had been added to the board early in the campaign, but the board generally shunned the limelight. They preferred to take a back seat, concentrate on building new foundations away from the pitch, and leave Bruce Rioch to be the club's mouthpiece.

Rioch was just as good a front man as he was an effective coach and he continued to feed me stories, all of them positive.

"I love this club," he told me again. It was something he kept repeating, and I believe he did.

In the December of that first season, Boro strengthened their administration team by appointing Keith Lamb as the club's new chief executive. Keith was a chartered accountant who had been working for a group of contractors in Hartlepool.

Keith was probably a rare such appointment in that not only was he a Boro supporter, he also understood the finer points of the game. He was well known in local football circles as both a player and manager in the Teesside League, and had been involved in the game in one way or another throughout his life.

I got to know Keith very quickly. He was usually happy to stand and chat at the gates of Ayresome Park while I was waiting for the players to shower after training. In our discussions over the next few years, Keith was forthright and expressed strong personal views on the team and the playing policies.

However, Keith's football opinions were merely part of typical Boro fans' everyday conversation. The new chief executive had enough on his plate in controlling the Boro's business affairs and making sure that the club was able to cope with its increasing standing within the game. As the Boro started to climb back up the divisions and the fans began to return to the terraces, the club increased dramatically in size and stature over a relatively brief period of time. It meant that Lamb and the directors had to plot a future route for the club much more quickly than might have been initially anticipated.

One thing Lamb believed in strongly was that the manager should be left alone and, as far as footballing affairs were concerned, his major contribution was in always trying to satisfy the needs of the manager. The total support for the man in control of the dressing room has long been a particular belief of Steve Gibson, too.

The bottom line of the Gibson-Lamb argument is: 'What's the point of appointing a manager if you don't allow him to manage?'

I agree that managers should be allowed to get on with the job for which they are paid. Boardroom interference on football matters should always be kept to a minimum.

While Gibson and Lamb have always tried to satisfy the demands of their managers, there has never been a suggestion that they believe managers should be untouchable.

Managers are paid a lot of money to carry out their roles. It is a fact of life that football managers must live or die by their own decisions and abilities, though many fans on Teesside may feel that one or two managers survived at the Boro longer than was necessary. However, that's all part of the bond and strong sense of two-way loyalty which is synonymous with the Boro.

Even so, all the managers who are covered by the first volume of this book, Willie Maddren, Bruce Rioch, Colin Todd, Lennie Lawrence and Bryan

Robson, were all sacked at the end of the day. So, while the level of loyalty persists from within the Boro's ivory towers, there is always a sense of pervading realism. The word 'sacked' may not always have been given to the media at the time of the managers' demise, but it is the realistic one to describe the end of the tenure of all of these five men once they were deemed to have reached the end of the line.

Not that there were any negative thoughts directed at Rioch in the 1986/87 season. In fact it seemed at the time that Rioch and the Boro were a match made in heaven and that Bruce would go on forever and become an icon on Teesside.

He was taking the team along at a faster rate than anybody could possibly have anticipated just a few months earlier, when we were merely celebrating survival on the day the Boro were reborn against Port Vale at Hartlepool in late August.

While the manager would have loved to have the opportunity to further strengthen with some reasonable cash outlay on new blood, the board were concentrating their efforts into balancing the books and ensuring that the club's financial foundations had depth and resilience. Boro's unexpected success on the pitch made it difficult for long-term planning difficult because Keith Lamb and the Boro board were having to try to match the team's progress by ensuring the club as a whole developed at the same rate and, without a sudden injection of funds, it wasn't easy.

I'm not going to suggest that Boro got everything right in those early days. The directors and many of the employees were all new to the situation with regard to running a football club and made decisions which did not always please the fans.

The *Gazette* had to deal with many individual complaints from supporters in the days following liquidation. But then the new board had no previous policies on which to base their decisions. They had to do things their way, based on the information they had in front of them.

This meant there were massive changes made, very quickly, in the way the club was run and the way in which fans were accommodated. There was not too much sentiment in those days, but a lot of hard business acumen. The ongoing priority was always the need to put the club first.

While directors, staff and fans were experiencing great change, so was the team. Now that Rioch and his players had got their game into top gear, there was no stopping them. Even without the extra players that the squad really needed, Boro were being carried along by a relentless tide of self-belief. Rioch's positive approach was working wonders. Nobody in the dressing room would entertain talk of defeat - they feared nobody and believed they could beat anybody.

The remarkable run-in to the end of the 1986/87 campaign, during which the team was unbeaten after mid-March, was one of the most memorable spells in my time of reporting on the club. Rioch had gelled the small squad into an effective fighting machine which had the respect of the whole division, and they swept all before them.

It was inevitable that they would return to Division Two at the first attempt.

Boro were promoted on an emotional night at Ayresome Park, when more than 18,000 fans watched a goalless draw with Wigan Athletic. Despite Boro's failure to score it was still a good game and everybody stayed until the end. After the final whistle the players came out to salute the fans from the directors' box. This wonderful moment fully emphasised the fact that the Middlesbrough had regained its pride.

With promotion in the bag, Boro had just one remaining game to fulfil, which was away at Doncaster Rovers. The supporters treated the occasion as a party day out and so did the local media. We pressmen were as keen as the fans to enjoy the day and hired a minibus to take us to Belle Vue and back. On the way we were given a taste of what the fans have to deal with, when we suffered the usual indignation of being searched by police officers when the bus was stopped at a roadblock just outside Doncaster. When we entered the stadium it was rather depressing. It was one of the most run-down grounds that I have ever seen. The main stand was scruffy, the terraces were a disgrace and huge clumps of grass and weeds were protruding through the concentre. When you consider that Doncaster were probably struggling financially almost as badly as Boro had done 12 months earlier, it made you appreciate how far Boro had come in a short period of time.

Boro were by far the better side on the day and won 2-0. Once all the interviews were in the bag, we pressmen returned to our minibus and stopped off at the Pied Piper at Osmotherley on the way home to celebrate the season.

The wine flowed all evening and so I can not remember too much about the night, except for one of the hands during a game of three-card brag. Gordon Cox was dealing and there was an obvious mistake as he passed out the cards, though we had drunk too much alcohol to complain and played on.

Afterwards I asked that the cards were re-dealt as they should have been, in order to see which hands we should have received. It was simple to re-deal them and it transpired I would have had three threes. I never did quite get over such annoying bad luck, especially as I've never been dealt three threes since.

CHAPTER 5

WHILE the 1986/87 season had been a remarkable runaway success for the Boro, against all the odds, what the team achieved in 1987/88 was nothing short of miraculous. Bruce Rioch squeezed every last ounce of energy from his senior professionals, while the rapid development of the younger players from boys into men was a major contributory factor in a second successive promotion campaign.

I never felt at any time at the start of that second season that Boro were capable of going up again - I don't think anybody did. The small squad had already over-achieved massively in winning promotion at the first time of asking. Consolidation was not a word you would have heard at Ayresome Park, certainly not from Rioch. But this was an opportunity for the Boro to cement the growing new foundations, gradually improve and increase the size of the squad and eventually mount a fresh promotion campaign within a couple of years.

However, the astonishing winning mentality which pervaded throughout the club in that first season following liquidation was infectious. Talk of defeat was no longer in the players' vocabulary. Every game was deemed winnable. Rioch told me before the campaign started that he had insisted to his players that they had nothing to fear in this league.

He said: "I've told them they are as good as anybody in this division. I've told them this because it's true. We have stepped up a division but there's no reason why we can't continue to look up."

Rioch was proved right, yet this second promotion, which took Boro on to the biggest platform in the English game, was achieved ahead of the progress of the club itself.

Colin Henderson and his small group of directors had strengthened during their first year in charge, yet the club still retained a thin financial base. Things were not made any easier for the board in the summer of 1987 because a lot of the cash which they generated over the first 12 months had to be re-directed into improving the safety standards within the 85-year-old Ayresome Park.

As a result, there was little money for Rioch to spend on team strengthening the team in the summer. His only outlay was in forking out £30,000 to bring in Aston Villa's reserve defender Dean Glover.

I liked Deano from the start and he was another astute signing. He fitted in perfectly into the dressing room. He was a wholehearted Brummie, who knew only one way to play the game. What Deano lacked in quality he made up for in sheer commitment and effort – which were typical traits of Rioch's side at the time.

In further familiar Rioch fashion, Glover was not utilised as a defender. He was pitched into the midfield and spent much of his career at the Boro in this role. The familiar Rioch defence of Parkinson, Mowbray, Pallister and Cooper remained largely unchanged all season. So Deano was handed a midfield ball-winning role in front of the defence. It was a role in which he performed admirably throughout the campaign and became a fans' favourite.

It meant that Glover and Paul Kerr were more often than not handed the central midfield roles, though neither was considered a midfielder at his previous club. Stuart Ripley continued to provide the ammo from the right flank, while the effervescent Gary Hamilton worked wonders on the left, even though this was not originally his best position.

While Glover was the only incoming player, there was a further change at Boro that summer. Henry Moszkowicz resigned his directorship, while retaining his 36 per cent shareholding. I had held several conversations with Henry during the first 12 months, in addition to all the directors, and I have to admit that I did find him different from the others. He was a very well-spoken Londoner who ran a successful stationery business in the capital. Henry had made a massive gesture to help save the club but, as I could see it, he had very little in common with traditional northerners like Steve Gibson and Graham Fordy.

Henry sent me a letter to announce his resignation and when I phoned him for further comment he was reticent to air his feelings in public. I did, however, have a chat with Gibson who said that he was disappointed that the board had fragmented so quickly. He said that Moszkowicz had expressed views at board meetings which occasionally were not in keeping with those of the other directors, but added that the last thing he wanted was for Henry to step down.

These disagreements had clearly frustrated Moszkowicz, especially as it appeared the other directors tended to hold contrary feelings to him whenever there was an impasse. This sense of frustration led to him taking the surprising decision to stop attending board meetings.

As the major shareholder, Henry retained a powerful presence in the boardroom because he still had the opportunity to make a telling contribution to the club's decision making. Looking in from the outside, as he now was, he was facing a difficult situation. However, Henry stayed true to the club and I can't recall any director ever telling me that Moszkowicz had interfered with the general boardroom policy over the next few years.

There were concerns expressed by some fans in the *Gazette* that Boro might be in danger of falling back into liquidation now that Moszkowicz had stood down. Henry was obviously aware of those concerns and he sent me a letter towards the end of the October which stated:

"In light of certain reports that have been circulating in the area I wish to inform the people of Middlesbrough that it is my intention to retain my shareholding in the club and assure them whatever happens my money stays in. I will continue to sponsor the Boro Juniors and give Bruce Rioch and his team my unqualified support."

These were reassuring words which reconfirmed Moszkowicz's ongoing commitment to the club. It was a pity that he did not have more in common with the other directors, but he made no attempts to rock the boat. Despite the fact he always held colossal power because of his massive shareholding. Several years later Henry was to be the significant player in the negotiations which eventually led to Steve Gibson gaining 100 per cent control of the club.

Rioch made sure that boardroom matters always stayed well away from the dressing room, though the team did not get off to the best of starts in 1987/88. They won just one of their first five Division Two games. The turning point came on September 8 when Kerr struck the only goal in a Boro victory at Villa Park.

I can remember Rioch trying to play down the win, but I could see from his face how much it meant to him going back to his former stamping ground and beating Aston Villa with a team of seasoned pros and rookie kids. It also meant so much to Kerr and Glover who, while never admitting as much in public, must have felt they had initially taken a step down when leaving a club with so much tradition like Villa to join the reconstituted Boro.

Despite the traditional hiccup after the New Year, Boro never really looked back after that win at Villa Park. The board stumped up more cash before Christmas for Rioch and he again went to Aston Villa in order to strengthen this squad. This time he snapped up Villa duo Mark Burke and Kevin Poole. Bruce's family home was in Sutton Coldfield at that time, which allowed him the opportunity to regularly watch Aston Villa reserve games on a midweek evening.

England youth international Burke was potentially a super signing; he had a good pedigree, lots of pace and he was dangerous in front of goal. He was still very young and inexperienced when he arrived on Teesside and was arguably one more for the future but, as much as I liked him, I always felt that he never really did himself justice at Boro. Mark went on to enjoy a long career in the game, at home and abroad, but never seemed to find the right slot in the right club which could have made him a big name.

Goalkeeper Poole was one of the quietest lads I have met in football. I don't think he ever put any real pressure on No1 Steve Pears, either through his performances or his personality. Kevin always gave the impression he was not the kind of pushy player who would knock on the manager's door at regular intervals, but he was still a canny keeper at that level.

Poole was also a significant signing because Boro had progressed very quickly in such a short period of time and Rioch was mindful that he needed two senior goalkeepers in his squad. Kevin did play his fair share of games with Boro and has gone on to enjoy a long and illustrious career. I'm delighted to note, at the time of writing, he was still playing for Burton Albion in the Blue Square Premier League.

With Brian Laws returning from his cruciate knee ligament operation and Bernie Slaven banging in the hat-tricks, Boro maintained the momentum which had begun in September and were in a promotion place before Christmas. Rioch had continued to put the accent on youth by preferring youngster Alan Kernaghan up front to the old stager Archie Stephens. It was a brave move, because Kernaghan was very raw, but he was wholeheartedly committed to both the cause and the club.

By this time Bruce knew every one of his players inside out. I can remember one player telling me that he felt that Bruce even knew what they were thinking. He did, in many respects. Bruce drew information about his players from all sources and had a useful spy in the camp.

Boro had two men kit men at the time, Ken Smith and Joe Hunt, both of whom were lovely. However, Joe had a hard exterior, he had been around the club for some time and took immense pride in his job. He did not suffer fools gladly and many a time I saw him ask journalists and members of the public to leave the premises in midweek when they did not have special permission to be standing within the metal gates at Ayresome Park. Fortunately I had struck up a strong bond with Joe and he always allowed me to stay inside and pick up my interviews.

Joe regarded many of the players as being rather juvenile in their approach to their jobs off the pitch and didn't have too much respect for most of them. So, accordingly, he was always quick to report any dressing room wrongdoings – and any wrong words – to Rioch.

Their bond was very strong because Rioch had paid Joe's wages out of his own pocket during the liquidation crisis. Rioch knew that the team needed to retain its back-up workers during this difficult period, when the provisional liquidator could not retain all the staff. It was a magnanimous gesture by the manager and Joe never forgot it. If Bruce was the captain, Joe was his lieutenant, and the unlikely but effective partnership helped Bruce run a tight ship.

As ever, the fixtures were not kind to Boro fans nor the local media over the festive period. The Saturday before Christmas took Boro to Bournemouth. The Cherries had not adapted too well to life in Division Two. Having been promoted along with Boro at the end of the previous campaign, Boro had thumped them 3-0 at Ayresome Park in September and Bournemouth were struggling in the bottom six. On a cold, featureless afternoon at Dean Court on December 19, Boro drew 0-0 to extend their run of unbeaten games to 13.

I had travelled down to the south coast with Nigel Gibb in his Austin Metro. Nigel is a Boro fan of many years' standing who can proudly say that he has a virtually unblemished record of watching the team in every game, home and away, since the Sixties. He also went on to win the FA's national fan of the year award and received his prize in London from Trevor Brooking.

With Nigel driving both ways unassisted, we had an uneventful trip to Bournemouth. We were making good progress on the way back home when Nigel announced, shortly after joining the M1 from the M25: "We're running short of petrol guys. We've been on the red for some time. I'm hoping to get to the next services at Luton but it's going to be touch and go."

We had not passed a petrol station for some time, mainly because there are none on the M25. Nigel's target was to reach Toddington Services, which were just north of Luton, in order to refuel there. There were five of us and all eyes were on the gasometer as we crept our way through every mile.

In the event, we didn't make it to Toddington. There was no warning; the engine suddenly died as the last drop of juice was consumed.

By the grace of God, we were travelling downhill at the time and the car's momentum kept us going forward at some speed. In addition, we had just passed the exit sign for junction 11, which we could see in the distance. It was touch and go whether we would make it, but the car kept going sufficiently for us to enter the increased gradient of the slip road, which gave us fresh momentum and took us down to the roundabout at the bottom of the bank. Just before reaching the roundabout, we got out and pushed the car half on to the pavement.

Nigel was an AA member, so he phoned them immediately. He was informed that demand was high and we would receive a visit from a patrol vehicle in an hour or so. I got out of the Metro to stretch my legs and watched the traffic haring around the roundabout.

After ten minutes or so, an AA van suddenly appeared. I flagged it down, and the driver pulled over. He was not personally aware of our predicament, but was happy to help – and had spare cans of petrol in his vehicle.

The first gallon of juice had no effect, probably because the car was on too much of a slant, half on and off the pavement. But the second gallon did the trick, the car roared into life. We were on our way again and completed the remainder of the journey none the worse for the predicament. It was not the worst problem I encountered on the road, but a gentle introduction of what was to come in the future.

Shortly after Christmas we faced another long trip south for the FA Cup third round tie against Sutton United. Gordon Cox drove this time and we parked up in Gander Green Lane without mishap. Sutton were in the Vauxhall Conference but still something of an unknown quantity. However, their manager Barrie Williams was a bit of a character on the non-league scene and was regularly interviewed on TV before the match, which helped to give the tie a bit of national intrigue.

The Borough Sports Ground was a pleasant enough little venue, if totally under-developed. If there was a press box, I didn't see it. I joined several national newspapermen, who had been sent to Sutton in the hope of witnessing a Cup upset, sitting on a wooden bench at the back of the only stand. I had hired a telephone, which was situated between my feet, while I had my notebook on my lap and positioned my stopwatch on a protruding metal beam which was sticking into my back.

The pitch was grassless but flat and Boro's young players showed no signs of nerves as they completely outplayed Sutton and led 1-0 at the interval thanks to a goal from Gary Pallister. I don't know what went wrong at the break, but Boro lost their way completely in the second half. They conceded the equaliser and could easily have lost it as Sutton bombed forward relentlessly. The final whistle was greeted with some relief.

Interviews were hectic afterwards as dozens of pressmen crammed themselves into the small area near the dressing rooms - but I managed to get everything I needed.

When we set off back to Teesside, I realised that I had left my stopwatch on the metal beam at the back of the stand. I phoned Sutton on the Monday morning to discover it had been handed in.

The Sutton secretary was brilliant. "No problem," he said. "I'll post it off to you today."

The stopwatch duly arrived in the post at the *Evening Gazette* in the post the next morning. What a terrific gesture.

The watch arrived just in time for me to use it for the replay, which Boro were expected to win quite comfortably. In the event, they struggled to break Sutton down and might easily have lost it when the non-leaguers hit the crossbar from close range.

Boro eventually scraped through when Paul Kerr scored the only goal just before the end of extra time. The fact that Boro did not celebrate the goal summed up their feelings. Sutton received a worthy standing ovation from the Boro fans at the final whistle.

It was a narrow squeak, but Boro were through and were now looking forward to a trip to first division Everton in the fourth round. This was a massive challenge for Bruce Rioch's team, who were playing in Division Three 12 months earlier. In the event, they were equal to the test at Goodison Park and another goal from Kerr early in the second half earned a replay.

The new Boro board had experienced a 20,000 plus crowd at Ayresome Park on just one occasion, when 23,536 fans watched a disappointing 1-1 draw against Blackburn Rovers on Boxing Day. The Blackburn crowd was around 2,000 short of the Ayresome Park capacity at that time, though it was still a surprise to me when Boro decided against making the replay against Everton all-ticket.

This decision turned out to be a huge mistake, because the match had grabbed the imagination of the Teesside public. The fans reacted to an appeal from the police for everybody to get there early and, in the event, the gates were locked 50 minutes before the kick-off.

There were 25,235 inside and thousands more disappointed supporters locked outside. The worst scenes were in the back street behind the Holgate End where many hundreds of fans were trapped for a long period without being able to move in any direction. The frustrations of those supporters outside the ground boiled over and there were several ugly incidents, leading to arrests and a lot of bad feeling towards the club.

But it was a watershed moment in the history of the new club because it indicated that there were many thousands of potential fans out there than had been originally anticipated.

Two years earlier Boro had been playing in front of crowds of 5,000 and there was a belief that the fan base had collapsed, but now the supporters were willing to return with the promise of successful times again. Boro were eventually to tap into this source of additional support, leading to regular 20,000-plus attendances at Ayresome in the first division the following season and the eventual move to playing in front of capacity crowds at the Riverside Stadium.

Those fans who were fortunate enough to watch the game against Everton witnessed an absolute classic. It was a terrific end to the game with Tony Mowbray forcing extra-time with an injury-time equaliser following Dave Watson's opener. Alan Kernaghan gave Boro the lead in the 99th minute and Boro looked to have done enough to beat their esteemed opponents, until the dancing home crowd was dramatically silenced when a header by Trevor Steven was deflected into the net off Colin Cooper in extra-time injury time.

Heads did not drop and the second replay, on a freezing cold, windy night at Goodison Park, was another classic. In the event, Boro were to lose under unfortunate circumstances when Tony Mowbray turned a cross into his own net in the closing minutes.

The wind reached gale force after the game and there was a wind tunnel effect generated outside the stadium. As I tried to make my way back to the car, I saw two people blown over by the force of the wind. When I reached the corner of the stadium, I suffered the same fate and landed heavily on my left elbow.

The pain was severe and eventually I took advice from my peers at the *Gazette* and went to hospital for X-rays, which were clear. However, the pain persisted for several months and I always believed that I had suffered a hairline fracture which had not been picked up by the X-rays.

The defeat by Everton did little to affect Boro's momentum. They had picked up the pieces in Division Two following a poor post-Christmas spell and grabbed the imagination of the national media sufficiently for them to be chosen to feature in a live match on BBC (wasn't this match on ITV??? Brian Moore and Ian St. John definitely do the commentary - look on YouTube!), when they entertained fellow promotion contenders Aston Villa on February 14. Despite the game being on TV, the Boro fans wanted to be part of the occasion, and the club's second biggest league crowd of the season of almost 17,000 turned up at Ayresome Park for the Sunday afternoon clash. They witnessed another classic. Boro's winning goal sticks in the memory, Mowbray diving horizontally to head home. The photos of the goal appeared everywhere the following day.

Even though Boro still had a relatively weak financial base, the prospect of a second promotion was not an opportunity that anybody at the club wanted to see go to waste. So the board made further cash available for Rioch to bring in another striker.

Rioch broke the mould of signing Aston Villa players by switching his attentions to Watford and striker Trevor Senior, whose goalscoring achievements in an earlier spell with Reading were legendary. Trevor was welcomed with open arms in the dressing room. He was a bubbly character, full of fun off the field and a clinical finisher on it.

He provided the added impact up front and scored enough goals to enable Boro to achieve their ultimate ambition of reaching Division One.

At Easter, Boro stuffed Sheffield United 6-0 at Ayresome with Senior scoring twice. They recovered from an out of character 4-0 defeat at Ipswich to win against Plymouth and Barnsley and leave themselves on the brink of promotion. All they had to do was to beat mid-table Leicester City at Ayresome in their final game.

The stadium was virtually full an hour before the kick-off and hosted the highest crowd under the new regime of 27,645. The atmosphere was terrific when I walked into Ayresome, which was long before the game started but, as I gazed around at the partying on the terraces, I felt that something was not right. The fans were celebrating a promotion which had not yet happened. There were painted faces everywhere, red and white balloons and constant chanting. It was as if the fans felt that Boro had only to turn up to be promoted.

I still didn't expect Leicester to spoil the party, but that's exactly what happened. Boro froze on the day and the Midlanders took full advantage and won 2-1. Having witnessed so much celebration before the kick-off, the feeling at the final whistle was even worse. Yet Leicester played very, very well on the day and Boro couldn't match them. It meant that Aston Villa pipped Boro for second spot behind champions Millwall.

So it was into the play-offs which were an unknown quantity for all of us and I didn't give Boro much chance of coming through them. There was a feeling of failure hanging over Ayresome Park following the defeat by Leicester and I wondered how Bruce Rioch could possibly lift the players sufficiently to come through them.

To make matters worse, Boro were paired in the semi-finals with Bradford City who had comfortably done the double over Rioch's men in the second division.

The first semi-final match was played on a Sunday morning at Valley Parade. It was a bright, sunny day and the City fans were up for the kill. But there was something special about the Boro that day. They played in an all-white strip which had been especially produced for the match. Whoever thought of the idea deserved a medal because two or three players told me afterwards that it made them feel different. It helped them to forget all about Leicester and they began to play again.

The match attracted plenty of press interest; so much so that I couldn't get a place in the crowded press box and was ushered away into a large room at the far end of the main stand. There were a few seats, but I didn't get one and I stood throughout the game, watching the events through the glass windows. The view was still ok, though there were a lot of us standing, with our notebooks, pens and phones in our hands. Yes, three hands that day.

Despite the Boro's impressive white strip, City still had the edge in the game and did much of the pressing. The decisive moment came when Trevor Senior scored a goal for Boro. City won 2-1 on the day, but that away goal gave Boro a fantastic psychological edge.

With a 25,000 crowd at Ayresome Park for the return leg, the atmosphere resembled that from the Leicester game, but this time Boro were really up for the game. Bernie Slaven scored to level the scores on aggregate, but City battled all the way and the game went into extra time. Gary Hamilton gleefully scored the second goal in the first period and Boro were on their way to the finals.

In that season, the rules stated that the lowest non-relegated first division team joined the top three second division contenders in the play-offs and Boro found themselves facing top-flight Chelsea in the finals.

The west London side had crushed Blackburn Rovers in the semis and were strong favourites to brush aside Boro and retain their Division One status. Like many Boro fans, I felt that this would be too difficult a hurdle for Rioch's boys to overcome and suspected they had reached the end of the promotion road.

Brilliant Boro climbed to a new level of performance in those two games against Chelsea. In the first leg at Ayresome they won comfortably by 2-0 with goals from Senior and Slaven. It was a remarkable team performance and there was no fluke about the win.

Chelsea took it particularly badly. I read several articles in the national media over the next few days where the Chelsea players claimed that the result was a fluke and that Boro didn't deserve even to be in front going into the second leg. In fact the general consensus of everybody connected with Chelsea, as well as the national media, was that Boro would be swept aside at Stamford Bridge.

It was a very hot Saturday afternoon in London for the decider. We had set off early from Middlesbrough, with Gordon Cox giving himself plenty of time to find a parking spot in what is always a non-friendly area for cars. The Stamford Bridge press box at that time was very high up at the top of the stand opposite where the players run out. It was a difficult, sweaty climb up the staircase to reach it.

However, I was relieved to be sitting in the press box and not elsewhere in the stadium. The pervading mood was decidedly ugly. In fact I can't recall witnessing a worse atmosphere at any game I have reported on. The intense feeling of hatred was everywhere in the ground. You could sense the home fans were baying for blood.

They had read the comments of their players in the national media and genuinely believed that Chelsea had suffered an injustice in the first leg.

There were constant flurries of activity in the seats below us, where it appeared that some Boro fans had been seated alongside Chelsea supporters, leading to friction and spots of bother. The press box was definitely the place to be. The main bulk of the Boro fans were to my left, standing behind a protective metal fence but could not be heard above the cacophony of the home supporters.

The atmosphere was just as ugly when the match kicked off. The whole stadium seemed to be willing on the blue shirts. Chelsea tore into Boro from the start. When Boro fell behind in the first 20 minutes to a goal from Gordon Durie it seemed only a matter of time before they folded completely.

The pressure was intense but the longer the game went on the more Boro looked capable of dealing with it. Chelsea were not as good as they thought they were and Boro looked increasingly comfortable. In the event, they held on for a mammoth victory with one of those never-say-die battling performances which you remember for all time.

The final whistle was greeted with hysteria from the Boro fans, and 'Ee-Aye-O' was much in evidence. Unfortunately the Chelsea fans in the Shed End could not stomach the loss of their first division status at the hands of northern upstarts. Hundreds of home fans came haring on to the pitch at the final whistle and raced across, unchallenged by stewards or police, to the Boro fans. They threw whatever they could find into the Boro section but, thankfully, could not scale the protective metal fence from the outside.

It took almost an hour for officials to clear the ground of angry Chelsea fans. Only then could the Boro players finally come out to celebrate their success with the ecstatic travelling supporters. We media men had stayed within the safety of the press box throughout this time. The wait was worth it.

Witnessing the Boro players celebrating the most unlikely of successes was a memorable moment in my life.

In many respects it was an occasion which was almost hard to take in considering that Boro had started virtually from scratch as a club only two years earlier. What was achieved by Bruce Rioch, Colin Todd and their small squad of players that season was nothing short of miraculous.

CHAPTER 6

I CAN vividly recall Bruce Rioch telling me that he feared that Boro might have been promoted too quickly. As he prepared for life in the heady heights of the first division in 1988/89, the manager was still operating with largely the same nucleus of players who had been using jumpers for goalposts during the liquidation summer.

The club were still not on a perfect financial footing and there had been little opportunity to significantly increase the size of the squad over the past two years. All the club's talented young players had been thrown into the battle from the onset, while Rioch had been able to bring in only three serious contenders over the two campaigns.

Rioch told me that, not only was the return to Division One going to test his best players, but also there was a danger that the step up would leave too many players behind. It was asking a lot of the fringe players in particular to make an impact in the first division. Rioch did not hide from the fact that a very small squad had become effectively smaller at this high and demanding level.

I suspect Rioch said nothing of the like to his players. He would make sure they were fully primed, as ever, for the start of the new campaign, and fearing no one. The fledgling Boro board had done their best to keep pace with the dramatic advances made by Rioch's army, but the club still had a relatively weak base from which to launch an assault on the first division. Matters were made worse by the fact that a lot of cash had, once again, needed to be spent on vital safety work on the East Stand as Boro prepared for life back in the top flight.

Defensively Boro still looked ok and in Steve Pears was a goalkeeper of rare quality, highly dependable and clearly a relative snip at £80,000 from Manchester United. In front of Pears, the back four had remained largely unchanged over the two years and was being led by example by the no-nonsense approach of skipper Tony Mowbray, who had taken everything in his stride so far.

Alongside Mowbray, Gary Pallister had blossomed into a cultured player whose timing was superb, while I felt the young full-backs Gary Parkinson and Colin Cooper could be relied on to give their usual 110 per cent and would cope with the step up.

Up front Boro had two prolific scorers in Bernie Slaven and Trevor Senior. I couldn't see any reason why either of them would not continue hitting the back of the net, even if neither of them had previously been tested at this level. The theory that good strikers can score goals anywhere was about to be put to the test.

I did make a note at the time that I felt Boro were potentially very weak in midfield. Two of Rioch's midfield men, Dean Glover and Paul Kerr, were a converted defender and striker respectively. Gary Gill, who could also play in midfield, was originally a defender by trade. Brian Laws, another midfielder converted from a defender, had elected to move on to Nottingham Forest under freedom of contract.

Winger Stuart Ripley, whose strong runs and telling crosses were a key part of the team's success over the previous two years, would be fine at this level, though there had to be worries about Mr 200 Per Cent Gary Hamilton.

The brave Scot was suffering pain from an ongoing knee problem and regularly needed injections to be able to take the field. In the modern era, and even if Boro had enjoyed the luxury of a bigger squad at that time, Hamilton would not have played so many games. However, not only did he continue to answer Boro's desperate call by turning out week in and week out on the return to the first division, but he performed personal heroics in playing virtually the whole season.

The potential problems in midfield were not lost on Rioch, though he didn't have the extravagance of a never-ending supply of cash with which to make a major difference. In the event, he was able to make just one signing in advance of the new campaign, when the board came up with the cash to buy Mark Brennan from Ipswich Town £350,000.

Boro desperately needed midfield experience, a fact not lost on Rioch. I felt at the time that Brennan was a risky purchase, especially as so much expectation was heaped on his young shoulders. The midfielder was only 22, which suggested he needed older players around him if he was to cope with so much responsibility in trying to hold the Boro engine room together. Mark had plenty of first division games under his belt and knew what life was all about in the top flight but, after arriving at the Boro, he never enjoyed the benefits of having the necessary level of quality and experience around him in order to make his move to Teesside a fully successful one.

Brennan was still welcomed into the dressing room, and fitted in well, but as far as I was concerned one new face was never going to be enough. Within a few games of the campaign getting underway, the situation became even tighter when the Boro squad lost another player.

Rioch called me into his office one morning and told me that he had been closely evaluating Trevor Senior. He expressed the belief that Senior was not good enough to play at this level and was not what Boro needed if they were to make an impact in the first division.

Senior had not scored a goal in four appearances in the top flight, and in fact did not score for the club at all in the first division. I was still initially surprised to hear Rioch's comments. Senior, for me, was quite capable of scoring for Boro given a run in the side and opportunities in front of goal. Though Rioch went to some lengths to stress that he believed this was not the case.

I was well used to the manager feeding me stories and I realised that this one was intended for publication, even though it was going to be virtually devoid of quotes. Rioch had made his mind up that Senior had reached the end of the Boro road. I also knew that he expected me to write the story exactly as he had relayed it to me.

So I returned to the *Evening Gazette* and wrote a huge story saying that Senior was available for transfer because he was not cutting the mustard. I tried to make it clear that the story had emanated from the manager's office, rather than the editorial floor of the *Gazette*, though it was not easy to support it without quotes.

The story was printed with a massive headline, and was another good exclusive for the newspaper. But the story was not accepted very well at the Boro, particularly in the dressing room. Trevor was a very popular member of the squad. He was one of those bubbly characters who made players laugh and he helped generate a good atmosphere. The other players also respected him as a player. Trevor had scored consistently throughout his career and had netted vital goals in helping Boro reach the first division and his team-mates believed in him.

One or two players had a dig at me about the piece, notably Alan Kernaghan, who was angry that I would even think of suggesting such a thing. He questioned my right to write the story in the first place and said the other players were not happy with me. I sympathised with Alan's feelings, but I had to publish the story because I knew that Trevor's days were numbered at Boro.

Sure enough, Senior was sold to Reading on October 10. Maybe the players were a little wiser after the event. One or two of them told me that Rioch did not enjoy Senior's training ground repartee and wisecracks, especially when the manager was trying to give a team-talk.

My personal opinion was that it was a clash of personalities which led to Senior's departure. He was potentially a threat to the manager's rigid control of the players. Rioch, who knew he had to keep his small squad swimming in the same direction, had made a ruthless decision to prevent the players from being sucked under. I would never want to question the manager's right to make any changes he deems fit in order to maintain his level of respect and have everybody pulling in the same direction, and the departure of Trevor Senior fitted this scenario. To quote the age-old Boro adage, there's no point having a manager if you don't back him and allow him to do things his way.

However, my own opinion, in hindsight, is that Boro would have had a much better chance of staying up if Senior had stayed. I feel that he would have scored sufficient goals to make a difference. Senior's eventual replacement, Peter Davenport, scored four goals in that season. I would have happily backed Senior to have doubled that tally. These extra goals could have made all the difference.

In the event, the Boro board backed Rioch to the hilt in supporting his planned changes up front, and stumped up £750,000 for him to sign English international Davenport from Manchester United in the November. It was a massive outlay and reflected a huge step forward. Not only were they playing alongside the big clubs, but they were also beginning to think like one.

Unfortunately the signing of Davenport was one which did not bring the anticipated benefits. Peter, a terrific goalscorer with United and previously with Nottingham Forest, was handed a huge responsibility at Boro but did not score enough goals. In this respect the gamble to fork out so much money on one player when the squad as a whole was rather thin, backfired.

Like everybody else, I would have loved to see Davenport score more goals. I liked Peter as a person. Despite having enjoyed experiences at two major clubs, he was not a big-time Charlie. He was a down to earth lad and as a result, fitted in well with the other players. In this respect Rioch had done his homework well.

However, I felt Davenport was unwittingly the catalyst for major changes into the dressing room mind-set. Maybe Senior, himself an experienced player with many years' football under his belt, started the ball rolling. Davenport's arrival contributed towards changes in the attitude of some of the players because he had tasted life at the highest level and could relate stories of how top players went about their business at other clubs, and how they were treated.

This gradual change in mental approach was inevitable at Boro as the squad grew in age and stature. Rioch had been able to keep his squad together as a result of a mixture of a paternal approach and a sergeant major mentality. But the boys were becoming men and it was increasingly difficult to maintain a rigid law and order regime.

Davenport must have found it very strange to enter a dressing room with such a regimented approach. The rules and regulations were many and varied and, while the young lads at Boro had never known anything else, a seasoned pro like Davenport had tasted different treatment elsewhere. He had come from clubs where players had occasionally questioned decisions from on high and had the opportunity to be more out-spoken.

Not that there was anything wrong with the way in which Rioch had imposed himself on the squad. He had assessed the situation from his early days at the club and reacted accordingly. Nobody could ever take away from the former Scottish international skipper what he had achieved with such slim resources on Teesside.

However, it was becoming increasingly difficult to extract such a high level of performance from a squad that was still wet behind the ears. The cracks were beginning to appear at the time when Davenport joined because the players were finding it increasingly difficult to maintain their above-standard performances every week. When Davenport arrived, Boro were in eighth position in the first division, but their early-season adrenaline as a result of their promotion was already seeping away.

Despite losing the opening three games, Boro had maintained a positive outlook early on. Boro went to Spurs in late September and played some great football on the quality White Hart Lane pitch, but I felt they were muscled out of the game in going down 3-2. Seven days later they responded to the Spurs defeat with a brilliant team effort at Coventry, where they won 4-3 after leading 4-1. Bernie Slaven scored a memorable hat-trick and went on to plug away relentlessly up front all season, finishing with a highly commendable 18 goals in league and cup.

In the next match, at home to West Ham, Gary Pallister was having an absolute stinker. The crowd were on his back and he seemed incapable of doing anything right. To make matters worse, Pally had received a standing ovation from the fans before the kick-off when he was officially presented with an international cap by chairman Colin Henderson having made his England debut against Hungary in the summer.

Pally's performance was so bad this particular afternoon that he was bright red in the face as one mistake followed another. Boro were struggling to impose themselves on the game too, until Pally decided to take matters into his own hands and make everything right again. He picked up the ball inside his own half, ran forward, evaded a couple of challenges, exchanged passes with Bernie Slaven, and then rammed home the mother of all goals from outside the box.

All that had gone before was suddenly forgotten. Pally was the crowd's hero after that goal, which proved to be the match-winner. I felt that Gary began to grow rapidly in stature as a player after that game and never looked back again.

The West Ham win was followed by a bad defeat when Boro went out of the League Cup at the hands of lowly Tranmere Rovers. Boro should have had the tie settled in the first leg, but they couldn't score and were held to a goalless draw at Ayresome.

They were out-battled in the return at Prenton Park and trudged off the pitch with their chins on their chests. It was a dreadful defeat and the manner of the performance was worrying. Rioch spent a long time with the players in a dressing room lock-in afterwards and did not appear for the routine post-match press conference. I was relayed a message from the dressing room that the players were not allowed to give any interviews.

I was standing at the foot of the coach steps when Rioch eventually came out of the dressing room with Colin Todd and strode purposefully on to the coach.

I asked Bruce for a comment as he started to climb the steps and he turned and said: "A picture paints a thousand words."

I'm not sure what that was supposed to mean but it is one of those comments you never forget. In the event I absolutely battered the team in the *Gazette* the following day and there were no complaints from anybody at the Boro.

Boro were fortunately faring a little better in the league. They won six out of nine games around that time and there were high hopes that they would dig their feet in and maybe just survive in the top flight. Unfortunately, they could not maintain this momentum.

First they had to settle for a run of drawn games, and then the defeats followed on behind. It was the first time I had witnessed a negative situation since Rioch took over and it was not enjoyable.

Just before Christmas Boro were held to a goalless draw at home to Charlton. Then we went to Everton for one of the many games against the Toffees they seem to have played over the years on Boxing Day. Boro went down 2-1 at Goodison and then drew 0-0 at Norwich City a couple of days later in what I regard as a traditional Boro festive fixture. It appears that every season Boro, and their fans, have to make an incredibly long trip to the other end of the country between Christmas and the New Year. It's amazing that the fixture list has never improved after in all these years.

Boro dug deep at the start of 1989 and managed to lift themselves to a new level at Ayresome Park, in front of their biggest crowd of the season of 24,411. On January 2 they beat mighty Manchester United by 1-0. The golden goal was scored by Peter Davenport, against his former club, his first for the Boro.

However, Boro were struggling for consistency and crashed to an appalling defeat the following Saturday. In 25 years of watching the Boro I've witnessed some great wins and some awful defeats. Their 2-1 loss at Ayresome at the hands of Fourth Division Grimsby Town in the third round of the FA Cup was the worst I have ever seen by any Boro team. It was worse than the defeat at Wrexham which was to follow in Bryan Robson's time.

The Grimsby defeat is a match which tends to have been generally forgotten in Boro's modern history, or maybe it has simply been brushed under the carpet. The Mariners were just an average fourth division side and three tiers below Boro when they came to Teesside. Boro's performance that day was both abject and alarming.

They did manage to lift themselves for the game at Southampton seven days later and won 3-1. I usually enjoy the long trips to the south coast and this was another memorable day out, even though it tanked down all day and was very cold. So it was a relief to be crammed behind glass in the enigmatic press box at The Dell, even if it was a potential death trap.

On all my visits to The Dell I could never understand how the press box ever received a safety certificate. It would never have been allowed by Boro's safety committee. It was incredibly narrow and was impossible to pass behind, or in front of, any reporter who had already taken his seat. If you were in any way claustrophobic then you had no chance.

There was a door in the middle of the press box which, fortunately, opened outwards, and the local media people seemed to deliberately arrive late so they had to be accommodated in the wider central part of the box. The two ends of the box narrowed as they reached the corners.

In fact if you were unfortunate to be allotted the end seats your face was pressed right up against the glass and the bench dug into your stomach. To make matters worse, whenever the Saints attacked, the fans in the back row would stand up en masse and it was difficult to see what was going on. Aye, it's a glamorous life this reporting lark.

Boro's victory helped to mask the damp, cold day, but then there are always nice people at Southampton. I once entered the reception area at The Dell and realised that I had completely forgotten to order my press pass. I suggested to the press steward that the fax with which I usually applied for my passes must have gone astray. The steward filled in a press pass for me without hesitation. You always appreciate the people at the clubs who try to look after you.

Boro needed someone to look after them following the win at Southampton, because the rest of the season just fell away in front of their eyes. After two successive draws in home games against Spurs and Coventry, which Boro easily could have won, Rioch took the players on a week-long break to Bermuda to try to blow away the cobwebs.

I would have loved to have been invited to fly out with the squad but no invitation came my way. Instead I had to ring Ayresome Park to obtain the club's Bermudan hotel telephone number in order to maintain a daily contact.

The team had been in Bermuda for a couple of days when I received a tip-off that Bernie Slaven had not travelled with them. I took two calls at the *Evening Gazette* from fans who insisted they had seen him in Middlesbrough.

It seemed unlikely as Rioch had said nothing when I spoke to him. He merely mentioned how the team was enjoying the break.

However, a call to the hotel proved that Bernie was not there. I asked for Slaven directly and spoke to his room-mate Gary Pallister.

Pally admitted Slaven was not there.

"Well where is he?" I asked.

"He's injured," said Pally.

It was a good try, but then Pally was not commissioned by the club to give away private information about the squad. I had a pretty good idea that Bernie was not on the treatment table at Ayresome Park, so the obvious story to write for the *Evening Gazette* was: "Where is Bernie Slaven?"

It was not until the team returned to Middlesbrough that Bruce informed me that Bernie had a fear of flying, and this was why he did not join the rest of the squad in Bermuda. I think I'm correct in recalling that Bruce told me that Bernie had been given permission to return home, which was understandable given the circumstances.

However, I had been receiving further calls from some well-informed fans. I had pretty good evidence that Bernie had returned from the players' London hotel base by himself, before the remainder of the party flew out to Bermuda. It meant that Bruce and the players must have had no idea where Bernie was when they boarded the plane.

I spoke to Bernie later and he admitted his fear of flying. He said it had surfaced during a previous pre-season trip to the United States, when the team were involved in a couple of really hairy flights.

"There were times when we were certain the plane was going to crash in the States," said Bernie. "I never wanted to go through that again."

I felt there was no disgrace in this. Most of us have phobias. I have long held a fear of heights, which fortunately has eased considerably in recent years, though I couldn't climb the Transporter steps to save my life.

From Bernie's point of view it was good that his fear was out in the open because it meant that he would receive plenty of support from the people around him whenever the possibility of having to catch a plane came up again. In fact I've flown with Bernie on several occasions and he's been great company, which suggests that, more often than not, he has conquered his demons.

Once the Bernie stories were all put to bed, it was back to concentrating on Boro's battle to get the ship afloat again. Unfortunately the vessel was beginning to let in water. The harder the players tried, the worse it got. In fact, following their 3-1 success at Southampton, they were to win just one further game in the whole of the remainder of the campaign, courtesy of two late goals from Slaven in a 2-1 mid-week win at West Ham.

Otherwise the players found it very hard going. They were in danger of losing the plot by the end of February. We went to Luton for a mid-week match and lost 1-0 and then went down 2-0 at Millwall three days later. They were two bad defeats on the road within a week. I could sense that the mood around the club was becoming tense. It was a relatively new experience for me with this squad. It was increasingly difficult to get interviews and hard for the players to talk positively.

Nobody at Boro wanted to see the team relegated, most of all the board. So they stumped up the cash for Bruce Rioch to go out and sign a new midfielder, which was the area where the team was having most problems.

Rioch brought in Mark Proctor from Sheffield Wednesday. Proc was a Boro lad through and through, having started his career with his hometown club before being snapped up by Brian Clough at Nottingham Forest. Proc had plenty of valuable experience and the ability to put his foot on the ball and help the team keep possession. Proc played well in the final ten games of the campaign, but was too late in arriving back on Teesside to slow up the slide.

Around that time, winger Mark Barham, who had been signed from Huddersfield earlier in the season and was trying to resurrect his career following a major injury, also broke into the side but Barham was to start only three games and had no opportunity to make an impact.

It was a mammoth task for any new players to try to lift the ailing team. Ironically the biggest impact in midfield at that time came from Gary Gill, who was restored to the side in mid March and produced a quartet of superb hard running performances which lifted the players around him. Gilly played in two memorable home performances against Everton and Southampton, both of which ended 3-3. Gary's impact was brief because he suffered the agony of a broken leg in the latter match, and that vital piece of added impetus was lost to the team.

In the event, Boro never gave up the ghost and stayed out of the bottom three until the very final game of the season. They went to Hillsborough on May 13 needing to beat Sheffield Wednesday to stay up. The Owls had also suffered from a disappointing campaign and were not completely safe themselves. It was not to be Boro's day. The home side always had the edge as drab Boro were beaten 1-0 and not only fell in the bottom three, but also into Division Two.

Despite the run of poor results, the Boro players had given their all to try to keep the club in the top flight, but lack of confidence in the second half of the campaign proved costly. Simply staying out of the bottom three all the way through to the final match was a major achievement in itself for such a small squad.

It brought to mind Rioch's portent at the start of the campaign when he stressed that promotion might have come too quickly for the team. It had been an exhausting season and Boro's lack of quality, mainly in the central area, had cost them dear.

So the crazy post-liquidation Boro roller coaster kept on rattling away. In the three seasons since liquidation, the up and down story of the club was unrelenting. Life was never boring supporting and following the Boro. Yet as time went on, the never-ending story would become bigger season by season.

CHAPTER 7

THE chill winds of change began to sweep through the corridors of Ayresome Park when Gary Pallister was sold to a British club record £2.3m in early September of 1989.

The fee represented a massive influx of cash into the club's coffers, but the loss of Pallister was a major blow for the dressing room. Pally had developed into a vital part of the bedrock on which Bruce Rioch's team was founded. The Pallister-Tony Mowbray partnership was as good as any young centre-back combination as you would find anywhere in the Football League. It had served the team so well since the club's rebirth from the ashes of liquidation.

Not that Boro allowed Pallister to leave without a fight. There's no way that Rioch wanted to see his effective centre-back partnership broken up, nor did the club's board of directors. Everybody is entitled to have their ambitions and the reality was that Pallister had set his heart on Old Trafford. The glory days of players longing for nothing more than simply to wear the Boro shirt were consigned to the past.

Most of the Boro squad were now much more worldly than they had been in the summer of 1986, when simply ensuring that a weekly wage continued to come into the household was the acceptable bottom line. The players realised there was a great big world out there, potentially offering much more lucrative employment than relegated Boro could offer. Moving away from Teesside was suddenly an attractive proposition for those who felt they were good enough to hack it elsewhere, particularly at bigger clubs.

Pallister was one of those players whose eyes had been turned and he already had two England caps under his belt. He had been outside Teesside, met top internationals from other clubs and had realised that if he wanted to make it big time, and recoup the cash and medals that went with it, then he would not benefit from staying at Middlesbrough for the rest of his career.

Speculation of Manchester United's interest in Pallister had started during the summer. There were regular stories appearing in the Sunday papers that United had lodged bids of up to £1.5m for the Boro defender. I checked out the stories with Rioch every time they appeared, but the manager dismissed them out of hand. Rioch certainly appreciated the immense importance of Pallister to his team and did not want to see reports appearing in the media which might suggest Boro were weak when it came to hanging on to their best players.

Rioch never admitted to me that United had made any offers for Pallister. In fact the 'offers' may well have been nothing more than enquiries during the summer but I knew from experience that the reports of United's interest were far from groundless. There is no smoke without fire in these situations. The fact that the stories continued to gather pace over a course of several weeks was a clear indication that United were desperate to sign Pallister.

However, Boro initially stood firm and Pallister began the 1989/90 season as a Boro player. In the event, he was to play only three games.

The rumours continued to grow stronger. Suddenly I began to hear whispers that Pallister was determined to get away. I didn't want to see him leave; I always got on well with Pally, and still do. As a football fan, I always prefer to see a player stay loyal to the club in these situations, but I could hardly blame Pally for being tempted by such a golden career opportunity.

Gary was well aware of the kind of money that was on the table at Old Trafford. It was a massive career move with potential financial security for life and the opportunity to put medals in his top drawer; the kind of step up the ladder that anybody would want to make in any walk of life.

In the event, the Pallister saga produced the outcome which we have seen on many occasions in football. Once a player with a high market value has made it clear he is not happy, it becomes inevitable that his club will eventually decide the time has come to cash in.

I was tipped off that Boro chairman Colin Henderson and his fellow directors had finally agreed to meet Alex Ferguson and his negotiating team. The meeting was arranged at the Cleveland Tontine. The object, quite clearly, was to try to hammer out a fee for the transfer of Gary Pallister. There was no way that I was going to receive an invite to the meeting, but I could hardly wait to check it out the following morning.

I rang Henderson first thing and he confirmed that not only had the deal been done, but Boro had secured a record fee for a defender of £2.3m, which at that time was absolutely massive.

Henderson took no pleasure in seeing Pallister leave, but this feeling of disappointment was countered by the huge amount of money which Boro had squeezed out of United.

Henderson revealed to me that the two parties had set up camp in two separate rooms at the Tontine and regularly came together for detailed discussions before temporarily splitting up and discussing the ramifications of what had just been said. Whenever Ferguson and his team returned to the negotiating table, they discovered that the fee had increased. This happened on several occasions. Henderson and Co were determined to squeeze every last penny out of United.

In the end they secured the kind of fee which United had never contemplated paying at the start of the talks. Boro insisted that United would have to pay dearly, and they did. The final fee was a negotiating coup from Boro's point of view.

Despite the immense fee, I knew the Boro fans would be disappointed to see Pallister leave. We had all watched him mature from a nervous, gangly youth into a cultured defender who always seemed to have that little extra split-second – always a sign of high quality. Pally was far from the finished product, as United were to discover during his first 18 months or so at Old Trafford. But once he found his feet, there was no stopping him. In the end not only did United get value for money but Ferguson had the last laugh when Pally was later sold back to Boro at a profit for £2.5m.

To make matters worse, Boro were never really to benefit from that £2.3m in the way they should have done. Even with money to burn, they initially faced a major problem in replacing Pallister. There were a lot of good defenders around at that time, but most of them were playing in the First Division. Unless you can pay obscene wages, which was out of the question, you can't attract current England internationals to a second division club. In this respect it was almost impossible to replace Pallister with a player anywhere near his level of ability.

Rioch was forced to look at players who were on their way up the ladder, rather than already at the top. Eventually he went to Mansfield Town for their young defender Coleman, in the hope that he might develop into a top-notch player.

Coleman certainly had his qualities and was a 110 percenter but he suffered injuries on Teesside and I felt he never really had the opportunity to get his feet under the table. He was a very personable lad who went on to have good career elsewhere, but he probably came to Boro at the wrong time. In any case, the task of stepping into Pallister's shoes was always going to place a heavy burden on the shoulders of his replacement.

Coleman arrived on Teesside towards the end of September. Rioch had already moved to strengthen the team's weakest area, which was the midfield, during the summer. He snapped up the experienced Trevor Putney from Norwich City and little-known winger Alan Comfort from Leyton Orient, and both players had little problem settling into the dressing room.

Putney in particular was a very bubbly character, always full of quips and a great guy to have around. I've bumped into him a few times on the media circle when Boro have been playing in the south, and he's not changed one bit.

Comfort was completely different to Putney, quiet and considered in his comments, and he displayed a high level of intelligence which you don't always see in footballers! Again, he was a highly likeable lad and a vital addition to the squad as he was the orthodox left-footed winger which Boro had needed for a long time.

While the new faces were desperately needed, it must still have been strange for the likes of Putney and Comfort coming into a dressing room where the air was still thick with the spectre of relegation. Even as the season was about to get underway, I could sense that a little bit of the edge had gone out of the banter of the players.

I feared that Boro might not bounce back to the top flight at the first attempt, especially as there were so many strong clubs in the second division, like Leeds, Sheffield United, Newcastle, Blackburn and West Ham.

At first it appeared my worries would be unfounded. Boro started the season in terrific style, stuffing Wolves 4-2. However, that little bit of luck which Boro probably needed early on, deserted them. Few of us who were at Elland Road for the second game of the campaign will forget that incredible Leeds winner in the closing minutes, when a tame low drive hit a divot and shot over Kevin Poole's shoulder and into the net. It was uncanny, Boro did not get the point they deserved that night. It was a signal that Bruce Rioch was no longer going to enjoy happy times as the managerial chair gradually became very hot indeed.

After Leeds, Boro went to Roker Park for a Sunday derby against Sunderland and again lost 2-1. Most derbies tend to be very close games, this was no different. However, Boro didn't give any indications that they were capable of winning on the day and I can remember feeling at that time that the spark was missing.

It was Pallister's final game for the club. I wondered if there was a possibility that Boro's performances would improve with the weight of the Pally-for-United speculation finally removed from the players' backs. In the event it got worse rather than better and Boro won only three games up until the middle of November.

Rioch's regular side now contained fewer than half of the players who had helped build such strong foundations after liquidation. The team was beginning to change but the bunker mentality was lost. Rioch's new-look line-up never really gelled that season and the manager eventually paid a heavy price.

In addition to struggling to find the right blend on the pitch, Bruce was not having the same effect in the dressing room. There were a lot more senior and worldly players in there than before, subsequently the manager's combination of tight rules and motivational talks were no longer having the same effect.

Boro were beginning to lose at home on a regular basis, especially to teams they would have stuffed out of sight two years earlier. Crowds at Ayresome Park were also dipping dramatically. When Boro went to Newcastle in early November they had failed to win in six games. In the event Rioch's men forced a battling 2-2 draw against the Magpies, but suffered a major bodyblow when winger Alan Comfort was carried off towards the end of the first half after being hurt in a tackle close to the dugouts. It was a setback for the side as a whole because Comfort had settled in well at Boro and, as he gradually got to grips with the higher standard of football, there was a belief he could become a genuine force in the second division.

Comfort never played again. After a long battle in rehab, he was eventually forced to concede defeat and retired because of the injury he sustained. I interviewed Alan on several occasions afterwards, both in the days following his injury and when it became obvious his playing career was over. At no time did he ever express remorse, regret or sour grapes over what had happened to him. As a thoughtful and deeply religious person, the injury probably further strengthened Alan's personal beliefs and his love of God.

It was no surprise, therefore, to see Comfort later join the ministry and begin a new life as a curate in a parish in London, quickly rising to vicar. The church has been his vocation ever since. Again, he's a player I have met up with on several occasions since because he has undertaken, and thoroughly enjoyed, local radio reporting assignments for north-east stations when Boro have played in the south.

The loss of Comfort was a blow because he was the only left-sided attacking player in the squad and his absence unbalanced the side. It created a dilemma for Rioch which he partially solved by pushing Peter Davenport out wide. The £750,000 striker went on to play a lot of his football on the left flank during the rest of the campaign.

In front of goal, Davenport was struggling more than ever to be the scoring threat he had been with Forest and United. He scored just three goals in the whole of Boro's Division Two campaign. While Peter did his bit as a team member, the goal contribution which Boro had expected from him on Teesside never materialised and he turned out to be a disappointing buy.

In early February of that season, in an attempt to solve the team's problems in front of goal, Rioch went out and bought striker Ian Baird from Leeds

United. On the face of it, the move made sense, and Baird was to play his part in the club's battle to beat the drop. The craggy Yorkshireman was a no-nonsense player who took no prisoners on the pitch, though he represented a different type of player to the less direct types that Rioch had previously preferred to bring into the club.

Baird was not a prolific goalscorer by any means, but there was a hope and belief that his physical presence would make it easier for those around him because he was one of those players who was happy to take the knocks. When I spoke to him for the first time, I realised that Baird was mentally very tough. He wasn't the kind of man who suffered fools gladly. He spoke as he thought and, while he wasn't the greatest ball player, he took his solid outlook with him on to the pitch.

Baird took over up front from Alan Kernaghan, who I felt was one of the few players to make any real progress in the 1989/90 season. Kernaghan was Boro through and through, but he was not usually in Rioch's first-choice team and had to work harder than most for his opportunities.

Kernaghan had done a good job in deputising at the back alongside Tony Mowbray before Coleman arrived on Teesside to replace Pallister. Then he had slotted in up front alongside key striker Bernie Slaven, leading to Davenport being utilised on the left. It meant that Kernaghan had to accept a utility role because he could also do a job in midfield. The bottom line was that Alan was happy just to be in the team. He was effective in whatever he did in 1989/90 and that's why it was the breakthrough season for him. His career was to take off spectacularly later under Lennie Lawrence.

Kernaghan's best moment of Rioch's last season came in late November when he scored a hat trick in a 4-2 midweek win at Blackburn. He played up front and his finishing was lethal. This was Boro's first win for two months but Kernaghan was never allowed to bask in the full extent of the glory which should have come his way following his achievement. Rioch banned the players from speaking to the media after the game.

Just before Christmas, a crowd of 11,000 watched Boro beat Leicester City 4-1 at Ayresome. Boro were still capable of putting together a good team performance on their day, but such days were becoming few and far between.

It was in the February that Rioch admitted to me that he had lost the support of the players.

We were chatting in his office one day when he suddenly told me: "I've lost the dressing room ... but I'll get it back."

Bruce's admission that the players were not responding to him any more was an honest and admirable comment to make to a local newspaper reporter, even if it was clearly not intended for publication. Rioch was worldly enough to appreciate the reality of the difficult situation he was having to try to deal with. In this respect it gave him a better chance of being able to deal with it.

However, I felt that Rioch might not be given the opportunity to try to turn things around. Even somebody like Bruce whose incredible post-liquidation contribution at the Boro could hardly have been bettered, was not above the unwritten rules of the game. The team's slide during the last six months had been horrific both in its speed and its nature. Now Boro were in grave danger of slipping back to the third division where they had started.

Boro were still a relatively fledgling club, because it was deemed that everything had started afresh in 1986, but the club was being run on careful lines as a business, and the spectre of a second successive relegation was not one the board could stomach.

Ironically, at that time, the club was on its way to Wembley for the first time in its history. The Zenith Data Systems Cup semi-final games against Aston Villa produced Boro's two most memorable performances of the whole season, and Ayresome Park was rocking at its foundations as Boro eventually triumphed after extra time in the decider, thanks to goals from Bernie Slaven and Paul Kerr against his former club.

This ensured Boro of their place in front of the Twin Towers. It hardly mattered that the Zenith Data Systems Cup was also known – by everybody who hadn't been good enough to reach the final - as the Mickey Mouse Cup.

While the cup success was something of a distraction, Boro were losing all too often in the league. Consecutive home defeats at the hands of West Ham and Watford in early March were very depressing and left the club in a very difficult situation. If results continued like this, then Boro would definitely go down.

It was a dire situation which was not lost on the board and they decided to take action. At that time Boro were training every day at the Maiden Castle sports complex in Durham City, which was linked to Durham University. It was an ideal training area for the team, being in beautiful surroundings with the River Wear running along one of its borders although Maiden Castle's location was not so good for the Middlesbrough-based media.

Initially I had driven up there every day from Middlesbrough, filed my daily report for the back page of the *Evening Gazette*, and then drove back again. It was particularly difficult making the two journeys every day that winter because the roads were regularly icy, and driving was problematic at times. This was not lost on the players either, who regularly gave me reports of prangs in which they had been involved as their vehicles skidded on the ice in the Durham area. In fact there was a grave danger of Rioch losing players as a result of these occasional car crashes.

Eventually the manager decided that my five journeys a week were unnecessary. So he had devised a system whereby he handed me four stories, all strong enough to make back page leads, every Monday. This effectively covered me for the first four days of the week. At that time Bruce was better at devising stories than I was. Only if a Boro story appeared during the week in another publication and needed immediate comment, was I to contact him. Bruce's new system worked very well, and as a result I was making personal visits to see him on Mondays and Fridays only.

It was on Friday, March 9 that I drove up to Maiden Castle for my regular visit. Boro were travelling to Hull City the following day and I was looking for team news. When I walked into the training ground's reception area, Boro assistant manager Colin Todd was pacing the floor. As soon as he saw me, Toddy approached and said: "Don't take your coat off. Get back in your car immediately and drive back to Middlesbrough because the chairman wants to see you urgently."

I had got well used to Colin and his wisecracks over the last couple of years. He was a wind-up merchant who was always looking to play a trick or two. I always felt Toddy was the perfect foil for Rioch because he was the vital link between the manager's room and the dressing room.

If Rioch wanted to hand out instructions which might not always be favourable to the players, then Todd would see that the players accepted them with a smile rather than a grimace. He had a lovely knack of dealing with the players and could always have a laugh and a joke with them and take some of it back. This was at a time when Rioch had to stay a little bit aloof because of his managerial position, and I always felt that Rioch and Todd were a near perfect combination.

However, when Colin told me to go back to Middlesbrough and see chairman Colin Henderson I laughed out loud. I'd fallen for too many tricks in the past. I told Colin that I was there to see Bruce and I'd stick to my original plan. But Colin insisted that Rioch wasn't at Maiden Castle and he handed me an address in Albert Road, where I was to meet the chairman.

I still wouldn't bite immediately, but Toddy was insistent.

"This isn't a wind-up, it's serious," he kept saying.

The longer Todd persisted, the more I suspected this was no jape.

Despite my constant contact with club officials, I had not received any off the record tips that Rioch's job might be in danger. Basic logic told me that Rioch could not carry on in the post forever while results were so poor, but there had been no official whispers from within.

If Toddy's words had been a wind-up, then the *Evening Gazette* would have had no story that evening because I would have been left up the creek without a paddle. In the event we got a massive exclusive.

I drove back to Middlesbrough and went looking for the offices in the address that Toddy had given me. It was no wind-up as Colin Henderson was waiting for me. He didn't beat about the bush and immediately informed me that Bruce Rioch had left the club and had been replaced as manager by Colin Todd.

I couldn't help but raise a smile. The system of appointing from within was a not a new one, but I wasn't sure that Toddy filled the criteria. Still, it worked elsewhere. Liverpool were the best club around at that time and they had a policy of replacing the outgoing manager with somebody from within the club's current coaching staff.

Despite appointing initial unlikely incumbents like Bob Paisley, Joe Fagan and Ronnie Moran, it had worked incredibly well for them. It ensured that 'The Liverpool Way' was always maintained.

Henderson made a reference to Liverpool in explaining the change of manager. He stressed how the board was determined to create continuity within the club, despite Rioch's departure, and in the way in which the team played football.

There was some logic there, but I had never seen Toddy as a manager. He was too close to the players. I could not see how they would respond to him if he started ranting and raving. In the event, I was to be proved wrong, because Colin turned out – in my opinion – to be a much better manager than I could ever have imagined. If things had been different in the long term, I think he could have been hugely successful at the Boro. Even so, at the time it seemed a strange appointment.

Henderson went to some lengths to publicly thank Rioch for what he had achieved for the club. He was keen to see that the manager did not depart under a cloud despite recent results. Certainly, without Rioch at the helm, it's difficult to imagine Boro being capable of climbing back up the divisions and regaining their self-respect as quickly as they had lost it.

Rioch made mistakes at Boro, like all managers. The huge outlay on Peter Davenport, the early sale of Trevor Senior and the massive responsibility placed on the shoulders of Mark Brennan are some which come to mind.

Despite that, what he achieved initially with such a wafer-thin squad was beyond compare, and I was delighted to see Bruce go on and enjoy success as a manager with other top clubs because he deserved it.

I rang Bruce for a comment and he was a little distant, and made it clear he did not want to talk on the record.

"I'll talk to you later, at a more appropriate time," he said.

However, once I had put the phone down I realised there was no more appropriate time than the present. So the Rioch sacking interview never took place, though Bruce has always been the best of pals whenever I've met up with him since then.

Rioch's departure from Middlesbrough, as relayed exclusively in the *Gazette*, came as a massive shock to the vast majority of the club's fans who had stuck solidly behind him despite the horrendous run of league results. I thought it was the correct decision to sack Rioch at the time, because I knew the players were no longer on his wavelength. I honestly believe Boro would have been relegated back to Division Three if he had stayed.

This was not a view which was universally popular. Many fans, most of them looking forward to the club's first ever Wembley appearance, could not believe that Rioch had gone. Within a matter of days I received dozens of phone calls from angry supporters, not to mention the huge deluge of letters which poured into the *Gazette*.

Many fans revered Rioch, and they had wanted him to stay in charge at Boro whatever happened on the field.

However, dropping back into the third division was not an option the directors wanted to face. The board had taken the logical decision under the circumstances, and also the right one. I felt that the decision to appoint Todd as his successor did not make sense at the time but during his brief reign as manager Todd totally transformed the club – even if he was to lose the dressing room under naïve circumstances 14 months later.

CHAPTER 8

IT was a magnanimous gesture when Colin Todd asked skipper Tony Mowbray to lead out the Boro team at Wembley in the Zenith Data Systems Cup Final.

Mogga was forced to miss Boro's first appearance in front of the Twin Towers through injury. So this was a superb way to give the popular captain a genuine sense of involvement for the big occasion.

The Redcar defender had become a big favourite with the fans, having improved from raw beginnings and developed both in ability and quality during the Bruce Rioch era. So there were no dissenting voices on Teesside when Mogga led out to the Boro for the clash with first division Chelsea.

In handing the task to Mowbray, new manager Todd was also aware of the fact that Boro had qualified for the Wembley showdown with the Blues as Rioch's team. Boro had beaten Port Vale, Sheffield Wednesday, Newcastle United and Aston Villa to reach the final, and Rioch was in control of the side for all of these games. In taking a back seat in the build-up, Todd was able to avoid the limelight and make it clear he wanted no personal glory for what the Rioch-led Boro side had previously achieved.

Todd told me several days before the final that Mogga would be leading out the team. It was an exclusive back page lead in the *Evening Gazette*. However, I recall that Toddy didn't really give me any reasons for his decision, even if they were patently obvious. As Bruce's right-hand man, and good friend, Colin clearly intended to make no comments which would invite comparisons to the previous regime.

I found Toddy generally much more elusive with his comments than Rioch when he was talking to me on a daily basis. That's despite the fact I got very close to him and still regard him as a good friend today. I knew from the start that Colin was happy to have me on board. We already knew each other so well. He never avoided an interview, even if he didn't always say what I wanted him to. He gave me plenty of tip-offs, but always left it up to me to fill in the gaps.

Todd was only three games into the management lark when Boro went to Wembley. So that was another reason for him taking a back seat on this ground-breaking occasion. With only ten second division games remaining in which to save the club from the dreaded drop, Todd really did have other things on his mind.

His first league game in charge of the Boro produced a half-decent performance, forcing a goalless draw at Hull City on a bone hard pitch. I can't remember too much about the game. In fact the most memorable part of the day was the fight between two journalists in the press box at Boothferry Park before the kick-off.

The wooden press box at Hull was reached via an open, rickety metal staircase which was situated behind the back of the main stand. As a person who dislikes heights intensely, I always found the climb difficult and even lost sleep thinking about it. The staircase's metal frame was ornate, with holes cut into the metal. As you tried to concentrate on making sure your feet landed firmly in the middle of every step, you could see the bare ground becoming increasingly distant beneath you, inviting you to slip through the gaps.

The climb was enough to put anyone in a sweat, but it was still a shock to the system to see two grown men fighting in a press box. As a boxing fan I enjoyed this little set-to, though the two lads hardly stuck to the Marquis of Queensberry rules. I'm not sure what sparked the fight, though it was definitely a domestic issue and didn't involve anyone from Teesside. I think the result of this little duel was a draw, with both egos remaining intact. However, as a result of the confrontation, the two contestants didn't speak to each other for the remainder of the afternoon. It must have made watching the goalless draw even worse.

With regular left-back Colin Cooper having suffered an injury-hit season so far, Todd made his one signing of the final 13 games shortly after the drawn game at Hull. He snapped up left-back Jimmy Phillips from Oxford United for £250,000. This was a more than useful signing because Phillips was experienced and a natural left-footer, something which was a rarity at the Boro at the time.

Jimmy was also a 110 per center, a true professional and a nice lad to boot. He was always happy to give interviews and I can't ever remember him having a bad word to say about anybody. Jimmy hardly missed a game during his time on Teesside and gave Boro good value for their transfer fee. So it was frustrating to see him receive criticism from the terraces towards the end of his spell at Ayresome, as I don't feel that he deserved it. I believe he was a better player than that.

It's good to see that Jimmy is still active in the game as he regularly accompanies Bolton Wanderers reserves on their annual trips to Teesside.

Jimmy's Boro debut, and Colin Todd's first home game, was not a memorable one. Boro were crushed 3-0 by promotion chasing Blackburn Rovers. It was a bad beating, but they had little time to lick their wounds. The team headed straight off to Dartmoor to settle into their base at Moretonhampstead ahead of the ZDS Final.

Boro were staying in a large hotel which contained its own sporting complex and was situated on the outskirts of the Dartmoor village. The facilities within the grounds ensured the players were able to train, and to relax, ahead of the league game at Plymouth Argyle on the Tuesday and the cup final the following Sunday.

After filing my match reports following the Blackburn defeat, I drove to Moretonhampstead in an *Evening Gazette* pool car. I had booked a room for four nights in a 16th Century coach inn. I was very impressed. My room was spacious, with ancient wooden beams forming the ceiling and a genuine log fire facing the king-sized bed. I could not fail to let my mind wander and imagined how many well known people might have stayed in this very room over the centuries.

However, I did not have much opportunity to enjoy my surroundings. This was essentially a hectic working trip. I needed to carry out lots of pre-cup final interviews with both manager and players, in addition to reporting on the Plymouth game. All the stories had to be filed to the *Gazette* on a daily basis to fill the newspaper's regular Boro slots and also the special cup final supplement which we were producing to commemorate the occasion. It was nevertheless a rare pleasure to have the opportunity to spend some time in such an historic and atmospheric inn, especially as the tab was on the *Gazette*!

Having never been to Dartmoor before, I drove through the centre of the moor the following day in order to reach Plymouth for the second division fixture. It was an exhilarating experience and required some careful driving as the famous wild horses regularly trotted across the road, oblivious to the traffic.

The game was also exciting, as Boro were a revelation that night. They played with plenty of freedom and were worthy 2-1 winners with goals from Ian Baird and Mark Brennan. It was three valuable points towards the relegation struggle and the players were in great heart afterwards. It ensured that I had no problems picking up my interviews in the build-up to the cup final.

The players left Home Park in their team coach and, having chatted to the driver before departing, he told me he was returning to Moretonhampstead via the A38, which was the major arterial road in the area. I much more fancied the trip across Dartmoor again and my passenger, Ray Robertson from *The Northern Echo*, had no problems with us taking the direct route. So I set off to link up with the B3212 which cuts right through the middle of the moor.

What I hadn't anticipated was the cloud of thick fog which engulfed us as soon as I started to climb towards the moor. It was a proverbial pea-souper. I am not exaggerating when I say that I could not see more than five yards in front of me.

I should really have turned back, and circumvented the moor on the A38 but, having travelled several miles already, I was stubborn and decided to stick with it. I can't remember Ray protesting, but I'm sure that he won't have been happy because company cars don't go slowly, even in thick fog, as anyone who drives one will know.

The B3212 was a narrow, winding road and it was near impossible trying to stay on the road, never mind sticking to the left hand side lane. But I persevered and left Ray to sweat through the experience. The 40-minute journey back to Moretonhampstead eventually took us around and hour and a half. I was fortunate because, as I recall, I rarely passed another vehicle coming in the opposite direction. But if any of the wild horses had strayed on to the road as I drove past, then there could have been a disaster and the *Gazette* would have had to send out a replacement reporter.

The remainder of the week on Dartmoor went well. Once I had filed my final interview to the *Gazette* on the Friday morning, I set off back to Teesside. I don't remember stopping during the long journey and was home just before teatime. I had something to eat, picked up the wife and kids and all our luggage and then drove all the way to Watford, where we was staying in a hotel prior to the cup final. It was a rather hectic day in which I had driven more than 600 miles but it was Boro's first appearance at Wembley after all.

The team travelled directly from Moretonhampstead to their pre-match base in London but must have left their souls behind on Dartmoor. I took the tube from Watford to Wembley with my family, full of excitement and anticipation, along with Boro's 35,000 fans. In the event the day was a huge let-down.

Boro could not handle the occasion and it passed them by. They went down 1-0 with Tony Dorigo scoring directly from a free-kick to give Chelsea the trophy. Boro hardly put two attacks together in the whole game. Even the fact that I had seen Boro play at Wembley for the first time could not mask my huge sense of disappointment. It was a long journey home that night.

After a couple of hours sleep, I was in the *Gazette* offices very early the next morning to write up all my reports. That day the *Gazette* carried the legendary headline "Just Because Someone In Blue Scored A Goal Doesn't Mean We Lost". I understood the sentiments expressed in that headline but could not agree with them. I felt badly let down; not because Boro had lost, but because they had failed to perform.

Colin Todd admitted to me afterwards that he was relieved to get the game out of the way because it had interfered with the team's main task, which was to stay out of the third division.

Boro did respond very well to their no-show at Wembley by beating Oldham Athletic 1-0 at Ayresome Park six days later with the winning goal coming from Bernie Slaven. The crowd was 17,000, which was not too bad for the time, but I couldn't help wondering where the other 18,000 Wembley fans had gone.

Unfortunately Boro couldn't maintain the momentum following the win against the Latics. They won just one of the next eight games, when Bernie Slaven and Ian Baird scored in a 2-0 home win against Bradford City. Bad home defeats at the hands of Ipswich and Barnsley suggested that Boro might not have the bottle for the battle as they edged ever nearer to the drop.

So it was all down to the final game of the campaign, at home to neighbours Newcastle United. The Magpies had enjoyed a decent season but needed to win to retain a chance of snatching automatic promotion, depending on the results of the other games. Boro would almost certainly be relegated if they failed to win. The newspapers were full of stories during the week claiming that the Magpies were going to send Boro back into the third division. Judging by Boro's recent form and the task they faced, you couldn't argue with them.

Todd had not been able to call on the injured Mowbray during any of his 13 games, while Trevor Putney was a long-term injury victim. Boro were also missing Gary Parkinson, Peter Davenport and Stuart Ripley. Twenty-year-old Owen McGee was recalled to the side but there were obvious weaknesses and, on paper, the Magpies held all the aces.

In the event, Boro went on to produce one of those memorable performances which will live for all time with those fans who were fortunate enough to be there. Boro defied all the odds, played some remarkable attacking football and won 4-1. Slaven and Baird both scored twice and there was no fluke about the result. Newcastle were overwhelmed.

As a result, Boro were safe and Colin Todd had helped to keep the club in the second division after only 13 games in charge. Boro won just four of them, but it was enough.

Slaven's brace against Newcastle took his goal tally for the campaign to 32 in all competitions, which was an incredible achievement considering that Boro had struggled badly at times. I felt that Bernie's contribution was the achievement of the season in the north-east, bar none. I argued that fact when I met up with my fellow judges when we met in Newcastle to select the winners of the Hennessy Player of the Year Awards.

The Hennessy awards night was the north-east's most prestigious football event at that time and I always felt that it was an honour for me to be part of the selection panel. We met at the Civic Centre in Newcastle at the end of every season and were always treated to an excellent meal while we discussed the merits of the various award contenders.

The meal was a food-tasting exercise because the same courses were served up to the gathered dignities and club representatives at the awards night at the same venue, though with one or two slight alterations which we may have suggested to the chef at the selection lunch.

Anyway, on this particular occasion, the judging was not to my taste. Despite my protestations in a heated debate, my fellow judges looked at St James's rather than Ayresome, and the winner of the main award was selected as Newcastle striker Mick Quinn. As I recall, Quinn had scored three or four more goals than Slaven during the campaign, but in a hugely more successful side.

United did not win promotion, despite Quinn's goals, while Boro would certainly have gone down without Slaven's goal contribution. The panel's decision to select Quinn as Player of the Year left a sour taste with me and, as a result, I rarely enjoyed taking part in future selection get-togethers.

WILLIE MADDREN – right manager at the wrong time.
Willie was a terrific judge of a player, but his attempts to take the Boro forward were hampered by the club's ever increasing financial problems.

BRUCE RIOCH – pictured here at Hartlepool in Boro's first match after liquidation, built a remarkably resilient team from journeymen pros and untested youngsters.

TELLING IT LIKE IT IS – Bruce Rioch sends instructions from the dug out, while his right hand man Colin Todd looks on. Todd went on to save the Boro from a return from the Third Division and then took the club into the play offs. Also pictured is physio Tommy Johnson.

LOOK I'VE SCORED – Colin Cooper, pictured after scoring against West Brom in 1987, typified the phenomenal young talent which benefited from Bruce Rioch's reign. Cooper went on to play for England and, in an illustrious career, is now on the coaching staff at the Boro.

WE'VE DONE IT! Ecstatic Boro chairman Colin Henderson hugs Bruce Rioch after the club reached the First Division following the dramatic events of the second leg of the play off final against Chelsea at Stamford Bridge in 1988.

TEAMS OF ALL THE TALENTS – Eric Paylor's last appearance in an 11-a-side game was against Steve Gibson's X1 at Billingham Synthonia. Paylor is pictured on the far left of the front row, while Gibson is third from the right on the back row.

JUST TRY AND STOP ME! Gary Pallister sets off on the blazing run which brought him a remarkable solo goal against West Ham in October 1988 and helped send his career in an upwardly mobile direction.

MAN INJURED REF! Alan Comfort lies badly hurt on the touchline at St James's Park while Bruce Rioch remonstrates to the ref. It was an horrendous injury which was to end Comfort's career, and also indicated that Rioch's luck was on the slide.

WE'RE ON OUR WAY TO WEMBLEY – Boro's triumphant players celebrate in the dressing room after beating Aston Villa in the second leg of the Zenith Data Systems Cup northern final in 1990. Back row: Mark Proctor, Peter Davenport, Tony Mowbray. Front row: Paul Kerr, Nicky Mohan, Owen McGee.

MORE AWARDS – Eric Paylor takes tight hold of two bottles of champagne which were later handed over to Tony Mowbray and Steve Pears, while the Evening Gazette competition winners look on.

MOGGA'S MOMENT – Boro's injured skipper Tony Mowbray proudly leads out the team for the Zenith Data Systems Cup Final at Wembley against Chelsea.

GREAT FRIEND AND CHAUFFUER – and not a sat nav in sight - Gordon Cox where he's most comfortable, behind the wheel of a car.

SIGN HERE PLEASE – Boro chairman Colin Henderson supervises the signing of Boro new boys John Hendrie and Robbie Mustoe in the summer of 1990.

TOP MAN – Boro winger John Hendrie receives his Man of the Match prizes from Eric Paylor and young fan Stephen Godfrey in September 1990.

PITY ABOUT THE MAC – Eric Paylor presents a Man of the Match award to winger Stuart Ripley on New Year's Day 1991.

I'M PLAYING FOR THE OTHER SIDE – Alan Kernaghan, on loan at Charlton Athletic, prepares to make a tackle on Boro striker Ian Baird during a match in South London in February 1991.

STILL HOT – Bernie Slaven gets in a shot against Watford at Ayresome Park in April 1992, but it was a rare opportunity for the free-scoring striker because his career at the Boro was coming to an end.

A NEW FUTURE – Boro chairman Steve Gibson poses with the new board of directors after finally settling the long-running shareholding wrangle by taking full control of the club. Also pictured are Graham Fordy, George Cooke and Reg Corbidge.

PREMIERSHIP BOUND – Boro boss Lennie Lawrence stands proudly with his triumphant team in the dressing room at Molineux in 1992 after Boro secured their place in the inaugural Premier League by beating Wolves.

WELCOME TO THE BORO – Boro's new signing Craig Hignett meets Ian Ironside, Jon Gittens, Andy Peake and John Hendrie following his arrival from Crewe Alexandra in November 1992.

SAFE HANDS – Boro skipper Steve Pears receives his Hennessy North-east Player of the Year award from Jack Charlton in May 1992.

WELCOME TO TEESSIDE – Boro's new boss Bryan Robson is greeted by Boro chief executive Keith Lamb on his arrival at Teesside International Airport.

THREE OF THE BEST – John Craggs, Stuart Boam and Willie Maddren are pictured as they walk around Ayresome Park with a host of other former players before the last game at the stadium against Luton Town.

CHAMPAGNE SUPER BORO – Bryan Robson is greeted with a bubble bath from his players as he arrives at Ayresome Park after Boro had won promotion in 1995.

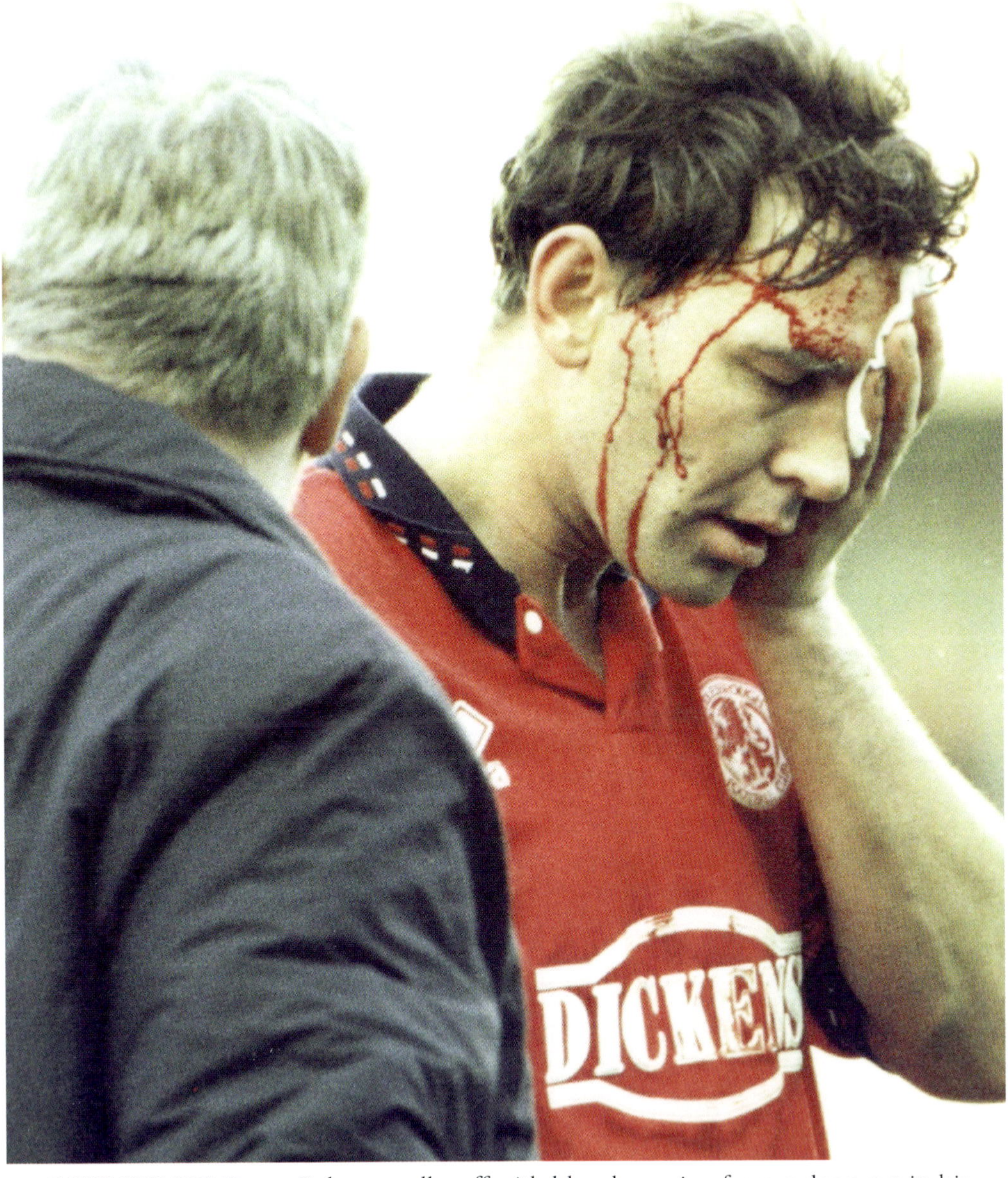

GORE BLIMEY! Bryan Robson walks off with blood pouring from a deep cut in his forehead after colliding with a post during a game at Millwall in February 1995.

IT WILL BE NICE WHEN IT'S FINISHED – Eric Paylor and Boro chairman Steve Gibson are pictured in front of the West Stand at the Riverside Stadium as work races on relentlessly to complete the construction in time for the start of the new season.

THE OLD AND THE NEW - The Ayresome Park gates in front of the Riverside Stadium, there's plenty tales from there in Volume 2

CHAPTER 9

COLIN Todd almost took Boro back into the first division at the first attempt. It was a startling effort from the former England international in his first full season in management.

I have always believed that Toddy did not receive the credit from the fans, and possibly not the directors, for what he achieved at Middlesbrough in such a short space of time.

The fact that Todd didn't take Boro all the way was partly down to himself. As Boro were preparing for crucial play-off games against Notts County, word reached the dressing room that the manager was planning major changes during the summer.

Several players were made aware before the play-offs - from whatever sources - that their futures at the club were in doubt. There was no official announcement from the club at that time but the players were left in no doubt that a clear-out was planned.

When Todd officially placed eleven players on the transfer list, following the second leg of the play-offs, nobody was surprised but the mood around the club was not very good to put it mildly and the play-offs were already lost.

I don't know whether the fact that players would be leaving was deliberately or accidentally leaked into the dressing room but a lot of senior players had reason to believe that their names were on the list, and it severely affected their personal performances against Notts County. The whole thing was a massive cock-up and ultimately cost Boro whatever chance they had of beating the Magpies. Too many senior players lost heart before a ball was kicked in the two games.

Todd's plans to completely overhaul the squad may have been in the club's best interests and may have had huge benefits - but we will never know. What is certain is that his plans were clearly not in the best interests of eleven members of the squad at that time. It is rather ironic that most of them ended up staying at the club while it was Todd himself who moved on.

I was waiting for the call when Colin rang me at the *Evening Gazette* after the play-off defeat to tell me that eleven players were available for transfer. I had been tipped off in advance by the players that they believed massive changes were in the offing. I could hardly have imagined, however, that so many players would be involved.

The attempted clear-out was a huge story for the *Gazette* at the time, and the names of all eleven players and their photographs were splashed across the front page of the newspaper.

I felt sorry for most of the players involved because I had a close relationship with them but I also believed that a manager must be given the right to manage, and if Todd insisted a clear-out was needed to turn things around, then that's the way it goes in football.

It was up to the club to back him or sack him and the Boro directors certainly did not sit back. In the event Toddy left the club that summer, without having the opportunity to make significant changes. I was disappointed for him because I felt that he had shown terrific potential as a manager, even though, for some reason, he never really hit it off with the fans.

Colin had surprised a lot of people by taking a previously ailing team to a higher level than might normally have been expected. The fact that he has since worked regularly both as a manager and coach is a tribute to the respect he has garnered within the game.

Toddy went on to prove himself elsewhere by enjoying a long career in management at Bolton, Derby and Bradford City. He won the first division title with Bolton and was Bradford's longest serving manager for 20 years. After leaving Valley Parade, Colin moved to the continent to take over the Randers in Denmark and was still at the helm there at the time of writing.

I always believed that Todd's ability to communicate with players on their level was one of his strengths as a manager, though one or two former Boro players may disagree with me. Despite my friendship with him, Toddy could be elusive with me and distant at times, though I always believed this was because he did not want to air every detail of the dressing room tittle-tattle with me, as Rioch had done so effectively on and off the record.

I've never met a manager yet who did everything right in his dealings in the transfer market, but I felt that Colin was a decent judge of individual ability and did relatively well with his signings, both at Boro and elsewhere. Again, this is open to interpretation, because it was the names on his list of transfer targets that summer which unnerved the Boro directors and led to his departure from Ayresome Park. He did not leave because he put eleven players on the transfer list.

When Colin took over the helm at Boro in March 1990, he was most certainly on a solid footing with most of the players. As first-team coach, he had been the one whose job it had been to put an arm around the shoulders of players who may have occasionally received the sharp end of Bruce Rioch's tongue for one reason or another.

It's not easy stepping up to manage those players that you have been a little too close to in the past, as Gareth Southgate must have discovered when he took over the Boro hot seat but Todd generally coped well with the task. Those 14 months in charge at Boro were very much a learning process for him, but he learned quickly before probably over extending himself in that fateful second summer.

Having guided Boro to last-gasp survival at the end of the 1989/90 campaign, Todd was given cash to strengthen the side in preparation for what turned out to be his only full season in command.

He made two terrific signings who were to give the club years of valuable service. Todd went to Leeds United and paid £500,000 for winger John Hendrie, and also snapped up the relatively unknown midfielder Robbie Mustoe from Oxford United for £375,000.

Hendrie was worldly wise and very experienced at the time of his arrival on Teesside, having already made a name for himself with Bradford and Newcastle, before spending 12 months at Leeds. The Scot was at Bradford at the time of the tragic fire in 1985 which cost the lives of 56 supporters and had a huge effect on John's life.

Hendrie was immensely popular with the Boro players because he was one of the boys and liked a laugh but he was a committed pro who always gave 110 per cent on the pitch. I found him great to interview because he maintained a healthy realism about the game.

Like Todd, I had been impressed with Mustoe when I saw him play for Oxford the previous season. Robbie was a non-stop running, bite-your-legs midfielder who could pass the ball to feet. He also knew where the goal was and turned out to be one of Boro's best servants of the modern era.

When Mustoe arrived on Teesside I found him to be still youthful and almost shy as a person, but he matured very quickly and was never out of his depth in any situation. He was not one of those players who always took the eye during a match, yet consecutive managers and coaches at the Boro always appreciated his massive and consistent contribution. As a result Mustoe was one of the first names on the Boro team-sheet throughout the nineties.

Todd's third major signing was to bring in the experienced Scottish international warhorse John Wark. There was little the 33-year-old had not encountered in the game and I wondered about his attitude when he was signed. In the event Wark came here to try to do himself justice and was a hard worker for the team. He always attacked the ball and had some great games for Boro, allied to a few disappointing ones.

There was no longer much power in the old legs and I felt he got by on commitment alone although Boro recorded 20 clean sheets in the second division that season so Wark's defensive contribution must have been very useful. I can recall Todd telling me that he believed Boro had never really made up for the loss of Gary Pallister, so Wark's experience was clearly a big factor in helping them fill that gap.

The fourth signing made by Todd was Martin Russell, a 23-year-old ball-playing midfielder from Scarborough. No doubt Todd brought Russell in as one for the future, but it didn't work out for the lad. He didn't adapt to life at the higher level and, while I never really got to know him, I believed that he found it hard at Boro.

For a team that had struggled the previous season, Boro got into the groove pretty quickly at the start of the 1990/91 season. Walk, Mustoe and Hendrie settled in swiftly and were regulars in the side throughout the campaign.

Boro opened with a goalless draw at home to West Ham and were then due to play at Plymouth the following Saturday. I had arranged to travel to Home Park with Gordon Cox as usual and we decided to leave Middlesbrough at 6am because of all the queuing traffic that we expected to meet in the West Country on the way. It was the last week of the traditional summer holiday period, which always seems to spark a late rush.

I drove round to Coxy's house and we set off in his car. However, we had travelled less than 15 miles down the A19 when the engine spluttered and died on us. It was not what we wanted to experience with the clock ticking and Plymouth 380 miles away.

Coxy was a member of the RAC and he phoned immediately for assistance. We had to wait a while and began to get a little nervous. The RAC officer eventually arrived and inspected the engine.

He poked his head up to say: "It's knackered, I'm afraid. I can't fix it here. I'll have to tow you back home."

Fortunately home was less than 15 miles away. The car was hitched up and we took our seats in the RAC van and headed back in the opposite direction from Plymouth.

It was 8.10am when we arrived at Gordon's house. We were back to square one, having lost more than two hours. Time was getting tight. We needed to get to Plymouth because we had a match to watch, and a job to do. It might have been possible for me to check with the garage staff at the *Gazette* in the faint hope there was a pool car available though, even if I was lucky, it would take half an hour or more to sort out.

There was no alternative.

"We'll have to go in my car, Coxy," I said.

Coxy was taken aback. He'd never been in my car before.

"You sure."

"What choice do we have?"

I've always maintained a personal dislike of using my own car to travel away from home to report on Boro games. I'm not one for buying new cars, so I've never fancied adding unnecessary additional miles to an already much utilised milometer.

There have always been alternative methods to get to away games, such as taking the train, driving a *Gazette* pool car, or sharing a lift with a highly competent driver like Gordon Cox who knows the way to every ground blindfold, not to mention his driving skills. In any case, travelling with Coxy was always my top choice because of the convivial company. The furthest I have ever driven in my own car in more than 20 years of following the team, apart from September 1, 1990, is to Leeds.

Here we were, within spitting distance of Ayresome Park, 380 miles from Plymouth, and stuck for both time and transport. There was no alternative. We had to use my car, however, much it went against the grain. I had a VW Golf at the time and it was a nice car. I've had a few of them over the years and always found them reliable, though I'd never blasted one for 380 miles without stopping. However, that's what we needed to do, and we set off at 8.12am more in hope than expectation of reaching Home Park in time for the kick-off.

I'm not a slouch behind the wheel but I'm no Stirling Moss either. I had been driving for around an hour and making only gradual progress when Coxy suggested that he should take over. In the event, he drove all the remainder of the way to Plymouth, and most of the way back again. The car seemed to respond better for him than it had for me.

It was a gruelling, hot day, not suited to long-distance driving, and we had a sweat on when we started to hit long, fume-laden traffic queues on the M5. We crawled past Bristol, where road works made progress even slower and more frustrating. There were times when we felt we were making good headway when suddenly we needed to break quickly behind a wall of stationary traffic which stretched into the distance.

On the several occasions I have travelled to Plymouth I've always felt as if it was on a different planet. It takes long enough to drive to Bristol, but when you get there you discover you've still got two hours to go before you reach Plymouth, dependent on a good run.

Unfortunately we didn't have a good run and at one time there seemed little chance of us making the kick-off. But Coxy kept plugging away and, following quick progress down the A38 after passing Exeter, we pulled up outside Home Park at 2.50pm. It was a terrific feat of driving on Coxy's part because I knew I couldn't have done it if I had been behind the wheel. With the sweat pouring off us, we jumped out of the car and raced into the stadium, taking our seats among the local bemused pressmen just as the game was about to commence.

Boro drew 1-1 that afternoon, thanks to a goal from Bernie Slaven. After the final whistle we picked up the relevant interviews and then headed back home. There was no time for playing bowls. We bombed back the way we had come, though this time we encountered few traffic problems. It was still half past one in the morning when I crawled into bed and the car had another 760 miles on the clock. I could not have possibly asked my employers at the *Gazette* for the petrol money for a 760-mile journey. So I had to write it off. But I felt a great sense of achievement that day and we did the job which, basically, was all that really mattered.

Two weeks later we were back on the road again to head south west for Boro's game at Swindon. Coxy's car had been suitably repaired by this time and we enjoyed a trouble-free trip, other than the usual long day on the road. Boro won 3-1 with some style. Having initially been happy to settle for mid-table obscurity, I felt for the first time that Boro might have a chance of turning things around in that season.

We were on the road yet again two days later for a night match at Port Vale.

Tiredness probably played a part in Boro's performance that night. I was certainly feeling it. Boro were lethargic and went down 3-1. They also lost at home to Oldham the following Saturday but these two defeats were only a hiccup and Boro hardly looked back after stuffing Leicester City 6-0 at Ayresome Park at the end of September.

The esteem in which the Boro faithful held Bruce Rioch was never more evident in mid-October, when more than 20,000 fans turned up at Ayresome for the home game with Millwall. Rioch had taken over at the London club immediately after leaving Ayresome and was leading his new team into action against Boro for the first time. Before the kick-off, Rioch was invited to the directors' box where he was presented with a fresh Scottish salmon by

Boro chairman Colin Henderson. It was a touching moment which earned a standing ovation from the supporters, many of whom still wished that Rioch was at the helm at Boro.

In the event, Rioch's team started well on the day and Boro were struggling to establish some control. The game was eventually turned on its head by John Hendrie who, picking up the ball on the edge of his own penalty area, ran all the way to the other end of the pitch, evading several tackles, before slotting the ball into the net to give Boro a 2-1 victory. Bruce would not have enjoyed the moment, because Hendrie carved Millwall apart, but no doubt he later savoured the salmon.

There were some more gruelling trips that season. We must have clocked up a massive mileage. Boro went to Wolves in midweek towards the end of October and lost 1-0, and then we headed off on the road again four days later to Brighton, where Bernie Slaven scored a scintillating hat trick in a 4-2 win.

The Boro directors experimented by running an executive coach to the Goldstone Ground and, as there were a couple of seats available, I was invited along as a guest. It was an excellent trip, with a pre-packed meal eaten and enjoyed by all in a lay-by just outside the Sussex town before the kick-off. On the way back to Middlesbrough we left the A1 in Yorkshire to visit a country pub where another meal was laid on, and a convivial hour and a half or so was enjoyed by all.

Boro made it three wins in a row by beating Barnsley at Ayresome, and then winning away at West Brom but things were not going too well in the next match at home to Charlton. Boro were struggling to put anything together and Todd made a change at the interval by bringing on substitute Stuart Ripley in place of Slaven.

I thought no more of it at the time, until a friendly steward whispered in my ear that Slaven had stormed out of the ground, jumped into his car, and gone home. It was a good story and gave me something decent to write about after Boro were beaten 2-1 by the Addicks. Colin Todd was not too happy at the press conference afterwards when asked questions about Bernie's AWOL disappearing act, especially as he had initially known nothing about it.

It made for another good story in the *Gazette* on the Monday but that's what you got with Bernie. He was a larger than life character and he had a habit of making the headlines, even if he didn't score. What made it better was that he usually did score. Bernie proved that fact when netting in each of the next three games following the Charlton setback.

The first of those games was at Portsmouth seven days later, and the Boro directors repeated the Brighton exercise by organising an executive coach. Again I was invited on the trip. I enjoyed the journey down, and the meal, though the return trip was not so enjoyable.

Boro director Graham Fordy had organised a game of Shut the Box at the back of the coach, and needed a fourth participant. I was invited to complete the quartet, and accepted the opportunity to have a bit of fun and avoid the most boring part of the journey.

I have always enjoyed the odd flutter on the horses, which I feel is a test of individual knowledge and skill but when it comes down to fortune, if it wasn't for bad luck I wouldn't have any at all.

Anybody who knows the game of Shut the Box will appreciate there is no skill involved whatsoever. It is all down to the dice. In the event these particular dice didn't like me one iota. On the whole of the 300-mile journey home I didn't win one game of Shut the Box. I lost every one and it cost me an absolute arm and a leg. The Paylor family went without food for a whole week (well, almost). Since that day, I have shuddered with fear at the prospect of playing Shut the Box, even when there is no cash at stake.

Boro won 3-0 at Pompey that day, which probably eased my pain, and seven days later there was another long haul for us to enjoy, this time to Oxford. The journey was forgotten as Ian Baird scored a hat trick in Boro's 5-2 success. The team had gelled well and the goals were beginning to flow.

Boro suffered the usual Christmas hiccup, though they won at Ipswich against all the odds on Boxing Day. It was another horrendously long trip at the worst possible time. I had to leave my family tucked up in bed sleeping off their Christmas Day excesses as I left the house to head off for East Anglia. The win helped to ease the pain and it was a memorable moment for Wark, finishing on the winning side against the club where he had enjoyed two highly successful spells in his career.

Any readers who believe that reporting on the Boro is an easy job should try to attend every single game, and find the time, fully sober, to carry out all the interviews and then write up the reports. Three days after the trip to Ipswich, Boro were at Bristol City for the Saturday game between Christmas and New Year which traditionally seems to take the team and the local media to the other end of the country. To make matters worse Boro were dreadful at Ashton Gate that day and lost 3-0.

I was back at Plymouth – twice – in the January. No rest for the wicked. Boro were paired with the Pilgrims in the third round of the FA Cup. Fortunately Boro's name was first out of the hat and, as they were at home, initially there didn't seem to be too much to worry about. Boro failed to fire on all cylinders on a drab afternoon and were held to a goalless draw. So it was off to Home Park again for all and sundry for the replay the following Tuesday.

This time I arranged to go to Plymouth by train, staying overnight in a hotel after the game. I set off from Darlington station with Ray Robertson from *The Northern Echo* and *Daily Express* reporter John Donoghue, on the appallingly slow cross-country journey which seems to stop everywhere in the Midlands and eventually terminates at Penzance. Both Ray and John always like a bit of a chinwag, so maybe this particular journey passed by more quickly than normal.

When we alighted at Plymouth station at around 4.30pm, Ray was approached on the platform by a man who assumed he was the match referee.

"Are you the officials for tonight's game?" he asked, eyeing up John and I as potential linesmen.

"No, we're not," said Ray. "But we'll stand in if you don't find them."

The confusion was no doubt aided by the fact that we were all carrying hold-alls, which we needed for our overnight stay. But the incident gave us something to smile about after our long sticky journey on the train.

We got a taxi to our hotel, enjoyed a pre-match meal and then booked another taxi to take us to Home Park. As soon as we arrived at the stadium, I did not have the chance to get my feet on the ground before we were informed by a fan that the game was off.

There had been torrential rain in the West Country that day and the pitch was waterlogged. Now we realised why Ray had been asked if he was the match ref.

Plymouth were keen for an early inspection.

I can't recall who the ref was but, following his inspection, he made the unusual decision to postpone the match for only 24 hours, in the hope the replay could take place on the Wednesday evening.

The postponement left us three intrepid reporters with a full evening to kill in a strange part of the country, and we were very grateful to the local Pilgrims reporter from the *Plymouth Evening Herald*, who took us under his wing. He took us to his local snooker club where we had a wonderful relaxing evening in a friendly atmosphere. There were one or two hardy Boro fans in there, too.

I introduced John Donoghue to the game of pool and he became immediately addicted. We went on to play frame after frame against each other until three in the morning, by which time I could no longer keep my eyes open.

The following morning we got a taxi to Home Park again, where the ref was staging a 10.30am inspection. It was obvious upon our arrival that there was no chance of the replay taking place. There were still large pools of water all over the pitch. The ref wasted little time in announcing a further postponement.

So Ray, John and I filed our reports and then made our way back to the station to return home on the next cross country train. We progressed steadily from Plymouth to Bristol Temple Meads station, where we seemed to be stationary for a rather long period of time. Eventually we were told by a steward to get off the train as quickly as possible – because the engine was on fire. Sure enough, as we stepped on to the platform, flames and thick smoke were emanating from the engine.

We had to await further information and spotted the station bar where we could get a welcome drink.

"Maybe there will be a pool table," said John, practising his break-off.

There was indeed a pool table. John immediately began fumbling for some change and we went on to play non-stop pool for another two hours. It certainly beats working for a living.

Eventually we heard the public announcement that a replacement engine had been found in order for us to continue our journey. It was rather late in the day when I reached home again and, as usual, I was up early doors the following morning to drive to the *Gazette* and pick up the new day's back page Boro story.

The following week we had to do it all again. We went back to Plymouth by train. This time the weather in the south west was fine and the replay finally went ahead. The trip was worthwhile because Boro won 2-1 with goals from Ian Baird and Paul Kerr. The return journey home passed without incident though this time we failed to fit in any games of pool.

However, I had another good story in the bag because Bernie Slaven had publicly expressed his displeasure to me at having to play on the left wing during the match. I could understand Todd's selection decision, because Bernie had such a good left foot and it was difficult to find genuine left-footers at that time. But I knew how much Bernie hated playing there and he did not hold back in voicing his frustrations.

Twelve days later Boro were in action in the fourth round of the FA Cup, when they travelled to Cambridge United. However, they failed to perform on the sloping, grassless pitch at the Abbey Stadium and went down by 2-0.

My main memory from that match was the alarming bias of the home reporters. When Cambridge scored their second goal, one of the home scribes leapt into the air, waving his arms around like a lunatic and almost doing cartwheels around the press box.

Cambridge were full value for the win, but the whole point of being a football writer is to bury your personal feelings and tell it like it is, warts and all. This guy had no chance of doing that. I didn't begrudge Cambridge the win because they deserved it, but this wild celebrating was the sort of behaviour you rarely witness in a press box, and that's why it sticks so vividly in my mind.

Boro finally got back on track in the second division in February, winning three games in a row, culminating in a 1-0 midweek victory at Charlton. I didn't make a note of what time I arrived home from that trip, but it was late – and, as usual, I was up again a few hours later to write up the report.

By this time Todd had added to his squad by bringing in loan signings Colin Walsh and Andy Dibble. Midfielder Walsh arrived on loan from Charlton and proved useful at times. While he didn't get the permanent move to Teesside he might have been seeking, he made a contribution to the promotion push.

Walsh could be in and out of games, like all players, and there was one particular home game against Bristol City where he was having a nightmare. Having lost possession at one end of the pitch, Walsh received a few brickbats from the fans.

However, he redeemed himself in terrific style, racing back to the other end of the pitch, getting into a defensive position and then taking a full-blooded shot in the stomach when the Bristol City player seemed certain to score.

Had City equalised at that moment, then Boro would not have qualified for the play-offs. Walsh paid a huge price for his bravery because he has down on the ground for some time, in some pain, and did not play again for the club because of an abdominal injury. I always felt that his courage was a defining moment in the season.

An injury to Steve Pears had led to Todd bringing in Andy Dibble from Manchester City. The Welsh international keeper was highly rated and did a great job in helping Boro reach the play-offs. Unfortunately, when Dibble returned to the club for a second spell during Bryan Robson's reign, he endured a personal nightmare.

A midweek trip to Millwall added to the miles I ran up that season, though this time I went by train and stayed overnight in a hotel near Piccadilly.

Cold Blow Lane was not the most attractive of stadia in those days. It was a dull, dingy ground even when the sun was shining. It was situated in the type of area where you were not too happy walking at night, especially when carrying a briefcase. After watching Boro draw 2-2, I gingerly made my way, along with *The Northern Echo* reporter Ray Robertson, through the dark streets to New Cross Station, from where we found our way to Piccadilly.

The following day I woke up feeling very ill. There was an intense pain in my head and I was sick. I don't know how I managed to file my reports to the *Gazette*, but once I had sent the final story I had to go straight back to bed. I phoned the office to say that I felt too ill to get up, and it was unlikely they would see me that particular day.

I learned later that my peers in the *Gazette* were a little dubious about my story. They suspected that I had gone on a jaunt around London and bunked off work for the afternoon.

However, I don't have a history of illness, save for a recent major operation, nor of taking time off work to which I am not entitled. So this did come a little out of the blue for all of us.

I managed to get some sleep, but had to vacate my room by noon. In the event I eventually struggled out of bed and made my way back to Kings Cross, and then home. I did not enjoy the travelling under such circumstances. It was not a pleasant experience and fortunately it was not one which was commonplace.

Boro's next away game was at Blackburn Rovers on Easter Monday and Coxy and I decided to take the usual route across the top on the A59. In the event there were extensive road works to circumnavigate, both at Blubberhouses and Bolton Abbey, and the journey was a nightmare. Blackburn is one of Boro's regular shortest away trips, and that's why it usually attracts such a good Boro following. It's just a short hop across the Pennines. But on this occasion we missed the kick-off, albeit by only a few minutes.

I can count on one hand the number of times we have missed a kick-off, so this was a very rare occurrence. The plan for every away game is to try to arrive two hours before the start. It's a target we usually achieve. Without the road works we would probably have arrived at 1pm, which gives some idea of the time we spent idling in bumper-to-bumper traffic.

With the games beginning to run out for the Boro, it was becoming touch and go whether Colin Todd's men would make the play-offs. We drove to

Twerton Park at Bath for the game against Bristol Rovers, which took place towards the end of April. It was a long journey for nothing. Boro went down by 2-0 in a particularly poor performance. The sloping pitch was bone hard and Boro simply couldn't handle it. It was John Wark's last game for the club and I can remember thinking how much he had struggled on a pitch where it was impossible to turn quickly.

In the event Boro regained their composure and took themselves to the verge of qualification by beating Wolves and Brighton in consecutive games at Ayresome. They could have earned a play-off place in midweek at Oldham and ran themselves into the ground in their efforts to take the points. They created a host of chances, all of which were spurned. In an end-to-end game Oldham took two of their chances to take the points, but the result did not reflect nor reward the Boro performance.

So it was all down to the final game. Boro travelled to Barnsley on the Saturday knowing that qualification was virtually certain unless results elsewhere went badly against them. Boro would have needed to lose 4-0 at Oakwell in order not to qualify. Barnsley still had a chance of joining them in the play-offs if they beat Boro and Brighton failed to win their final game.

The Oakwell showdown produced a tight tussle and, while there was never any chance of Boro losing 4-0, Colin Todd's men seemed to settle for a damage limitation exercise and went down 1-0. This ensured Boro of their place in the play-offs and the travelling fans enjoyed themselves at the final whistle.

At the same time Barnsley were awaiting the result of the Brighton game in order to ascertain their own fate. When the Brighton result was broadcast as a draw by a local radio station, hundreds of Barnsley fans raced on to the pitch and started celebrating in front of the main stand. It was party time at Oakwell. Their fans were absolutely ecstatic. I was trying to file copy at the time and could hardly hear myself above the din.

At the same time I had been informed by another reporter, quite correctly, that Brighton had won their game, thanks to an injury-time winner. It meant that Barnsley had failed to win a play-off place after all.

Having personally not heard the earlier radio announcement, I had no idea why the Barnsley fans were celebrating in the first place. It seemed ludicrous to me that they were so happy after failing to reach the play-offs under such circumstances.

As the time went on, the celebrations continued apace. Nobody from the home club seemed to have the courage to announce to the partying fans that Barnsley would be winning nothing that season. After half an hour or so, to my utter amazement, the Barnsley players then walked out of their dressing room to stand in the directors' box and acknowledge their delirious supporters.

It was obvious to me that the Barnsley players knew they had not qualified but the only way to prevent ugly scenes, as the home directors probably saw it, was for the players to celebrate with the fans. It was one of the most unreal things I have ever witnessed in football. Eventually the Barnsley players returned to the dressing room and their fans went home happy, still ignorant of the true outcome that afternoon.

Even so, those Barnsley fans probably had a more enjoyable evening than Gordon Cox and I. We were heading home along the A1 towards Wetherby when we were involved in a pile-up on the outside lane. We had a full car at the time and I was in the back seat and dozing when I became aware that Coxy had slammed his foot on the brakes in attempting to make an emergency stop.

I managed to sit forward and dip my head behind the seat before the impact. There was the sickening noise of crunching metal as we hit the back of the car in front. It transpired we were the last vehicle in a four car pile-up. Thanks to the grace of God, none of us in the car were hurt, not even from whiplash, while I can't recall anybody being seriously injured in the other vehicles.

Coxy exchanged addresses with the other drivers under the watchful eyes of hundreds of gaping faces as the rest of the A1 traffic crawled past us in the inside lane. When Coxy was eventually able to back away from the pile-up, our car was still driveable despite being extensively damaged at the front. So we were able to limp home with nothing more than a bloody nose for the car.

It was a close shave, and brought home the fact that it's a gamble every time we take to the road for away games. I've done so many away games, and clocked up thousands of motorway miles, and am still in one piece to tell the tale. It's remarkable that I have encountered so few incidents on the road, and long may it remain that way.

While the season ended with a bang for us press men, it might have had a different outcome for Boro, too, but for the bad feeling that quickly developed after the players became aware that Todd was planning major changes in the summer.

His forward-thinking plans might have produced terrific results for Boro if he'd had the opportunity to put them into effect, or they might have turned out to be a disaster. The last thing that Boro needed at that time was for the players to know that several of them would not be part of the club's future, whether Boro beat Notts County in the play-offs or not.

In the event, the Boro players were unable to produce their best in the two play-off games and were beaten deservedly by a team which on paper, probably not quite on Boro's level.

The first game at Ayresome, in front of 22,000 fans, was a particular let-down and sowed the seeds for Boro's exit. Todd's men managed to salvage a draw thanks to a late goal from Jimmy Phillips but had not looked the part during the game.

We went to Meadow Lane for the second leg three days later and, again, County were much more up for the game. Boro did play better than they had done in the first meeting, but were second best on the night and went down 1-0. There was a feeling of emptiness at the final whistle. In neither game did Boro perform to the standard that might be expected from a team which had such a golden opportunity to win promotion.

Bruce Rioch had taken Millwall into the play-offs but, like Boro, they also succumbed in the semi-finals at the hands of Brighton. Notts County went on to beat the Seagulls in the final.

Within days, Toddy phoned me at the *Gazette* with his retained list. I was a bit taken aback by the list of names but Colin insisted to me that he was determined to completely overhaul the squad ready for a bigger promotion push next season. He gave me the names of some of the players he wanted to bring in and, while those names have now gone out of my head and were never written down, I can recall that they contained some ambitious targets and some that were not so exciting.

Todd clearly felt the changes were necessary, but there were some surprise names missing from his retained list. Bernie Slaven, who had scored 19 goals in all competitions that season, and fellow striker Ian Baird, who had managed 15, were both on the transfer list. Gary Parkinson, Colin Cooper and Alan Kernaghan, all of whom had been with the club since liquidation alongside Slaven, were also up for transfer.

Coops had been switched to right-back from his regular role at left-back by Todd, but had been injured for much of the second half of the campaign. Kernaghan, who was employed in a variety of positions by Bruce Rioch, had been used solely as a defender by Todd. Another centre-back on the list was John Wark, along with another of Todd's signings, midfielder Martin Russell.

I believe that Todd was keen to spend in the region of £1m to bring in new faces and, at first, I got the impression that the board were ready to try to back him. Initially, none of the transfer-listed eleven left the club, while nobody came in.

Then, out of the blue, Toddy rang me to say he had been sacked. He inferred interference from the board, though it was not until later that I discovered there had been problems regarding his list of new targets. In typical Toddy fashion he made it clear that he had no axe to grind with the directors.

Toddy was relatively upbeat about life in general. I never saw him downcast or depressed after a bad result, and this sacking was no different. He was chatty on the end of the phone and answered all of my questions, again without giving away too many of the finer details.

Shortly afterwards I received a call to go down to the Boro boardroom for the official announcement. There was no particular reason given for the parting of ways, and chairman Colin Henderson wished Toddy every bit of luck for the future.

The general feeling looking back is that Todd's ambitious plans to overhaul the squad were maybe a little too far-reaching. It created a situation which made the directors uneasy that summer and any attempts which they may have made to tone things down were clearly met with resistance from the manager's chair.

So the two parties agreed to split. At that time I don't think the directors had anybody in particular in mind as Toddy's replacement and so the guessing game started in the *Gazette* and elsewhere.

CHAPTER 10

I HAD to hand it to the Boro board of directors in the summer of 1991. They carried out their negotiations with potential new managers in complete secrecy.

I did my best to pick up titbits; and who might be their likely first choice. What I did know was that their initial list of targets included around half a dozen names. One of the men on the list was Port Vale boss John Rudge, who was one of the top lower league managers around at the time. In fact Rudge, as far as us media men were concerned, had emerged as the likely favourite.

In fact when I turned up at Ayresome Park for the press conference for the official unveiling of the new Boro boss, I was not the only one who expected to see Rudge walk through the door along with chairman Colin Henderson and chief executive Keith Lamb.

I was rather taken aback, therefore, when it was Lennie Lawrence who walked in alongside the Boro officials. I recognised him immediately. Lennie had been one of the names on the short-list that I had been working from and it turned out later than he was always the directors' No.1 choice.

I had received a couple of tip-offs that Lawrence would get the job, but then I'd also been tipped off that it would be Rudge. So it was difficult to be certain exactly what was going to happen, especially as there was nothing official coming out of the boardroom. The Boro directors had been tight-lipped all the way through.

Lennie Lawrence was otherwise known rather affectionately by the media as 'Houdini'. He acquired the tag after engineering a handful of remarkable last-ditch survival campaigns at his previous club Charlton Athletic. Every season the Addicks seemed certain to drop out of the first division, but Lennie managed to keep them up thanks to a sudden late surge of results.

While I recognised Lennie, the reporter next to me leaned across and asked: "Who is he?" I won't reveal his name because of potential embarrassment, but Lennie was certainly not the high-profile boss that many might have expected and I wondered what the immediate response would be from the fans.

I was happy to see Lawrence handed the Boro job. However, I had seen him plenty of times on TV and he always came across very well. The main task for me, as ever, was to establish a working relationship with him as quickly as possible, in order to make sure I maintained a finger on the club's pulse.

After filing the story of Lennie's appointment to the *Evening Gazette*, I had the opportunity to chat with him afterwards. I liked him from the start. Lennie made it clear that he called a spade a spade and he also promised he would take me into his confidence as long as I did not do the dirty on him – a point he strongly conveyed. He said he understood that I had to write things the way I saw them, but pointed out that if I misrepresented anything he told me then the relationship would be in trouble.

I had no problems with this. I've always appreciated the need to try to project a story just as the interviewee would want to see it. There's nothing to be gained from putting words into people's mouths.

If any Boro manager stopped talking to the *Gazette* then we would have serious problems in trying to get the daily news stories in print across to the fans. It's the same rule when applied to the players. If one player stops talking to you, the rest of the squad could follow suit in empathy. So I was happy with Lennie's ground rules and I found him a great guy to deal with over the three years he spent on Teesside.

The daily arrangement was that I rang him at home every morning before he set off for Ayresome Park. I had to time it right, catching him in between his morning shower and leaving his house in Egglescliffe.

Lennie was both honest and forthright in his quotes, even though he did not always tell me everything that was going on at the club. He never lied to me if I put a story to him which previously had not been in the public domain, however. This made him different from any other manager I have dealt with and I always regarded it as a great credit to him.

There are managers who brush certain questions under the carpet if they don't want to make a comment - but not Lennie. If he realised that I was aware of a particular story, he would give me his views on the situation because he realised that I would print what I knew anyway. I believe that Lennie's policy was that the more I knew about the situation the more likely I would get the facts right.

So Lennie was a lot more open with me than Colin Todd had been. In this respect he was also being open with the fans, because whatever he told me went straight into the pages of the *Gazette*.

Lennie had been installed at Ayresome Park for less than a week when he confided to me that he had to take Boro into the top flight at the first attempt. "If I don't do it this season, then it won't be as easy next season when the players have become used to me," he admitted.

Lennie's theory made sense. He also achieved his aims because he delivered in his first season in charge. Boro were promoted on that champagne afternoon at Molineux the following May.

Lennie wasted no time in getting to grips with the job. He delved into the background of the players he had inherited and actually started the season with a smaller squad than Colin Todd had done.

Some of the players that Todd had placed on the transfer list, such as Ian Baird, Colin Cooper, John Wark, Martin Russell, Kevin Poole and Trevor Putney eventually moved on, along with Simon Coleman. In fact eight players left very quickly.

Only three experienced players were brought in. Lennie went to Watford and signed midfielder Willie Falconer and striker Paul Wilkinson for a joint fee of £800,000 and also brought in goalkeeper Ian Ironside from Scarborough as cover for Steve Pears.

Falconer was a half-decent player who established himself as a regular in Lennie's side, despite missing several months of his first season on Teesside because of injury. I always felt that Willie could have been an even more successful box-to-box player had he had a touch more pace because he knew the way to goal.

Wilkinson, like Falconer, was just approaching the peak period of his career. He was a young striker at Everton when they won the first division in 1987, subsequently growing stature and experience during successive stints at Nottingham Forest and Watford.

Boro got excellent value in particular for their outlay in Wilko. He scored 22 goals in all competition in the promotion campaign and got another 16 when Boro were in the inaugural Premier League season 12 months later.

I found Wilkinson easy to get on with and straightforward in his comments, though he had an edge to him. He always took me to task if I had written something about him with which he didn't agree. If I'd said that he missed a few gilt-edged chances, Wilko would grab me the following day and explain exactly why the chances were not gilt-edged. I liked his direct approach and, as I have said, the more you know the better the chance you will get your facts right.

Lawrence had no problems blending Falconer and Wilkinson into the side. It was a great piece of business for the club. In fact Lennie swept his way through the squad with a new broom and lifted spirits. He wasted little time in dispersing the clouds which hung over the dressing room following the failed attempt to win promotion via the play-offs.

Lennie's hardest task was in dealing with the futures of some of his defenders. He spent a lot of time convincing Alan Kernaghan to stay on Teesside, but won the battle in the end. Kernaghan, who was one of Todd's eleven transfer-listed players, had spent a long spell on loan at Charlton, under Lawrence, the previous season. Kerny had been very successful with the Addicks, and the spell in London had not only boosted his confidence to new levels, but had focused his mind on moving away from the Boro.

Naturally, Kernaghan was hoping that Lawrence would take him to Charlton during the summer, and no doubt Lennie would have had the same idea if he had stayed in south London.

However, Lennie's switch to Teesside threw Alan into a state of confusion. He clearly knew nothing about Lennie's impending move to the Boro until the manager walked into the Ayresome Park dressing room for the first time.

Lennie told me: "I bumped into Kerny outside the dressing room. He looked at me and said 'What are you doing here?' I told him I was the new manager of Middlesbrough Football Club. He couldn't believe it."

With several players already on their way out of the Boro, Lennie desperately wanted Kernaghan to stay because he wanted him to be a key figure in his defence. It took some negotiating, but Lennie eventually convinced Alan that he had a big future on Teesside. Kernaghan agreed to stay after all and Lennie slotted him in alongside skipper Tony Mowbray at the start of the season.

Not only did Kernaghan continue to progress in leaps and bounds, but he went on to become a Republic of Ireland international and was eventually sold on by Boro for a healthy £1.66m - which is a lot more than his likely valuation in the summer of 1991.

Lennie admitted to me that he could see the funny side of the struggle to keep Kernaghan, after having previously spent several weeks in convincing him to leave Middlesbrough. It was a battle he was relieved to win.

One struggle which Lennie lost was in trying to tempt Colin Cooper to stay at the Boro. Coops had missed a few games through injury over the past two seasons and, having been played arguably out of position at right-back by Colin Todd, had set his heart on a move and a clean start somewhere else.

Eventually he went to Millwall for a relatively cut-price £300,000. Lennie expressed his disappointment at this loss because he was well aware of Cooper's qualities and would have loved to have kept him. But he told me that Coops was fully focused on leaving and had turned down all of Lennie's appeals for him to stay.

In the event Lennie got through a tremendous amount of business in a short space of time before the start of the 1991/92 campaign. Most of them were outgoing deals. However, while the Boro squad may have been small at the start of the season, it looked slick. Paul Wilkinson slotted in nicely up front as an ideal foil for Bernie Slaven, who went on to finish as top scorer in the second division campaign with 16 goals. This was one more than Wilko, though the former Watford man grabbed another seven goals in the cups.

Lennie's side took a short time to gel, losing two of the first three games. Then the players clicked into gear and won six in a row. As a result they were always in the thick of the promotion chase.

Boro set the tone in early September by winning two long away trips within four days. We went to Oxford on the Wednesday and saw Boro win 2-1 thanks to a Slaven brace. The team repeated the winning scoreline three days later at Watford, where Wilkinson and Falconer got the goals against their former club.

Boro opened their League Cup campaign against Bournemouth, which isn't the perfect draw for even well-travelled journalists. Boro drew the home leg 1-1 and then we went down to Dean Court for the decider.

It was a stay-over in a hotel for me, fortunately, the prospect of which was made even better when the game went into extra time. Gordon Cox was driving back after the game and I can recall the look of utter disgust on his face at the end of 90 minutes when he considered the prospect of losing another 45 minutes' sleep. Boro still went on to win the game, grabbing the winner in extra time thanks to a Gary Parkinson penalty.

Dean Court is not exactly in the centre of Bournemouth and I can recall waiting an extraordinary length of time before finally hailing a taxi back to my hotel. It was in the region of 2am when I finished writing my reports and crawled into bed. I was up five hours later to shower and eat a quick breakfast before filing copy. At least I was able to doze on the train all the way home.

The following Saturday, Lawrence handed a first league start to highly-rated teenager Jamie Pollock for the home game against Wolves. Pollock had been pushing strongly in the latter part of the previous campaign. In fact Colin

Todd had told me on several occasions what a good player Pollock was going to be.

In the event Toddy was able to give Pollock just one game as a substitute, but the lad continued to progress quickly and Lennie felt he was ready to cope with the rigours of first-team football by mid-October. Pollock's no-nonsense, hard- working style of play was to prove beneficial for Boro. He went on to play a lot of football throughout the remainder of that campaign, becoming a big favourite with the fans.

Pollock was blessed with physical strength allied to mental power and he coped well in a man's world from the start. He had a strong temperament both on and off the field. He was good to interview and was never one to hold back if I had written something with which he did not agree. I had a couple of run-ins with him, as I did with several players over the years, but I always respected both his frankness and his determination to highlight stories with which he was not happy.

I had a liking for Jamie, as I did for most home-grown players who wore their heart on their sleeves. Unfortunately he did not have the chance to play for Boro at the peak of his career, having moved on elsewhere. I always felt his time in football might have gone on a little longer than it did, but eventually he set his heart on a new career and I was delighted to see him established in the family business back on Teesside.

Seven days after Pollock's first start, Boro were at Grimsby. I went with Coxy by road. We got to Cleethorpes a little early and so Coxy suggested that we went for a walk on the beach, which seemed to stretch for miles in every direction. I agreed, but it was a bracing October day, so much so that I was shivering and shaking all the way through the game, which Boro lost 1-0.

Soon afterwards Lennie told me that he was negotiating for Tony Mowbray to leave the club. I don't think that Mogga had played anywhere like his best football under Lennie, but it still came as a bit of a shock. Mowbray had been the bedrock of the club for more than five years and was still the main man in the dressing room.

It was almost impossible to imagine the Boro without Mogga. He epitomised everything that the club, and its supporters, stood for. He was a local lad who had come up through the ranks and who placed the club above everything else. He would run through a brick wall for the Boro when one or two other players were happy merely to get through games unscathed and continue to pick up their wage packets.

Despite his obvious talents as a footballer, Mogga had not yet achieved any real success in the game. He had played for England B but never got close to the biggest stage of all. I was devastated at the prospect of him leaving but I realised that it was a natural progression for the big defender. There was a danger that he would have seized up by staying on Teesside. In any case, like all players, Mogga was ambitious and had no guarantees of achieving these aspirations with Boro.

I did not speak directly to Tony in his last couple of weeks with the Boro, though Lennie's impressions were the same as my own.

He said: "Mogga's feeling stale. I've seen it before in players and the best outcome in these situations is to help him to move on. He's still a good player, but he needs to move on for it to come through again."

Lennie revealed that the two had been involved in several meaningful discussions and both agreed that the skipper's career would benefit from a move and therefore the manager was not going to stand in Mogga's way.

The news that Mogga was probably on his way out of Teesside eventually leaked out, and it became clear that the away game at Barnsley on November 5 would be his last for the club. It was a poignant night and lacking in fireworks because Boro lost 2-1. Mogga's impending departure was confirmed by the way in which he waved to the Boro fans at the final whistle.

Within 24 hours, Boro had completed a £1m deal with Celtic for Mogga to move to Glasgow. It was the end of an era in Boro's history.

I was fortunate to keep in occasional contact with Tony for a long period following his departure from the Boro. As much as he was a Boro lad through and through I always felt, as he did, that he had left the club at the right time. However, his life did not always work out well for him. He had to overcome personal tragedy while at Celtic with the sad death of his wife Bernadette. One can not imagine what a loss of this magnitude has on a young man, though in Tony's case it led to him strengthening his religious faith and becoming a Roman Catholic.

After almost four successful years with Celtic, Mowbray moved on again and was a tower of strength at the back for five years with Ipswich. He finally hung up his boots after helping them to promotion in 2000. Mogga then became a coach at Portman Road, learning his trade under George Burley and becoming Burley's right-hand man.

Management always beckoned and Mowbray went on to prove his spurs in the hot seat at Hibernian, before replacing former Boro boss Bryan Robson at West Brom. There are those fans who believe that Mogga's destiny is eventually to manage the Boro.

I'm not so sure, but I'm delighted to see him proving to be so successful within the game.

Lennie Lawrence did not use the £1m windfall from the sale of Mowbray to replace the defender from outside. Instead he handed the job to Middlesbrough-born youngster Nicky Mohan, who had been on the verge of the team for some time having initially made his Boro debut as a teenager in the first division under Bruce Rioch.

Lawrence was unsure about Mohan at first. So unsure, in fact, that he accepted an offer of £200,000 from Plymouth for the Teessider. Mohan turned down the move to the south west and he had good reason to feel that he had made the right decision when he found himself playing regularly in the Boro first team.

In many respects Mohan was similar to Mowbray in terms of wearing his heart on his sleeve. He loved his hometown club and took personal delight simply from putting on the red shirt every week. Nicky made mistakes early on, as all young players do, but he went on to play his part in the push for promotion.

Nicky was a highly likeable lad, always happy to give an interview. I felt he was very unlucky to lose out in the defensive purge which took place following the diabolical 5-1 friendly drubbing at Lincoln City the following summer. Yet injuries allowed him the chance to get back in and continue to do a job for the club.

Mohan did go on to enjoy a half-decent playing career. He left Boro to join Leicester City but regularly moved clubs for various reasons before ending up in non-league football a few years ago. I still bump into him from time to time in Middlesbrough and he's as friendly as ever.

While Mohan came into the side in November, so did Curtis Fleming. The young Irish defender was Lawrence's fourth signing of the summer. He was snapped up for £50,000 from St Patrick's Athletic after impressing in a trial during Colin Todd's time. Curtis had been gradually coming to grips with life as a full-time pro but progressed rapidly and went on to establish himself as one of the club's major stalwarts throughout the nineties.

Curtis was off the top shelf as a man, as honest and straight as the day he was born. Like Bernie Slaven, he was one of those players who adopted Boro as his home and came to love the club like any local-born player. He was to witness many changes during his time with the Boro, and you always wondered whether he would be one of those players who might be left behind as Boro strove to climb the ladder ever higher season by season in the nineties.

However, Curtis always grasped the nettle and proved he was capable of dealing with the next step up. He dealt with whatever was thrown at him and experienced the highs and lows of the legendary Juninho-Ravanelli period at first hand.

Instead of signing another defender, Lennie used the Mowbray cash on a striker. He swooped to bring in Andy Payton from Hull City for £750,000. Payton had been a prolific scorer for the Tigers and, at the time, this seemed an excellent deal for the Boro and another good piece of business by the manager.

I had the feeling that Payton was regarded as the long-term replacement for Bernie Slaven, especially as I had learned from experience that football managers tended to prefer players they had brought in rather than those already in the squad. I believed that Lennie saw a Wilkinson-Payton partnership as the team's future, though he was wise enough to know that he needed to have a squad of forwards rather than just two individuals to choose from.

At that time Lennie had never given me any negative comments about Bernie but I had the feeling that he was not Bernie's greatest fan. In any case Payton was a top-notch signing and the team had nothing to lose and everything to gain from having increased competition for places up front.

The Wilkinson-Payton partnership might have been the preferred choice had Andy not suffered an injury on his debut against Bristol City. He scored an early goal in that match and looked a hugely talented player. However, Payton succumbed to the injury and was never the same player again, scoring just two more goals for the club.

It was dreadful luck for both Payton and for Boro, because they never saw the fruits of their investment in him. It meant, however, that Slaven survived that particular threat to his place in the side but the crunch was not too far away for Bernie. The dirt was to hit the fan later in the season, in the reverse match against Bristol City in fact.

Shortly after signing Payton, Lennie went out again and snapped up Andy Peake from Charlton Athletic. The midfielder was 30 at the time of his arrival on Teesside but, despite a lack of pace, I felt that he was very effective in the side. He was vastly experienced and had always produced the goods for Lennie in the past. Andy was a ball-winner who rarely wasted possession, and not surprisingly became a regular in the team.

Peake was a relatively quiet guy away from the pitch, but knowledgeable and realistic. He was also mentally solid, and at the end of his playing days he returned to his home area in Leicestershire and joined the police force.

In the December, Boro took part in an amazing League Cup match against first division Manchester City at Ayresome Park. Thick fog descended during the first half and long before the interval, it was impossible to work out from the press box what was going on. I could not understand how the game survived all the way through to half-time without being abandoned. It seemed certain it would be called off during the break and I later discovered that both managers, Lennie and City's Peter Reid, were keen to see an end to the farce.

In the event there was a near miracle during the ten-minute half-time interval. The fog lifted as if it was swallowed up en masse by a giant suction machine. Within a few minutes conditions that were previously unplayable transformed into a perfect environment. So the teams came out again and finished the game without any problems, with Boro winning 2-1 thanks to goals from Robbie Mustoe and Paul Wilkinson.

Much of the remainder of the football that month was wiped out by frozen pitches but Boro went to Newcastle United on Boxing Day and won 1-0 against the odds. The Magpies started the game as hot favourites but Boro took advantage of a breakaway goal from Paul Wilkinson in the howling gale conditions to take the points.

Two days later we were on the road for the traditional long trip between Christmas and New Year by heading for the south coast for the clash with Portsmouth. Boro obviously did not enjoy the long journey and went down 4-0 on a bone-hard, grassless pitch, in another gale. Lennie was particularly incensed after that game by the team's performance and told me that heads would roll if there was a repeat.

In the event, Boro got stronger and stronger, despite a slight hiccup when they went down 2-0 at the hands of Millwall at Cold Blow Lane. I drove down to south London with Gordon Cox and had high hopes of a chat with Millwall boss Bruce Rioch after the game, but it turned out he wasn't there. Bruce was ill at home trying to shake off a bout of German measles.

A couple of weeks later we were all back at Portsmouth for an FA Cup fourth round tie. This time Boro improved on their league showing by forcing a 1-1 draw. They did let themselves down in the replay when Pompey played out of their skins in winning 4-2 at Ayresome Park, but otherwise Boro were never turned over again for the remainder of the campaign – not even by Manchester United.

CHAPTER 11

LENNIE Lawrence's second division Boro hopefuls were paired with mighty Manchester United in the Rumbelows Cup semi-finals in the lengthening winter days of the 1991/92 season.

It was both a massive and daunting prospect, but well deserved, even if Boro had only just scraped past gritty Peterborough United from Division Three in the previous round.

Boro were rather fortunate to hold on for a goalless draw at London Road in the quarter-final. The stalemate ended in the replay when they edged into the semis thanks to a clinical finish from Stuart Ripley in front of almost 22,000 fans at Ayresome Park.

The home tie against United – Bryan Robson, Gary Pallister and all – was another tight affair with few chances created at either end in front of a full house at Ayresome. The game ended goalless and, bearing in mind the extent of the task facing them in the second leg, it looked as if Boro would be on their way to a comfortable defeat at Old Trafford.

However, there was a new-found confidence within the Boro squad by now. There was a level of belief which had not been witnessed for some time. Boro went to Manchester and shocked United. A goal from Bernie Slaven ensured that Boro forced extra time following 90 pulsating minutes of football. Even though Ryan Giggs scored United's second goal in the 106th minute and Boro eventually went down 2-1, they gained terrific mental benefits from their performance.

If nothing else, Boro regained their pride that day and new respect from the national football scene.

There was no official press parking at Old Trafford then and, having driven there with *Gazette* photographer Nigel Roddis, we had parked up in a private car park close to the ground. We left Old Trafford at 11pm to discover that the police would not allow any cars out of our car park because of the massive amount of traffic which was hardly moving on the roads outside. The only saving grace was that some of the unfortunate drivers around us in the car park had been sitting in their cars since around 10.15pm, when I was still in the stadium collecting interviews.

As everybody left their car engines running, our *Gazette* pool car was soon full of exhaust fumes, which we had to breathe in for an unnecessary length of time. Eventually we got away from the car park shortly before midnight. It was 2am when I was able to crawl under the covers and naturally I was up with the larks to write my reports.

While everybody had enjoyed the battles with United, Boro were concentrating all their efforts into maintaining their promotion push. We were off on the road again the following Saturday for my first ever visit to Southend United, where Boro won 1-0 thanks to a Bernie Slaven penalty. I found Roots Hall a strange place. There was an open market in full swing outside the ground until shortly before the kick-off, and the vendors were still busily putting their goods away into their vans while the main bulk of the home support was arriving.

To enter the press area of the ground you had to walk over a little bridge, a rarity in itself, and then you took your seat in a small glass-enclosed press box. It was warm and cosy but when the door was closed you could hardly hear any sounds from outside. It was like watching a game on TV with the volume turned right down.

However, I never had any problems with the hospitality at Southend and it was particularly civilised after the match when we reporters were allowed to stand outside the dressing room door waiting for our quotes.

A female national newspaper reporter who was standing alongside me outside the door certainly seemed to enjoy it. She never moved from her spot at the front of the press pack, possibly because there was a mass of naked male bodies on view every time somebody went in and out of the dressing room.

Three days later we set off for Cambridge for a Tuesday night match, celebrating the fact that Stephen Pears had been called up for England's friendly match against Czechoslovakia. It was terrific for Pearsy and well deserved, as he was a top-class keeper who had proved his abilities over several seasons. Maybe he had been largely overlooked in the past because he had spent just the one season in the top flight.

Pearsy's call-up was a great story for the *Evening Gazette*, but it was to end in tears because he suffered a fractured cheekbone in the match at

Cambridge. As a result he later had to drop out of the England squad and to make matters worse never got back in again.

His injury was a setback for everybody concerned with the Boro, and affected me too, because it was to lead to a brief fall-out with Steve. As a rule, he was one of my best pals in the dressing room and never turned down an interview request. When the news broke that he had been forced to drop out of the England squad, it was a big story in the *Gazette*. I wrote the story as Steve would have expected to read it, but I was let down by a *Gazette* caption writer who wrote a few words underneath the photo which accompanied the story, which suggested, very unfairly, that Steve had not deserved to be in the England squad in the first place.

Steve was naturally angry the following day and came out of the dressing room to remonstrate with me. In fact he was spitting blood, probably because somebody had been winding him up in the dressing room. I could only apologise profusely over the totally unnecessary wording of the caption, even though it was something which was beyond my control.

As I have said, I have had my fall-outs with players, and there are some disagreements which have festered throughout certain players' whole careers on Teesside. This particular incident was quickly brushed under the carpet and Steve and I were soon the best of pals again.

Four days after the trip to Cambridge, a Bernie Slaven hat trick in a 4-0 win at home to Brighton kept Boro on course for the Premier League. Soon after, the team lost their way slightly and failed to win any of the next three games, the last of which was a 2-1 home defeat by Watford.

Lennie was keen to stop the rot before it got any worse, and Stuart Ripley and Bernie Slaven were left out of the side for the next game, which was a night match at Bristol City.

As there was no press room at Ashton Gate at the time, I took my seat in the wooden main stand quite early. It was a relatively mild, pleasant night, though not so on the touchline. As I sat there I was amazed to see Lennie Lawrence and Bernie Slaven emerge and have the mother of all arguments pitchside.

I was too far away to hear what was being said, but it was quite clear that Bernie was absolutely livid and was making his points very forcibly. I could only assume that he was having it out with the manager because he did not agree with being left out of the team. The head-to-head disagreement was quite heated at times, and there were several occasions when Bernie was pointing his finger at Lennie.

I'm aware that many arguments between managers and players have gone on over the years at the Boro, but it's very rare that you have the opportunity to witness one in public. To make matters worse for the two protagonists, the bust-up was also witnessed by several thousand people as the ground gradually filled up with fans.

As a reporter this was good stuff, but as a Boro fan it was not so good. I did not feel this was the place or time for the two to have such a storming argument. Boro went on to draw the game 1-1, but the main story for me was always going to be the touchline bust-up. Lennie tried hard to play down the incident when I spoke to him afterwards, but it still received a massive headline in the *Gazette*.

While Lennie did not say too much on the record, he told me off the record that the incident was unacceptable and I knew that it was certain to have repercussions for Bernie. I got the impression that Bernie would have to keep his nose clean for a long time if he was to build bridges with Lennie. On the other hand, knowing Bernie as I did, I felt that this was unlikely to happen. While I knew he would always give his best for the club given the chance, his forthright way of talking to the manager would do him no favours, and on this occasion threatened to get him into deep trouble.

For his part, Bernie was happy to go public on why the argument had taken place and I appreciated his frankness. He made it clear that he was unhappy with Lennie's selection policy and felt that he had rather unfairly been made one of the scapegoats for recent results. Again it was a great story, but I felt there would be only one outcome.

Managers usually win in these situations – even if Colin Todd didn't - and I was not surprised that Bernie made just two more starts in the remainder of that season, including the crucial last-gasp win at Wolves.

The following season Slaven was not a regular in the Boro line-up and eventually moved on. I would have liked to have seen him stay longer, as I felt he was still capable of scoring goals at the top level. However, if managers have a dissenting voice from within the dressing room they normally deal with it in the usual manner. As passionate as Bernie was about the club, he was always going to be the loser in football terms. Lennie was attempting to keep a tight ship with everybody focused in the right direction, and any player who was rowing a different way would be deemed surplus to requirements, whether it was Bernie Slaven or anybody else.

It didn't mean that Lennie's decision to leave Slaven out was the correct one, but it emphasised that the manager made the decisions and the players must live or die by them. As I say, Slaven eventually moved on as a result. My own opinion is that it's dangerous to allow any striker with a good goalscoring record to leave any club and sometimes you can cut your nose off to spite your face. I'd never release any player who had proved he could score goals for you.

In Bernie's case I genuinely believe that it was not just down to the much-publicised arguments. The bottom line was that Lennie didn't rate Bernie and preferred other players instead.

Despite the draw at Ashton Gate, the games were beginning to run out and Boro were in no way obvious automatic promotion candidates. They had lost a lot of unnecessary points lately - it was going to be tight.

In the event, Lennie engineered one of the typical rousing end-of-season runs for which he was renowned. Boro won six of their last eight games and snatched promotion on the last day of the season.

They went to Tranmere for a Friday night match after Bristol and won 2-1. On my way into Prenton Park I was stopped by a young fan who asked me, in a strong Scouse accent, if I was Eric Paylor. I had never seen him before but I replied that I was, and asked him how he knew me. He said that he had attended Boro's home game against Tranmere in September and remembered me from seeing my photo in the matchday programme.

As the home game had taken place seven months earlier I thought it was pretty impressive memory work. Gordon Cox was bemused to hear the conversation and always regards that moment as my 15 seconds of fame.

Old boy Peter Davenport scored the winner for the Mackems with a peach of a goal as Boro were beaten at Sunderland on Easter Monday, but consecutive home wins against Bristol Rovers and Grimsby set Boro up for that crucial final game at Wolves.

Before the trip to Molineux, I drove up to Newcastle Civic Centre for the Hennessy Player of The Year voting luncheon. I felt that Steve Pears was the obvious choice as the north-east's top player that season but it was a hard battle to convince the whole of the five-man panel. Sunderland's John Byrne was also a popular choice and the arguments continued into mid-afternoon. Eventually, and thankfully, we settled on Pearsy on a three-two majority.

Two days later I drove back to Newcastle, this time with Lennie Lawrence and Alan Kernaghan in tow, for the Journal Player of the Year dinner. Malcolm Crosby, Boro's current assistant manager, was there on behalf of Sunderland, along with John Byrne while Gavin Peacock represented Newcastle. A pleasant meal and convivial chat was enjoyed by all.

All that was remaining to complete the season was Boro's final game against Wolves. Molineux had been the subject of major rebuilding work over a long period of time and the work had reached the halfway stage. It left the stadium a weird mixture of old and new football styles.

The old main stand was still to be replaced by a new one, though a few yobs helped it on its way by setting fire to it in the early hours of the morning before the game.

Most of Wolverhampton's fire engines were called to deal with the blaze, while the situation was made worse at daylight by the discovery of several incendiary devices buried in the centre circle. Naturally further investigation of Molineux was needed and for some time there was a doubt whether the game would take place.

We hung around on Teesside for some time, waiting for news. We did not leave Middlesbrough until 9.50am, after I had filed a back page story detailing the facts of the fire. Gordon Cox and I had to set off at this point to make sure we would be there on time if the match was on, and we were an hour into the journey before we heard the news on the radio that the green light had been received.

We arrived in the Black Country to find an intense atmosphere outside of Molineux. There were Boro fans everywhere, though most of them were agitated and were having regular conversations with Wolves supporters. It transpired they did not have tickets to get into the game.

I'll never forget the faces of those long-serving Boro fans in Eindhoven who had travelled to the UEFA Cup Final against Sevilla without tickets. Many of them had turned up in the hope they could get one, through whatever means, having failed to get one from the Riverside despite many years of proven support. I was constantly approached and asked if I had any spare tickets when I walked around the ground in Eindhoven, and this upsetting experience brought back vivid memories of the scenes outside of Molineux.

There were hundreds of Boro fans at Wolves without tickets and they were all desperate to find a way in. The attendance at Molineux was much reduced because of the rebuilding and this was one reason why so few tickets were available. In the event the vast majority of ticketless Boro fans were to be disappointed, which was a major shame because it was a great game and an even better result.

Such was the lay-out outside of Molineux that several fans found they were able to stand close to a nearby supermarket and see up to one-third of the pitch through a gap in the stands. It was better than nothing, though probably only added to their frustration.

I was not too close to the pitch either, because the press box was situated in the new stand opposite the main stand. The pitch was still in its original position, being close to the main stand, but far away from the one opposite. This was a temporary measure while the rebuilding continued but it was from a distance that I watched the game, though fortunately still with a clear view of events.

It was a big day for Ian Ironside. The former Scarborough keeper made his league debut for the Boro in that game, because of injury to Steve Pears. It never ceases to amaze me how some goalkeepers can accept they are the club's No.2, certainly in interviews in public, spend months without getting close to the first team, and then perform to an exceptionally high standard on the odd occasions they get a call-up. Ian, yet another highly likeable lad, was one of those players and he never let Boro down in the game at Wolves, nor when he had his chances in the Premier League the following season.

However, at first the game at Molineux did not go well for Boro. They were in trouble when they trailed 1-0 around the hour mark and then had Nicky Mohan sent off. The Premier League was a million miles away at that stage. However, on-loan defender Jon Gittens from Portsmouth forced the equaliser and then Paul Wilkinson headed in a late winner following great thinking from Jamie Pollock and the victory was Boro's.

I was fortunate to get on to the pitch at the final whistle and joined in the celebrations. Lennie was carried around shoulder high, having achieved everything that he had set out to do in his first season at the Boro.

Boro's promotion success was commemorated at the north-east Football Writers Association at their annual dinner in Durham City on the Sunday, when I was there with Stuart Ripley as my guest. Steve Pears won the main award and two days later picked up the Hennessy award in front of another packed house in Newcastle.

I travelled to the latter event at the Civic Centre on the Boro executive coach, after physio Tommy Johnson had given me a lift to the departure point at Ayresome Park.

In order to get home afterwards, I accepted a lift from a journalist friend, Arthur Pickering, who also gave Hartlepool chairman Garry Gibson a ride to his home in Sedgefield. On the way back we got a puncture. While still wearing our tuxedos, Arthur and I had to change the wheel on the side of the A1 at 1.30 in the morning, with Garry on stand-by.

CHAPTER 12

WHEN Boro stepped into the inaugural Premier League season in 1992/93, they still had some ground to make up as a football club in order to enter the big time.

The still fledgling board of directors had done a relatively good job in gradually building new foundations, despite the rollercoaster form of the first team and the demand to continually strengthen the squad. Now they faced the challenge of trying to finance a second attempt to get a foothold among the country's elite.

Boro probably had enough resources to compete among the lower echelon of the teams in the Premier League, even if they were well behind the big boys in terms of playing squads and resources. It was all about trying to stabilise at this level and in this respect survival remained the major target when Boro started the new campaign in this much-publicised and newly rebranded competition.

If anybody could keep Boro up, then surely Lennie Lawrence was the man. His record in winning survival battles at Charlton Athletic was second to none. Charlton were arguably a smaller club than Boro and it had been many years since the south Londoners could generate sufficient resources to match the big guns. So the fact that the Addicks had been able to compete and survive alongside the Manchester Uniteds and Liverpools over a number of seasons was a remarkable achievement.

That's why Lawrence had been handed the nickname 'Houdini' by the media, having displayed an uncanny knack of inspiring last-ditch survival efforts at the end of every season, just when Charlton were looking doomed to relegation.

Lennie had achieved his success at Charlton on a relative shoestring. He was not frightened to spend money, but he regularly told me that he tried to be prudent with the club's resources and spent money only when it was absolutely necessary.

The Boro board did what they could to provide sufficient backing at the start of the 1992/93 campaign. Lennie told me, during our pre-season chats, that the money was there if he wanted it. Yet he carried out few transfer dealings early in the summer, and in fact had made the club a transfer profit by the time the players settled into pre-season. Lennie was happy to keep much of his available spending money on the back burner, and wait to see what happened as the campaign developed.

Lennie had lost one of his most effective players during the summer in Stuart Ripley, who was keen to test himself elsewhere and was sold to Blackburn Rovers for £1.3m. It was a sizeable fee and reasonable business for the club, while it turned out to be a good move for Rippers because he went on to win a Championship medal with Blackburn.

Rippers had been the source of many Boro goals over the last few seasons and Lawrence knew he needed to replace him, so he went out and bought winger Tommy Wright from Leicester City for £650,000. The Scot had scored 22 goals for Leicester in the previous season and at the time this seemed to be an excellent piece of business for the Boro, especially as they had made such a big profit on the two deals.

It would have been a good deal if it had worked, but the goals dried up for Tommy when he arrived on Teesside. He scored just five Premier League goals for Boro, and added another in the FA Cup. Overall he was not a success at the club.

The other early summer signing was Jon Gittens. It was a signing which surprised me because I had always been given the impression that Lennie didn't really want the central defender. Gittens had been on loan from Portsmouth at the end of the previous season and, although he had done a reliable job, he had not set the club alight.

So the decision to sign Gittens could well have been the result of a gentleman's agreement. I was told from within the club that Gittens had been promised a permanent move to Teesside if Boro were promoted. Boro not only went up, but Jon grabbed one of the goals in the crucial win at Wolves on the final day.

In the event Boro paid £250,000 to complete a permanent deal with Portsmouth. At that stage Boro were certainly not too well off for defenders, and the fee didn't break the bank. It was not a massive gamble, but Boro never received any benefits from the signing. In fact the outlay turned out to be a relative waste of money. Gittens was out of the first team line-up before the season started and Lennie never rated him highly enough to give him a run in the side.

With the friendlies approaching, Lennie was ready to go into the new season with just Wright and Gittens as his summer signings. He believed he could afford to wait, knowing that he had the back-up money to strengthen any areas which showed signs of weakness.

In the event, Lennie was to spend most of the available kitty just before the season got under way. His change of plan appeared to hinge on a dismal defeat in a friendly game at Lincoln City two weeks before the start of the new campaign.

I drove down to Lincoln with Alastair Brownlee because my regular travelling companion Gordon Cox was watching his 'second side', Hearts, entertain Celtic at Tynecastle. It was a warm day, ideal for football, and the well-grassed pitch at the rebuilt Sincil Bank stadium was spot on. Third division Lincoln certainly appreciated it. Lawrence fielded his full-strength side but the Imps ran amok and Boro were humiliated 5-1. They were absolutely awful on the day. They hardly raised a sweat and Lincoln were made to look like world-beaters.

As bad as it was, I've never been one to take too much notice of results in friendly games. I've seen Boro both brilliant and dreadful in pre-season games over the years, but a pre-season string of results can never be taken as a guideline once the serious stuff starts.

While Boro hardly lifted a finger at Lincoln, it was difficult to believe that the same players would not do themselves justice once the league campaign started. We Boro fans know too well how the team have failed to perform against lesser teams, being apparently surprised by their opponents' unbridled enthusiasm, and then themselves played out of their skins against the likes of Manchester United when the tables were turned. As a rule Boro enjoy being the underdogs, but are not so happy when they are expected to win.

While everybody in the team was poor at Lincoln, Lennie told me that the game was a clear indication that his defence was not going to be good enough for the Premier League. He was probably right, but the defence was given no support from elsewhere in the team and I felt that there were just as many problems in the other departments.

In the event, Lennie concentrated on revamping his back line and did not wait for the new campaign to get under way. He went out immediately and spent £1.5m on two international defenders to try to bring about an improvement.

He opened negotiations with Celtic over Derek Whyte and Chris Morris, and the new boys were paraded at Ayresome Park with the new season just two days away. Record Boro signing Whyte cost £900,000, while Morris was £600,000. Boro striker Andy Payton, who had failed to make a major impression at Ayresome Park in his few months at the club, was thrown into the deal and went the other way.

The double swoop represented a huge outlay for the Boro and I was surprised both by its sudden nature and the amount of cash involved. I spoke to a couple of Scottish journalists to try to find out why Celtic were so happy to sell two defenders with the new season upon them, and the general comment was that Celtic could not afford to turn down the money.

While the joint fee must have been attractive to Celtic, I felt they must have been on a healthier financial footing than Boro. So the timing of the double deal continued to leave me wondering.

The two new signings brought a combination of experience and promise to Teesside.

The 28-year-old Morris had previous top-flight experience in England with Sheffield Wednesday so he would know what to expect in the Premier League. Whyte was a lot younger, and had at one time been seen as Celtic's future, though Scottish reporters told me that he had not been playing well recently and had been offered a far from brilliant contract extension at Celtic.

While I had my doubts about the deal, Whyte and Morris proved to be two of the nicest men ever to play for the Boro. I can't ever remember them complaining about their lot, even when they took a lot of flak from fans and team-mates alike during the Juninho-Ravanelli era. Neither player ever gave less than 110 per cent for the Boro, and Morris, born in Cornwall, initially put roots down on Teesside and went on to be handed a benefit game against Nottingham Forest. Whyte recovered from a slow start with Boro to gain in stature and win further Scottish caps.

Even so the timing of their arrival on Teesside is still one of the strangest deals I can remember. The whole deal gave the impression of being a panic double-signing, though it would be unfair to suggest that Lennie was not already aware of the availability and abilities of the Celtic duo or he wouldn't have been able to move so quickly. But why they were not signed earlier, or why Lennie did not wait a little longer to see what happened at the start of the season, will always be a mystery for me.

The double deal was also the first time that I could remember an agent being so prominently involved. Raymond Sparkes negotiated the contracts and travelled down to Ayresome Park for the unveiling. I found him very personable and spoke to him on two or three occasions over the next couple of years.

After recovering from the debacle at Lincoln, Boro looked a lot better in their final warm-up games, which took place in the two-day Newcastle Exhibition tournament at St James's Park. Boro went down 1-0 to Newcastle on the Saturday in pouring rain, and then lost the third-place play-off game on the Sunday when being pipped on penalties by Real Sociedad after drawing 3-3 over 90 minutes.

Andy Payton missed the decisive penalty, which was his very last kick for the club. At that time he gave no indication that he was aware of any potential move to Celtic, and when I phoned him for quotes that evening I was amazed to discover how much the spot-kick miss had affected him. For me it was a meaningless match but Andy felt he had let down his team-mates and I was struck by his comments.

The season was only a few days away when I upset Lennie with a story which I wrote about a potential transfer target. I was informed by a correspondent that Boro were chasing Russell Beardsmore at Manchester United and I wrote the story in good faith. I never agree to any Boro story being printed in the *Evening Gazette* unless I feel that the information is genuine. Unfortunately, in this case, obviously I was given a duff tip.

I'd developed a reasonably strong bond with Lennie but he took this particular story very badly and was upset that it had been given such big headlines. The Beardsmore story was totally untrue, as it transpired later, and Lennie had every right to be annoyed.

You never know what reaction you are going to get from managers in any given situation. All managers react in their own way to circumstances and there is no golden rule. Some managers don't care how many players you link them with, as long as you don't do anything which unsettles any current members of the squad. Other managers are angry when you link them with players in which they have no interest.

You never know which way it is going to go, but in Lennie's case he made it absolutely clear that he was very angry with this particular link. He even had a blast at the *Gazette* on the local radio. If nothing else, this particular incident helped to guide my decision in future situations because I was keen not to fall out with Lennie completely.

Lawrence had no problems whatsoever when I got the exclusive on the Whyte-Morris story and printed it 24 hours ahead of it being officially announced. It was a big story for the *Evening Gazette* and gave the fans a boost with the season almost upon us.

Boro went on to lose their opening Premier League match at Coventry as they took the field in their new ICI logo shirts for the first time. However, the campaign was quickly up and running when Boro recorded two scintillating back-to-back wins which suggested they might be good enough to hold their own in the Premier League after all.

Two goals from Bernie Slaven brought Boro's first Premier League points against Manchester City at Ayresome. Then Boro produced one of their best team performances from the last 20 years when they smashed reigning champions Leeds United 4-1. It will remain one of my most memorable and enjoyable Boro games of all time. Boro ran Leeds ragged with Paul Wilkinson scoring twice and Tommy Wright and John Hendrie also netting.

After Leeds, Boro were due to play at Southampton the following Saturday. Under normal circumstances I would normally have travelled to The Dell and back on the same day. However, for reasons which I can not recall, I set off on the Friday with Ray Robertson from *The Northern Echo* and TFM radio duo John Murray and former Boro star David Mills, who is back at the Boro again following a scouting post at Newcastle United.

John drove, and we headed directly for a Travel Lodge at Nuneaton where we were booked in for the night.

John had personally handled the booking arrangements and we arrived to find we had been allotted two doubles rather than two twin rooms. It came as a bit of a surprise to all of us. I didn't fancy spending the night in bed with any of the other three and was relieved to discover that the sofas in the rooms easily converted into another bed. So I had the sofa for the night and allowed my room-mate Ray to enjoy the double bed by himself.

In the event it was a good idea to halve the journey with an overnight stay, because once we reached the south, the traffic was horrendous. It was late August and the usual last-minute rush at the end of the summer holidays was reaching its peak. Even though we had left Nuneaton in good time, there was still some doubt whether we would make it in time for the kick-off.

Fortunately, as I have family and friends living in the area, I know Hampshire quite well and was able to take us through the back roads in order to arrive at The Dell around two o'clock. I met members of my family outside the ground and they were ticketless, so I was grateful for Lennie Lawrence doing me a big favour by coming up with the goodies at the last minute.

The match didn't go too well for Boro because they went down 2-1. On the way back we four reporters stopped off at Trowell for a curry, and I eventually arrived home at quarter past midnight.

Boro bounced back from that defeat by beating Sheffield United in early September and then completed the double over Manchester City. It might have been three wins in a row, but Slaven missed a last-minute penalty at home to Ipswich which would have given Boro all three points. Bernie raced out of the ground afterwards without giving me an interview, which was most unlike him. But I knew that he was both frustrated and embarrassed to have missed such an important kick.

Lennie still had cash in the bank and, despite the outlay on Whyte and Morris, felt that the time was right to further strengthen while the team was going reasonably well. He opened negotiations to sign midfielder Rob Lee from his former club Charlton Athletic. Lee was a good box-to-box player and would be ideal for Boro. I wrote several stories about the impending arrival of the player and Lennie gave me every indication that it was close to being a done deal.

However, I was sitting in the press box at Loftus Road reporting on Boro's match at Queen's Park Rangers in late September when Andy Peake, who was suspended, told me that Lee was signing for Newcastle. No doubt Peake had been helping Lawrence to try to convince Lee to come to Boro, because he was a former team-mate at Charlton, so Andy had a bit of inside info. I wrote the story for the *Sports Gazette* that evening, but was still surprised and disappointed that Boro had missed out on their target.

Lee had been shanghaied by Newcastle United boss Kevin Keegan, who had told him that Newcastle was closer to London that Middlesbrough. This was based on the fact that there are more flights to Newcastle airport from London than there are to Teesside. However the ploy worked and Lee signed for the Magpies, even though it was actually further away from London. It also meant that Lee did not get the opportunity to play Premier League football immediately, because Newcastle were in the first division at the time.

When I spoke to Lennie the following Monday I could see how bitterly disappointed he was to have missed out on Lee. Lennie knew all about the player's capabilities because he had him in his squad at Charlton and told me that Lee would have done a great job for Boro. Lee went on to play more than 300 games for Newcastle and is one of their most revered players from the modern era.

If Lee had joined Boro at that time, he might have provided fresh impetus which would have made all the difference at the end of the season. If Boro had been able to record two more wins they would not have been relegated.

With Lee lost and the promotion adrenaline beginning to wane, Boro could not maintain their terrific start to the campaign. They were in the lead three times at QPR before having to settle for a 3-3 draw. Rangers' equaliser came in the dying seconds and Lawrence was absolutely fuming afterwards at his side's lack of professionalism. It was a frustrating setback and marked the turning point as it was the start of a run of eight games without a win.

To make matters worse, Boro were comprehensively beaten at home by Keegan's Newcastle side, including Lee, in the League Cup during this winless spell.

Lennie was still desperate to find a strong-running midfielder and looked at a potential replacement for Lee. In early November, Bulgarian Nikolay Todorov, who played for Cannes, spent a few days on trial with Boro. He looked OK in training and was granted permission by the FA to make an appearance as a trialist in a reserve game against Derby County at Ayresome Park.

It made a good story for the *Gazette*, though my attempts to converse with Todorov in my pigeon French fell on deaf ears. So I was grateful when he gave me the phone number of his interpreter. I was playing five-a-side football on the night of the reserve game and hurriedly showered afterwards before racing to Ayresome. I walked into the stadium with 25 minutes already gone to discover that Boro were 3-0 down. In the event Todorov never got a kick and it was obvious long before the final whistle that this was a deal which was never going to happen.

I picked up an even better story during the game when I was tipped off that Bernie Slaven was going on the transfer list, but my hopes of keeping my exclusive to myself were wrecked when Lennie announced the news to the waiting media after the reserve game.

I was not surprised to see Bernie transfer-listed because I knew that the pair didn't have the best of relationships. Bernie had told me on several occasions that he didn't have much respect for the manager while Lennie had told me that he didn't think Bernie could consistently hack it any more at this level.

I've seen many situations where players come to the end of the road at certain clubs and this was one of them. Lennie wanted Bernie because he felt he would not score enough goals and that he was not a player through and through.

The manager had also taken exception to some of the things that Bernie had said to him, both in public and in private, and felt it was not helping harmony in the dressing room to have a frustrated Bernie on the fringe.

For his part, Bernie hadn't lost faith in his own ability and believed it was his job to score goals for the team. Given the chance, he believed he would continue to get them.

That's where the major difference in opinion occurred. Bernie felt he could still do it, Lennie felt he could not and the manager usually wins in these situations. He is paid to make decisions and ultimately lives or dies by them. It had been obvious for some time that the parting of the ways would come and that Bernie would move on. In the event the duo did bury the hatchet for a few weeks after Bernie was transfer-listed, though it only delayed the inevitable.

Results were getting no better and a run of crippling injuries made matters worse for Boro. Lawrence was finally able to use up the last of his cash when bringing in Crewe Alexandra's midfielder Craig Hignett. He was a similar player to previous target Rob Lee, having a good engine, getting from box to box and scoring goals.

Hignett, who cost £425,000, represented more of a gamble than Lee at that time, because it was a bigger step up in class for him. He was still a relatively young player with no top-flight experience and would need time to settle in.

The talent was definitely there and Higgy looked a half-decent player from the start but didn't pull up any trees in his first season. However, he eventually made a huge impact and his signing was a fine legacy from Lawrence. Hignett went on to give Boro many superb years of service and scored many vital goals.

I got to know Higgy very well and have maintained a good relationship. He is a typical Scouser with an eye for a joke or two off the pitch, but was always looking to make things happen on it. He was another player who came in from outside and fell in love with the club and that's why he put down roots in the area at the end of his career.

Hignett's arrival in the dressing room made it easier for Lennie to ease Slaven out of the firing line and there were definite signs that the

Glaswegian's illustrious career with Boro was about to come to an end. The bust-up at Bristol City from the previous season was something which was never going to be forgotten.

Lennie would still have selected Bernie on a regular basis if he felt he would produce what he was looking for, but the manager felt he had better options elsewhere. Slaven took his lack of games badly and this only further emphasised his lack of respect for the manager. The easy way for Lennie to end this 'atmosphere' was to move Bernie on.

Lennie had made some major changes to the squad since his arrival 16 months earlier and this was just another part of the overhaul. The last thing that Lennie wanted was to see the team go down just 12 months after winning promotion and I knew he was working hard to maintain the morale of the squad. It was not just his pride in his work; his job at Boro could be on the line if he failed.

However, results were slowly beginning to go the wrong way. A John Hendrie hat-trick brought a 3-2 win against Blackburn in a downpour at Ayresome at the start of December, but Boro failed to win again that month. At the end of the year they suffered a dreadful 1-0 defeat at the hands of Crystal Palace at Ayresome Park.

Five days later I was watching Palace again when they played Hartlepool in the third round of the FA Cup. I went along to the Victoria Ground to take in a game because Boro were inactive that Saturday afternoon. Their Cup tie against Chelsea, due to take place on the Sunday, was eventually postponed because of frost.

I had a pass, but could not get a seat in the Hartlepool press box and ended up watching the match by sitting on the cold concrete steps in front of it. It was a very cold day and I didn't particularly enjoy the experience. Neither did Palace, because this time they were beaten 1-0. Pool put a lot more enthusiasm into their game than Boro had done five days earlier which suggested to me that morale was low at Ayresome Park.

Boro continued to go from bad to worse when they lost 1-0 at home to Queen's Park Rangers. After the match the club was host to *The Northern Echo* football writer Ray Robertson's retirement evening and many Boro players past and present were in attendance, including former boss Willie Maddren, Eric McMordie, Gordon Jones and Tony Mowbray. Lennie Lawrence, despite his frustration over the day's result, was there along with chairman Colin Henderson and chief executive Keith Lamb.

It was a good night both for Ray and for me because I had the opportunity to quiz everybody about the latest state of affairs and also talk about the good old days.

Lennie confided in me that he felt the QPR defeat was a significantly bad result for the team. If Boro had won, it would have given them a shot in the arm, but defeat against relatively mediocre opponents with more difficult fixtures to follow only threatened to wipe away what little self-belief was remaining within the squad.

With vital home points having been thrown away, Boro were on a desperate slide. In fact an horrendous run of 12 defeats in 15 league games left them with a mountain to climb. I saw Boro concede five goals in a league game for the first time in a heavy defeat at Aston Villa and they looked all over a relegated side.

In late January I got a call from Bernie Slaven asking me to meet him at Ayresome Park. I arrived at 9.30am to find Bernie waiting for me. He told me, following a meeting with Lennie Lawrence the previous afternoon, that he was coming off the transfer list. I was pleased for him, but was not sure how long it would last. However, it was a good story for the *Evening Gazette* and, as usual, I got plenty of good quotes from Bernie to back up the story.

Lennie did return Bernie to the line-up, albeit briefly. Bernie desperately needed to score during this spell, but it didn't happen for him. The team was struggling and not creating chances. Bernie failed to score in three starts and two appearances as sub.

Inevitably he was left out again and his frustration boiled over. There was another fall-out which this time led to Lennie handing Bernie a free transfer. It meant that the striker could talk to any interested clubs and select the next step of his career himself.

I half expected Slaven to return to Scotland, where I knew there was plenty of interest. Hardly a day went by where I did not receive a call from some Scottish journalist or other, telling me that their club was interested in Bernie. He virtually had the pick of the teams in the Premier Division north of the Border.

However, Bernie resisted the temptation to go back to Scotland and in the end opted for Port Vale who were pushing strongly for promotion from Division Two. There was the opportunity to link up with Paul Kerr and Dean Glover again, and no doubt Bernie chatted to both players before making his decision. I still thought it a strange choice at the time because I felt that Bernie could have done better.

I knew how much the Boro meant to him and I always felt he was more likely to score goals for the club than anyone else. However, he was such a good finisher that he would score goals in any team which had players clever enough to put the ball in the right area for him. In the event he did okay at Port Vale but I felt he might have scored goals at a higher level.

I disagreed with Lennie in that I felt Bernie could have gone or for longer at Boro, especially as he left at a time when the team desperately needed goals. It did not make sense to me, allowing a striker to leave during a relegation battle.

On the other hand I also knew that Lennie felt that the atmosphere in general would improve if Bernie moved on. I'm not sure that it did, but then even Bernie would have struggled to make a contribution for Boro in the closing weeks of the campaign because chances were not being created.

I was sorry to see Bernie go because I had a good relationship with him, which has been maintained to this day. He is now one of my closest friends within the media circus. But nothing stands still in football and his departure from Ayresome Park was something even Bernie Slaven could not avoid in the end.

Boro were in action at Leeds in late January and I travelled with *Gazette* photographer Steve Elliott, because Gordon Cox had gone down early on a coach with a team of Boro Junior Reds. The Junior Reds were playing their counterparts in Leeds before going on to watch the match. I walked into Elland Road to discover that Leeds had installed new press facilities. Not only had the press box moved from the right-hand side of the main stand to the left, but it was now encased in a glass dome. It was state of the art, especially the seating, which was luxurious and the first truly comfortable press seat I had ever sat in.

One of the problems with being a reporter at matches is that you can't jump up and down and clap your hands to keep warm. Football is a winter game and, as you are sitting still without moving, often for up to three hours at a time, you lose the feeling in your limbs on cold days.

So I was over-dressed at Leeds as usual, with around 18 layers of clothes to keep me warm. I didn't need any of the extra baggage in such salubrious surroundings as the new Leeds press box, and had to start stripping off the layers. But if this was the future of reporting, I wanted more of it.

Not that Boro were any different on the day as Leeds stuffed them 3-0. I had arranged to get a lift back to Teesside with Alastair Brownlee because our photographer did not need to hang around after the game. Once we had completed our interviews, I walked with Ali to the old Leeds greyhound stadium, where he had parked his car.

When we arrived at the gates to the car park, we discovered they were locked. We could see Alastair's car, standing forlornly alone in the middle of a sea of mud, but we could not get it out of the car park. We walked right around the stadium fence and, although the fence was decrepit and badly rusting, there was not a gap wide enough through which to drive the car.

Neither of us had a mobile phone at that stage, so we had to walk back to Elland Road, where the receptionist suggested we phoned the police for advice. The police were helpful, fortunately, and eventually managed to make contact with the idiot who had locked the gates, leaving Ali's car inside. We returned to the gates to await the culprit's return and had to stand outside for some time in the cold night air before he returned with the key to let us out.

When the idiot turned up he claimed: "Sorry lads. I didn't know there were any cars still in there."

He was blind as well as stupid.

It was 7.55pm when we eventually drove away from Elland Road. By the time I got home, my wife was beginning to think I had run away.

It's a romantic life being a sports writer.

CHAPTER 13

EARLY in 1993 I was aware that all was not too well in the Boro boardroom. The board of directors who had emerged from the chrysalis of the consortium which saved the club after liquidation was on the verge of fragmenting further.

The post-liquidation Boro board was now six and a half years into its existence and had done a great job in helping the club to rise from the ashes. Boro had been promoted three times during that time, reached the play-offs on another occasion and been relegated twice. Not in one single season could the word 'consolidation' be applied.

It had been a difficult time for the directors, trying to establish the club on a higher level without cast-iron financial foundations or guaranteed success on the playing field. They had given Bruce Rioch and the managers who followed every possible support, though Boro had been unable to operate with anything other than a relatively small squad of players since liquidation.

The original 1986 board consisted of chairman Colin Henderson, Steve Gibson, Henry Moszkowicz and Graham Fordy. All were either shareholders, or represented shareholdings. Moszkowicz was the leading shareholder, while Henderson, Gibson and Fordy represented the shares of ICE, Bulkhaul and Scottish and Newcastle Breweries respectively. Reg Corbidge was later co-opted as a second director representing the Breweries' interests.

Within 12 months the boardroom lost a member when Moszkowicz stepped down because of ongoing disagreements, though some level of stability followed. Board meetings had continued apace without further changes to the personnel.

Now there was a fresh level of disharmony. The spectre of a second successive relegation from the top flight was bringing renewed pressure throughout the club and people were pulling in different directions. Colin Henderson was now quite clearly now operating from one camp, while director Steve Gibson was at the head of the second camp, and had the support of Fordy and chief executive Keith Lamb.

To make matters worse, the Football League had called in the bond which the consortium directors were forced to agree to at the time they saved the club. The bond was called in because the directors had failed to pay off all the creditors of the old company in full. All the shareholders were surcharged as a result, which involved a considerable extra financial outlay for Moszkowicz, ICI, Bulkhaul and Scottish and Newcastle Breweries.

Shortly afterwards, the Breweries decided to withdraw from their involvement with the Boro. They offered their 200,000 shares for sale, pro rata, to the remaining shareholders. All of the other shareholders took up their options, leaving Moszkowicz with 396,000 shares, which represented 48 per cent of the total, ICI with 265,000 and Bulkhaul 164,000.

This considerably reduced the number of players in the boardroom drama and potentially put Moszkowicz in a very strong position if he wanted to take things further. The London-based businessman was only three per cent of the shares away from having a controlling interest.

The gradual boardroom fall-out in the 1992/93 season created a bit of bad feeling and there were no board meetings during the middle of the winter, at a time when Boro were starting to struggle badly on the pitch.

In mid-February I had a long chat with Lennie Lawrence in his office and he was very open and forthright. While he stressed that he was doing everything in his power to keep the team in the Premier League, he felt it would be very difficult with the current squad. The team had started well, but was beginning to struggle badly.

Now dressing-room morale was low.

One of the points Lennie made to me was that he did not believe he was getting the level of backing from the boardroom which normally might have been expected. I didn't believe he was as close to the directors as Bruce Rioch and Colin Todd had been, and clearly this did not help.

I'd had a couple of fall-outs with Lennie during the season but I always felt he was an honest and honourable man. I wanted to see him do well and hopefully turn things around but it was a bleak time because there was a resignation of relegation in the air and nobody you spoke to believed that Boro would stay up. I supported those views. I had a feeling that Lennie was not going to enjoy the charmed life with Boro that he experienced with Charlton.

Coincidentally, the day following my heart-to-heart chat with Lennie I was called into a special meeting with chairman Colin Henderson which included the rest of the local media. I had requested the meeting because there had been no public comment from the boardroom while the team was going backwards. I'd hoped to put Colin under a bit of pressure and find out what the board was doing to make sure the club was not relegated.

However, Colin was too clever a man to allow himself to be pushed into a corner and he concentrated on making a series of points he originally planned to make.

Once Colin had given us the view from the boardroom the meeting turned into more of a debate than a media interview and things became a little heated at times. We local media men are all Boro fans and we were desperate for some answers which would give us hope for the survival battle.

On the record, Henderson went to some lengths to point out that Lennie had spent a lot of money in reshaping the team. He said that the board had come up with the cash which had been requested, but so far there were no signs that the investment in new players was producing results.

Colin made it clear that only Lennie and the players could save the club at this stage. He left the ball firmly in the hands of the manager and his squad. It was fair comment but I still came away feeling rather deflated. Colin had spoken well but I did not think that Lennie and the players alone could save the club. I did feel that a couple of new faces in the dressing room might make all the difference. However, as the chairman stressed, the money had more or less been spent.

Henderson prepared several strongly-made points which he intended for publication. I wrote up the story the following day in the *Evening Gazette* as he would have wanted it to appear. Colin's comments were not necessarily too kind on Lennie and made it clear that the board expected a mammoth effort from everybody in and out of the dressing room in the remaining three months.

When Lennie read the article in the *Gazette* he was livid. Initially he pointed the finger at me because he felt that I had taken sides and stuck the knife into him, but all I did was print what the chairman wanted to say. Once Lennie had cooled down he accepted this fact and confided in me that now he knew exactly what the board was thinking. The chairman in particular was putting him under pressure to produce results.

Shortly afterwards, Lennie was able to bring in another new face when Chris Kamara joined the club on a month's loan from Luton Town. I had spoken to Chris on a few occasions in telephone interviews in the past and felt that I already knew him well. As a Middlesbrough-born professional he was also well known in the town and held the claim to fame that he was a former schoolmate of Boro director Steve Gibson.

This was the first time I had met Chris face to face and he was as friendly as I expected him to be. I've maintained occasional contact with him ever since, including his spell in management and am delighted to see him make such a successful career for himself in the media.

The players were also impressed with Kamara upon his arrival. After a brief training session, Chris emerged from the Boro dressing room with – unbeknown to him – 'The Saviour' chalked on the back of his leather jacket.

Kamara's arrival virtually coincided with Gary Parkinson's departure. The right-back was no longer getting anywhere near the first team because of the form of Chris Morris and Curtis Fleming. When I bumped into Gary at Ayresome Park he was leaving to sign for Bolton Wanderers on a free transfer.

I was disappointed to see Gary go. He was one of the Rioch youths who had helped transform the club after liquidation and I'd always had a friendly relationship with him. I'm delighted to say he has continued to work in football and he was employed on the youth side with one of the north-west clubs when I last met him.

Kamara tasted victory in his third Boro match when the team went to Ipswich on a freezing evening in early March and won 1-0 thanks to a goal from Paul Wilkinson. I had double cause for celebration because I had backed Boro to win the game 1-0, at odds of 12-1. However, the return journey to Teesside was not too enjoyable. It was ten to three when I got to bed.

Boro's reward for their victory was a short break in Marbella, which saw me scrambling around for player interviews before the squad left for the sunshine.

However, I was able to ring Lennie on a daily basis at the team's hotel on the Costa del Sol.

When Boro returned home they faced a Tuesday night trip to Wimbledon. I travelled down to London on the train with John Murray from TFM Radio and Clive Hetherington from *The Northern Echo*, though all three of us were staying in different hotels. I was in the Bloomsbury Park Hotel just off Russell Square. There were problems with the mainline rail traffic and we were late arriving in London.

I decided to go without an evening meal which was just as well because the underground network was chaotic. I was delayed in getting to Victoria and I finally arrived at Wimbledon just half an hour before the kick-off.

It was hardly worth it as Boro were awful and lost 2-0. After the game I was grateful for a lift back to the city from Alan Comfort, the former Boro winger who had recently been accepted into the ministry. Alan had just started his training as a curate. I was delighted to be offered the ride because I might have otherwise been stuck at Wimbledon. After being dropped off, I was able to hail a taxi in the city and was back at the Bloomsbury Park within a couple of minutes.

However, I had further problems on the trains on the way home the following day, missing connections at both York and Darlington. It was 2.30pm by the time I finally got back to the office.

Bernie Slaven completed his move to Port Vale before the weekend which left Steve Pears and Alan Kernaghan as the only remaining members of Bruce Rioch's team. I phoned Bernie a week after his move and, while he appreciated the chat, he was clearly not enjoying himself at the time. He'd previously been a one-club man in England and I could tell that he wasn't too happy. It's always difficult for players to get their feet under the table at new clubs, especially when they have to spend the first few weeks in a lonely hotel room.

The players Bernie had left behind on Teesside were also in a state of depression. They were beginning to accept the near-inevitability of relegation. It was difficult to get interviews because the players had nothing positive to say.

On the Ides of March I was given a clear indication that things were beginning to happen at boardroom and director level. Henry Moszkowicz phoned me from London to publicly issue his demand for places for both himself and his wife Rosemary on the Boro board. The same demands, naturally, had been posted to the board.

Henry had resigned from the board in 1987 following a series of disagreements but had never lost his love for the club. At no time had he ever considered giving up his massive shareholding. He was the leading shareholder and as a result his opinions were important, though not necessarily in the Boro boardroom. His request for two directors' places for himself and his wife was refused.

The fact that Henry had made this move suggested that there had been developments behind the scenes. The power struggle was beginning to move into gear and, at that stage, it was impossible to predict the outcome. It seems ridiculous to admit it nowadays but there was no evidence from the *Gazette*'s point of view in early 1993 that Steve Gibson would definitely win the battle for control of the club.

While Steve had the support of fellow director Graham Fordy and chief executive Keith Lamb and was being busy putting together a list of ambitious plans for the Boro, he still held the smallest shareholding.

The outcome of the relegation battle was much easier to predict. I drove down to Chelsea with Gordon Cox in early April and watched Boro stuffed 4-0. We stopped on the way to place a Grand National bet and had been hoping to brighten up the day by watching the National on TV at half-time during the match. But the race was delayed and delayed and we had to return to the press box for the second half of the match before the horses were on their way. We discovered later that the National hadn't been run at all. This more or less summed up a frustrating day and, to cap a wasted trip, I arrived home at midnight in pouring rain.

Lennie still managed to squeeze something extra from the squad in the closing games when he staged his usual Houdini-style survival attempt. A goal from John Hendrie beat Arsenal 1-0 on the Tuesday after the Chelsea debacle, but then Boro lost their way again for a spell when beaten at home by Everton on Easter Saturday and 4-1 at Crystal Palace on Monday. That long trip to Selhurst Park on a public holiday was one of the most depressing football days of my life. Boro were murdered on a grass-free pitch and we got stuck in the holiday traffic in London as we attempted to drive home afterwards.

Relegation was nigh on inevitable but Boro gave themselves a chance when beating Spurs by 3-0 at Ayresome with two goals from Tommy Wright and another from Paul Wilkinson. However, it was only a faint chance. Boro were left needing to win at Sheffield Wednesday in their penultimate match and then keep their fingers crossed that other results went their way.

The Boro directors were pretty certain that the battle for survival was lost because the battle in the boardroom kicked off again on April 30, the day before Boro were due to go to Hillsborough.

On the morning I was summoned to an office in Queen's Square by Colin Henderson. He gave me the exclusive news that he was standing down as Boro chairman. He demanded a total restructure of the boardroom, greater shareholder involvement on the board and the reinstatement of leading shareholder Henry Moszkowicz. Colin told me he would be staying on the board but I realised that he was now virtually at war with Steve Gibson in the battle to control the future direction of the club.

It was a good story for the *Evening Gazette* but there was a further twist later in the day when Steve Gibson called me to his offices at Bulkhaul. When I arrived, chief executive Keith Lamb and director Graham Fordy were also there. Gibson was well aware of Henderson's resignation and filled me in with his side of the story. The rift was confirmed, while Gibson made it absolutely clear that this was a battle which he must win.

I don't think boardroom battles do much for the image of any club and the quicker they are sorted out the better. If you don't have harmony at the top, then you won't get it further down the ladder. The stories of the rift may have been good enough to sell a few *Gazettes* but I knew that the struggle needed to be resolved as soon as possible.

As I have said, at that time I did not know which was the stronger side in the battle, or which would be better equipped to guide the club into a bright future. Both sides clearly wanted the *Gazette* on board but it would have been foolish for the newspaper to take sides while so many things were still bubbling in the melting pot, so I treated every interview with a straight bat.

Boro were relegated, as expected, at Hillsborough, even though they won the game 3-2. Young keeper Andy Collett enjoyed a memorable debut in goal, having been pressed into service because of injuries to Steve Pears and Ian Ironside. Boro still went down because other results went against them on the day.

It left one game remaining, at home to Norwich City, but before then the boardroom battle kicked off big time.

On May 4 I was called to the Bulkhaul offices again where Steve Gibson launched a strong attack on Colin Henderson's role in the increasingly bitter struggle. Gibson gave me a statement which he wanted me to print in the *Evening Gazette* in full. When I arrived back at the *Gazette* with the statement, our editor at the time believed that there might be libels within it. So it was passed on to our solicitors who agreed with the editor. At the same time I had contacted Colin Henderson to give him the right of reply to the statement. He told me he would get a warrant to stop us from printing it.

Both sides had good reasons to both attack and defend their corners in the struggle for control of the club. I was stuck in the middle. I received several calls from both parties, and counter calls, during the course of the day but on every occasion I was unable to take any action.

The following day the *Gazette* solicitors suggested several amendments to the statement. I contacted Steve Gibson and told him of the recommended changes. Initially he agreed, though very reluctantly, and so the editor printed the revised statement. As soon as the *Gazette* was on the streets I had to deal with calls from both Gibson and Lamb complaining bitterly that the changes had considerably watered down the points they had wanted to make. I agreed with them, but the matter was above my head.

That evening the Hennessy player of the year awards evening took place at Newcastle Civic Centre. Steve Gibson and Colin Henderson were both in attendance, though they were seated at separate tables. The main award went to Newcastle midfielder Lee Clark.

The day before Boro's final game, the club sent me a statement which revealed that Lennie Lawrence had been awarded a year's extension to his contract. I was on a day off but I wrote up the story and filed it to the *Gazette*.

Lennie's original two-year deal was on the verge of running out and so the club needed to make a decision one way or the other. It was probably a good time to make the announcement and it answered a lot of questions because I had felt that Lennie had been on a little bit of stony ground in the closing months of the campaign. I had wondered whether he would survive the relegation and so, too, did many fans.

I noted in my records that it put Lennie under a lot of pressure to bring Boro back up at the first attempt, but that was probably not a bad thing. In any case, the constant striving for success is the nature of the game.

Boro's final game, at home to Norwich City, turned out to be a 3-3 thriller. It left Boro on 44 points which under normal circumstances was a pretty good tally and, in another season, might have kept them up.

Lennie Lawrence was philosophical about the relegation. He told me that the players had given their best under the circumstances and felt that it might have been different if the injuries had not been so severe.

He also told me that he believed he could have received slightly better support from the boardroom. Lennie claimed there had been no board meetings between November and March and, as the team was on the slide at this time, felt that the dire situation should have been under more regular discussion.

CHAPTER 14

IF there is one significant period in the recent history of Middlesbrough Football Club which stands out above the remainder and can be regarded as a watershed, then it is the months which covered the second half of the 1993/94 season.

Many Boro fans will not agree, because it was also a season where attendances at Ayresome Park fell dramatically as a result of ongoing frustrations felt over a lack of success on the field.

After a whirlwind start to the campaign, Boro lost their way and went on to play some dreadful football in the run-up to Christmas. Even though Boro picked up considerably in the second half of the season, many fans had simply had enough of Lennie Lawrence's management and subsequently deserted the club in droves. It was patently obvious they had no plans to return until there was a change at the helm.

However, it was hardly a disastrous season, bearing in mind that Boro had almost dropped straight through to the third division following their relegation under Bruce Rioch. There was little cash for strengthening the squad in 1993/94 yet, all things considered, Lennie managed to steady the ship and avoid a complete collapse on the pitch.

If Boro had been able to finish the season more strongly, they would have had a chance of scraping into the play-off positions. In the event they finished eighth which was something of an achievement in itself.

However, while I can try to argue that the team's standard of football and the overall level of achievement looks better than we all believed at the time, this is not the reason why this season was particularly significant.

1993/94 is special because it witnessed the emergence of stability at the top. This was the season when the saga of the boardroom battle was finally sorted out once and for all. It allowed the club to escape from its shackles and finally move forward.

Steve Gibson completed his coup d'etat by buying up the whole of the club's shareholding during the campaign. It gave him 100 per cent control and allowed him to begin to lay the foundations for the football club which we now accept as the modern Boro.

After months and months of internal bickering, at last the fall-outs and petty arguments from the boardroom were laid to rest and the club was given a solid direction. When we look back at everything Boro have achieved since, then 1993/94 was indeed a watershed season and hugely important in the history of the club.

Unfortunately the boardroom battle was no closer to being resolved when that season got under way and the veil of uncertainty behind the scenes made it very difficult for Lennie Lawrence to make a fresh impact. Looking at my *Gazette* cuttings from that era, I did try to get across to the fans the full extent of the difficult circumstances that Lennie and his players were working under when they began to struggle to maintain their bright start to the campaign.

However, when you have paid good money to watch the team on a regular basis and both results and performances do not meet your expectations, then you have a right to complain. The tirade of bitterness which built up towards the manager from the terraces that season was overwhelming and, without sufficient backing, I always felt he was working with one hand tied behind his back.

This was evident in the summer of 1993 when Lennie told me there was little cash in the kitty to strengthen the squad. I can't imagine what the reaction would be from 20,000 or more Boro season-ticket holders next season if Boro failed to add to their squad during the summer, but this was how it was at the start of that campaign.

Boro did have a much smaller season-ticket fan base in 1993/94, but it was still a body-blow to both manager and supporters. Lennie told me that if he wanted to buy new players, he had to sell from within his current squad in order to generate some cash. It was hardly an ideal way in which to prepare for a campaign, especially one where Lennie knew full well that anything short of promotion would be seen as a failure in the eyes of the fans.

I agreed with Lennie that the squad needed considerable investment if he was to turn the tide and, at the time, I felt that the board should have been doing more. On August 12, two days before the season got underway, I wrote a comment piece in the *Evening Gazette* complaining about the club's lack of summer activity in the transfer market.

Both Steve Gibson and Keith Lamb were absolutely livid about some of the things that I said and the way in which the article was written. Lamb rang me the same day to complain and Gibson was on the phone the following day.

Both made it absolutely clear that the manager had been backed all the way by the board with him being offered and signing a new contract, but the provision of significant funding to strengthen the squad was simply not possible. The duo stressed that the major responsibility of the board, as ever, was to ensure the future survival of the club.

Gibson and Lamb pointed out that there was plenty of experience within the squad and that they expected both the manager and the players to play their part and bring about a decent season.

Lennie wanted to do whatever he could to brighten up the squad and so, soon afterwards, he started the selling process in order to generate some vital spending money. The first player to leave Ayresome Park was left-back Jimmy Phillips who rejoined his hometown club Bolton Wanderers for £250,000. Lennie still regarded Jimmy's departure as a huge loss to the squad - so did I. Phillips was experienced and dependable, though I suspected it was a deal with which the fans were generally happy. The defender was not too popular on the terraces and had been the crowd's 'boo boy' from the previous campaign.

Philips was followed out of the club by midfielder Willie Falconer who was sold to Celtic for £450,000. Falconer would surely have done a good job for the team that particular season, so it was another disappointing loss which left Boro less effective in two areas of the pitch.

While Boro started the new campaign two players down, it soon became three when Alan Kernaghan moved on to Manchester City for what was a massive fee of at the time of £1.66m. Despite being a relatively slow developer throughout his Boro career and having been converted from a centre-forward to a centre-back, Kernaghan was quite clearly now regarded as Boro's biggest asset. So his loss created another big hole in the squad.

To make matters worse, Lennie told me that he would not have sold Phillips and Falconer if he had been able to find a buyer for Kernaghan first. His plan had been to sell Kernaghan and hold on to everyone else but, as City were slow to come in for Kernaghan, Lennie had no choice but to agree to the other sales when the offers came in.

As Lennie did not get his hands on anywhere near the £2.36m which the club obtained from the three outgoing transfers, clearly he generated some useful cash generation without too much benefit to himself nor the team. What Lennie did was boost the club's coffers and help make up for the lack of revenue through the gates during what proved to be a difficult season.

With the squad now considerably weaker, Lennie had little option but to start the season with a few kids in the team. Not only did they begin the season in the first team but they stayed there. Fortunately, the likes of Alan Moore, Jamie Pollock and Richard Liburd quickly developed as key personnel. Pollock in particular, who was still only 19 at the start of the campaign, assumed a terrific amount of responsibility in the midfield engine room and became one of the team's crucial members.

Liburd, also 19 when the campaign kicked off, had been a professional for only a few months having been signed from non-league football at Eastwood Town. Liburd was right-footed but was handed the job of replacing Phillips at left-back in an emergency. He did a great job under the circumstances throughout the whole of the campaign and you've got to hand it to Lawrence for giving him his chance.

However, it was 18-year-old Moore who grabbed all the early headlines. The Dubliner looked every bit a wonder kid in the opening games. It seemed that Boro had suddenly unearthed a sensational young player. Alan was a revelation when the campaign got under way, scoring goals and creating them while looking a clinical match-winner.

In the event, the headlines in the national newspapers probably did nothing to help him keep his feet on the ground. Alan was rather unfortunately compared with the great George Best on the back pages of the tabloids. This was a tag which hung around his neck like a noose and did him little good, career-wise. Alan did find it difficult to maintain his sparkling early-season form which took the gloss off some of the newspaper headlines. In fact, despite some great moments, Moore never repeated his early-season form from 1993/94 on a regular basis throughout the whole of his time with Boro.

Boro started the campaign at Notts County on the back of lurid revelations in *'The Sun'* newspaper that morning about Craig Hignett's private life. It was the day when names were introduced on the back of players' shirts and Lawrence emerged from the dressing room to tell me that Hignett was to have 'The Rat' embroidered on the back of his shirt. The fact that Lennie was able to joke about the story, minutes before the big kick-off, was an indication that it probably did more good than harm in the dressing room. The players had no doubt been cracking a few jokes about the story, and forgetting their pre-match nerves.

As a result, Boro were fired up from the start on a red-hot day at Meadow Lane, none more so than Moore, who scored twice and made the other as Boro won 3-2.

The club's new captain was John Hendrie. He had taken over from Alan Kernaghan, who had been stripped of the role, having turned down the offer of a new contract and effectively been available for transfer all summer.

I ghost-wrote a Captain's Column in the *Evening Gazette* at that time and had been speaking to Kerny on a regular basis previously. I rang Kerny that night to tell him that, as he was no longer captain, the *Gazette* would be taking on Hendrie as the new column writer.

I was both taken aback and embarrassed when Kerny replied that not only was he now ready to stay at Ayresome but that he had been officially named by Lennie as team captain for the opening day at Meadow Lane, while Hendrie's role was to be club captain.

The revelations pushed me into a corner though, as the *Gazette* had already made a binding decision to take on Hendrie for the season's column, I had to tell Kerny that we had switched camps regardless of the circumstances.

Kerny was unhappy to receive the news, because he felt that it was his job to give me the information for the column on behalf of the dressing room. Eventually, following some delicate discussion, he agreed to stand down, though it was an awkward situation for me. In the event Alan moved on to Manchester City within weeks – though we weren't to know at the time that the transfer would come about – and the *Gazette* stuck with Hendrie as its column writer.

Three days later I was summoned to see Steve Gibson at his Bulkhaul offices. He gave me the latest information on the developments in the boardroom, as he saw them, and also went to some lengths to explain the workings of his own business at Bulkhaul. I found it both interesting and informative, but I felt that the whole session was generated as a public relations exercise to make sure that I stayed on board during what Gibson clearly envisaged as a difficult few months ahead.

Steve had been very good to me during the liquidation crisis and I will always be grateful for that. On the other hand I think he also appreciated the power of the press and the value of positive publicity in the local paper. Steve did not want to lose me and I certainly did not want to lose him. In any case, the bottom line for Steve has always been the Boro and future progress of the club. He has never, ever made a decision on behalf of the club which did not always put the Boro and its supporters first. For the first time, I came away from our meeting feeling some guilt that I might not be making the right decision by sitting on the fence while the boardroom battle rumbled on.

Boro built on their success at Notts County with successive wins against Derby, Barnsley and Wolves followed the latter two away from home, and Boro were suddenly well clear at the top of the league with maximum points before the end of August.

Molineux's rebuilding was now complete and both the ground and the fittings behind the scenes were state of the art. I was not used to being treated so well during away games, but Wolves were making a major breakthrough in terms of media relations. There was a steward who repeatedly asked me if I wanted a sandwich or a drink and who was reluctant to take 'no' for an answer. Wolves were one of the first clubs to take this step into modernisation both in respect of buildings and attitudes towards their media guests and I felt it was a refreshing step in the right direction.

Before the month was out, Boro made their first foray into the Anglo Italian Cup. It was only at Grimsby Town, in the qualifying round on a Tuesday night, but it was still a step into the unknown for me. I went with Gordon Cox and, as he was late in picking me up, we had to try to make quick progress by blasting our way down the outside lane.

Everything was OK until we reached Ferrybridge, where we came to a standstill on the A1. By the time we reached the M18 we were struggling, but Coxy hammered the car and we completed the final 43 miles in 28 minutes. The thing about Coxy is that he doesn't like to miss a single kick. We walked into Blundell Park a little flustered just as the referee was blowing his whistle to start the game. Unfortunately Coxy's effective use of the accelerator hardly seemed worthwhile because Boro went on to lose a boring match 2-1.

However, those Boro fans who wanted to see the club in Europe did not have to worry because, seven days later Boro qualified for the main stages of the Anglo Italian from their round-robin group. They did so when beating Barnsley 3-0 at Ayresome Park. Like everybody else I struggled to work out whether or not Boro were definitely through, so confusing were the rules. But it was Gordon Cox who assured me, and Lennie Lawrence for that matter, that Boro had reached the international stage of the competition.

While we all looked forward to the prospect of a little detraction against Italian second division teams, unfortunately the tide was about to turn in the league. Four first division wins in a row had created heavy expectations which Boro were unable to fulfil.

I set off for Southend United with Coxy dropping off his pal Ian at Doncaster for the St Leger meeting. We still managed to get to Roots Hall in good time, despite horrendous road works at Basildon which delayed the arrival of other reporters. Sunday newspaper writer Brian McNally didn't get there until half-time. He had flown down to Heathrow and picked up a hire car, but got stuck in the roadworks.

Again, our efforts to get there in good time for the kick-off were barely worth it as Boro were poor and lost 1-0. On the way back we picked up Ian outside Doncaster Station at ten to nine. He had enjoyed a better day than us, backing the St Leger winner and then going to the cinema while he killed time awaiting our arrival.

Two days later Steve Gibson rang me at home to say that he had accepted the vacant chair at Ayresome Park. For the very first time since accepting the offer of a directorship at Ayresome Park in 1984 he was finally in the hot seat with the chance to make an impact within the club. He had been chairman very briefly during the liquidation battle, when his main quest had been to ensure the club's survival, but this was different.

Steve talked very positively about the future and would not entertain questions about the possibility of him failing to win the boardroom battle. I could tell how determined he was to gain eventual full control of the Boro and accepting the chairmanship was a step in the right direction.

However, while there was progress at boardroom level, things were beginning to go wrong for the team. The following day Boro lost to Stoke City on a saturated pitch at Ayresome Park. Three days later Alan Kernaghan was sold to Manchester City and soon afterwards goalkeeper Ian Ironside moved to Stockport County on a free transfer, leaving the squad further depleted.

Before the end of September, Steve Gibson asked me to drive to Bulkhaul for another chat. He revealed, for the very first time, that he had opened negotiations for a new stadium to be built on Teesside to replace Ayresome Park. It was awesome news and came completely out of the blue. I was flattered to be handed such information at that early stage of developments. The new stadium project indicated how determined Gibson was to push forward with his ambitious plans, even though he did not yet have control of the club.

On October 12 I had my first taste of Boro playing in Europe. Boro were at Pisa in the Anglo Italian Cup. It was a great opportunity to see the Leaning Tower, but I knew that the task of reporting the game might not be as pleasant. Not only was I working in a Continental country for the first time and with no knowledge of the Italian language other than the word 'spaghetti', but I also had a lot of copy to transmit back to England. I was expected to send reports and interviews to our sister paper *The Journal* at Newcastle, in addition to the *Evening Gazette*.

I rose at 5am and half an hour later a taxi arrived to take me to Teesside Airport. Armed with 92,000 lira and a Pisa tour guide I met up with fellow pressmen Alastair Brownlee, John Murray, David Mills, Clive Hetherington and Dave Roberts at the airport, along with Teesside referee Jeff Winter, who was travelling to work alongside Alastair as BBC Radio Cleveland's expert pundit. We were joined by a handful of fans on the shuttle plane to Heathrow from where we caught a flight directly to Pisa.

As soon as we stepped on to Italian soil, we were hit by the high level of humidity. It was extremely hot, especially for that time of year. My shirt was sticking to me within minutes. Fortunately the hotel was air conditioned, and my room – which I was sharing with Clive, reporting for *The Northern Echo* - was fine. A three-course meal was waiting for us upon arrival, which was just as well because nobody in the hotel spoke any English.

There was plenty of time remaining that afternoon for us to have a look at the Leaning Tower. Clive assisted me by taking the usual pictures of me standing and pretending to hold up the Tower from a distance. Unfortunately when I arrived back home I discovered that the film in the camera had not connected properly and the whole of the roll was blank. Che peccato!

By the time Clive and I returned to our hotel, there was no time to eat and I can recall we paid an extortionate amount of money for two colas. When we got a taxi to the Arena Garibaldi we met up with the remainder of the press brigade, but when we tried to gain admission at the official entrance we were refused entry. As far as the Pisa staff were concerned, we might have come from a different planet.

We could not make ourselves understood to the stewards, none of whom spoke any English whatsoever. It was a shock to the system to realise how difficult it was going to be to get this particular job done and just the start of the many problems which I would encounter in Europe with the Boro over the years.

The stewards sent us from gate to gate, so all seven of us lumbered hopelessly around the stadium in the intense humidity. For a long time it appeared that we would be refused admission completely.

As I recall, it was around 40 minutes before we heard the divine tones of an English-speaking voice from within at one of the gates. It emerged that the Pisa officials were expecting a group of English media but had forgotten to tell the stewards. So, at last, we were welcomed in and handed our media passes.

The stadium was typical Italian, being 100 per cent concrete with a main stand and three open sides. It was also sparsely populated and was a clear indication to me that this revived competition – which had attracted low attendances in Boro's English qualifying games - had not grabbed the imagination of the fans at home or abroad.

Mobile phones were in their infancy at that time. The normal process in reporting a match was to hire a landline in advance from an agency. I had spent some time during the past week speaking to an Italian news agency to make sure that they had received my order for a phone. They had provided me with the number of the ordered phone. When I clambered up to the press box I discovered that the phone was not waiting for me. Nor was Clive Hetherington's landline anywhere to be seen. I was not particularly impressed, especially as we could not make ourselves understood to any of the local Italian pressmen.

So we were up the creek without a paddle. I had no phone with which to send a match report to *The Journal*, and Clive could not service *The Northern Echo*.

In the event both Clive and I were saved by Clubcall journalist John Temple who had recently taken control of that most wondrous of items, a mobile phone. His particular phone was a huge thing, big and bulky, and nowadays it would be in great demand as a collector's item but it worked, even in Italy, and did the job for the three of us. Not only was John able to file his updates, but also Clive and I fitted in between the showers to send truncated reports ourselves. Without John's phone, we would have faced an impossible situation.

Lennie fielded a mixed team with quite a few young faces in action for the first time and Boro lost 3-1. While few Italians were in the stadium, the travelling party of 100 or so Boro fans could be heard singing non-stop through the game.

After the match the Italian journalists suddenly began to speak English. A rather pleasant guy with a better command of English than most of us Teessiders, approached and asked me to do an interview for Italian radio. I can't imagine what the Italian listeners made of it but I was happy to do it, especially as the radio guy provided me with free use of a phone afterwards. It gave me the opportunity to send the post-match quotes to The Journal.

The stadium was deserted when we left and I had to walk the two miles or so back to the hotel while most of the other lads went for a welcome birra. Upon arriving in my hotel room I had to start writing up the reports for the *Gazette*. I got to bed shortly before two o'clock while it was some time afterwards when Clive came back from the ristorante.

The *Gazette* copy typist rang me at ten to eight for the reports which were duly filed before breakfast. We had time for a morning walk in the hot sun before the coach arrived at one o'clock to take us back to the airport where we met up with Lennie and the players. The result had been disappointing but Lennie told me he was just happy to get the game out of the way without any injuries.

We had a fun flight back to Heathrow. Alastair Brownlee made the mistake of going to the loo just as his meal arrived and Jeff Winter and Dave Roberts took a bite, or a drink, out of every item on his plate before he returned.

After a long delay at Heathrow for the shuttle flight I got home at 10.45pm with 38,000 lira still in my pocket. Although the following day was officially a day off, I was writing follow up reports until 2.30pm. Ah, the romance of journalism.

A 4-1 victory against Sunderland the following weekend lifted the spirits but it was to be the last league win for two months. A season of great expectation quickly changed to one of sheer frustration.

CHAPTER 15

BY the middle of October 1993, Boro had slipped out of the top three and there were growing fears that the squad would not be capable of sustaining a push for promotion.

Lennie Lawrence was operating with a smaller number of players than in the previous campaign, and a run of injuries had stretched his squad to the limit. Several young kids had already been called up to try to fill the gaps, but it was not the answer.

Boro had won just two of their last eight games, but worse was to follow as the team went on to a draw a blank until the week before Christmas, leading to growing concern on the terraces.

New players were needed to try to prevent Boro from slipping further down the table but, although Lawrence had some money at his disposal, he did not have an open chequebook. Lennie felt had he had just enough cash to make one effective signing and was desperate not to waste it.

Boro were at Millwall towards the end of October and it was a great opportunity for me to check out the Lions' new purpose-built stadium, The New Den, ahead of Boro's plans to build a new ground.

I travelled down with Gordon Cox and we got to the stadium in good time, despite getting stuck in horrendous traffic which was snarled up throughout London. My first impression was that the outside of the new ground was a bit basic, without any frills, but clearly it was designed at the right price to serve a purpose. It was a much better facility than Cold Blow Lane, but then Millwall were unable to move from their cultural surroundings and the new stadium was hardly erected in the most salubrious area of south London.

Once inside The New Den I was immediately impressed by the infrastructure. The press facilities were a joy. Just as Wolves had done a few weeks earlier, Millwall had taken the media lounge facilities into a new era. Not only was there a large lounge with tea- and coffee-making facilities, but also separate phone and interview rooms. It seemed like a dream. This kind of facility is bog-standard these days but at that time it was ground-breaking.

What made it even better was that there was a passage giving access to the door of the players' lounge. Not only did Millwall look after you, they let you do your job as well - it was wonderful.

The game ended as a 1-1 draw, Boro benefiting from an own goal. Nobody likes to hang around in London on a Sunday, so we got a flyer. Coxy drove through London on the way back and over Tower Bridge but then he really motored up the M11 and A1 and we arrived back on Teesside before nine thirty.

The following Friday I was in action myself. Steve Gibson had challenged me to field a team against his recreational side for an eleven-a-side game and he kindly provided all the necessary facilities at Billingham Synthonia. I had played Sunday football for 17 years but retired from the eleven-a-side game some time previously. I played in midfield against Steve's team and the game more or less passed me by but I enjoyed the experience and so did my pals. Steve fielded a side of old pros and, although my team generally had youth on its side, the Gibson XI won 4-1.

Gibson scored one of the goals for his side, while Ray Train, George Shipley and David Mills netted the others. The Gibson XI also included the likes of Pat Cuff, John Pickering, Terry Cochrane and club physio Mark Nile, while Keith Lamb also played the second half.

Unfortunately the club's senior team was struggling. After a 1-1 draw at home to Peterborough I travelled to Portsmouth on the train to see Boro lose 2-0. The injuries were beginning to bite by this time and Lennie handed debuts to youngsters Michael Barron and Ian Johnson. Both did well at Fratton Park with Johnson hitting the post with a screamer in the first couple of minutes. Overall, however, Boro were second best and Lennie was very, very angry afterwards. It was rare to see him as upset as this but he gave me some great quotes for the *Gazette*.

The injuries were biting hard and the squad was stretched to the full. Lennie had been promised some cash to spend but nowhere near the £2.36m which he had generated in sales. Attendances were dropping dramatically at Ayresome Park and with the directors keeping one eye on the future, the manager could not hope to be handed anywhere near that amount of money to strengthen. He was already pitching in the kids and was well aware of how difficult the season was becoming.

When *The Northern Echo*'s Clive Hetherington and I came out of Fratton Park, we were struggling to hail a taxi to get to our hotel. So we were grateful for a helping hand from a Boro fan called Mick, who was working in Portsmouth, who offered us a lift. We had a drink together in a bar next to the hotel and then I finally retired to my room to start writing up my reports.

The journey back the following day was a nightmare because a lorry had apparently crashed into a bridge near Peterborough (how often does that happen?) and the main line was blocked. We sat on the train for ages without it moving, though the delay gave me the opportunity to write up several advance stories without having to worry about the shaking of the train. It was 4.30pm by the time I arrived home.

When I went to Ayresome Park the following day John Hendrie grabbed me and complained that I had printed a story which he had given to me earlier than I had promised. I can't recall what the story was about but I can remember that John was very upset. I didn't agree with him but I didn't argue because the circumstances had clearly annoyed him.

To make matters worse, John was injured and seemingly out of action for some time, so it was a frustrating period for him. These fall-outs with players happened from time to time, with some leaving a bad atmosphere for a few weeks. John wasn't the type of guy to bear a grudge and I knew it would soon blow over.

Hendrie's injury was a massive blow for both Lennie and the rest of the team. He had been converted from a winger to a striker to good effect by the manager. Hendrie's absence left Boro with only Paul Wilkinson as an experienced front runner and they were beginning to struggle for goals.

Lennie was also worried about the falling attendances. He asked me to put a special coupon in the sports pages of the *Gazette* asking stay-away fans to give their reasons. How many managers under pressure would make a suggestion like that? I was happy to publish the coupon, and was staggered by the huge response. I had to work several hours of unpaid overtime checking the coupons, putting them into different categories and counting them.

The results made for interesting copy in the *Gazette* but at the end of the day did nothing for Lawrence's credibility in the eyes of the fans, because he was heavily criticised in the coupons. Many fans were already calling for his head. I was speaking to Lennie on a daily basis and I knew how hard he was working behind the scenes to try to turn things around, so I did feel some sympathy, especially as he had authorised the fans' poll himself.

However, Lawrence's team was now lacking a spark. Boro lost 1-0 at home to Bristol City on the Saturday and were dreadful and I battered them in the *Gazette* on the Monday. My comments angered Lennie who criticised me in a radio interview, later snapping at me in a conversation soon after. It was out of character but I had no problem with that. I knew that Lennie was basically cool, calm and collected, and a good man. However, we are all human and the pressure on him to improve results was hitting hard.

The following day I travelled with Alastair Brownlee and Gordon Cox for Boro's Coca-Cola Cup replay against Sheffield Wednesday. When we alighted from the car outside Hillsborough, Coxy realised that he had not only forgotten his overcoat but his jacket as well. I was wearing plenty of layers of clothes but as it was a cold evening I could not bring myself to hand him one, as he shivered his way through the game in his pullover.

The match went to extra time, Boro eventually losing 2-1. Afterwards Coxy insisted on finding a fish and chip shop in order to warm himself up through the contents of his stomach. But we drove around the suburbs of Sheffield for ages, desperately seeking a chippie without success.

In the end we set off for home with Coxy's stomach rumbling louder than the car engine. Eventually I succumbed to the rattling and allowed both Alastair and Coxy a couple of bites of my turkey sandwich and corned beef slice which I had saved for such an emergency.

Bruce Rioch was back at Ayresome Park in Boro's next league game, bringing his Bolton Wanderers side in a match which was shown live on TV. The match went ahead despite a layer of snow on the pitch. Boro were awful again and lost 1-0.

Afterwards I had a pleasant chat with Rioch who rather politely refused to comment on Boro's current plight when asked the pertinent question by Gordon Cox.

There was another layer of snow the following Tuesday which gave me concerns that I might not reach Teesside Airport in time to catch the plane for Boro's next Anglo-Italian Cup away tie which was at Ascoli the following day. In the event the taxi which was due to pick me up was late, and my concerns increased. The A19 and A66 were at a standstill because of the snow but, fortunately, the wily driver knew the back roads and I arrived at the airport just in time to check in.

This time I flew with the team, whose coach arrived soon afterwards. We flew to Heathrow and then caught a huge Alitalia plane to Rome. The plane was two-thirds empty, which meant we could all stretch out over three seats. After arriving in Rome we boarded a coach which took us on the long journey over the Apennine to Ascoli which was on the other side of Italy.

It might have been a spectacular journey but it was dark, and all we could see was the snow which covered the road verges and made driving difficult at times for our driver. It was also freezing and so it was not an enjoyable four-hour trip. The driver's misery was complete when we arrived at our hotel and he skidded on the ice and drove the coach into a top of the range Audi car.

I was rooming with Alastair Brownlee and after a shower and a meal we retired to the bar with Boro's amiable coach John Pickering who was leading the trip while Lennie stayed at home on Teesside. I ended up staying up until 2.30am in the bar with directors Graham Fordy and Reg Corbidge who gave me one or two little titbits.

I phoned over my match previews the following morning and then went for a walk around the town with Alastair. Ascoli was a typical sleepy non-tourist Italian town, but very pleasant.

We left for the stadium after lunch and found it to be the usual statium; all concrete, three sides uncovered stadium. However, it was a 34,000 all-seater and much bigger than I had anticipated. This time we had an English-speaking tour guide called Alba, so the match reporting was a doddle compared with what I had experienced in Pisa. Alba was very helpful and so we encountered no problems.

Ali was working by himself for BBC Radio Cleveland so I stepped in as the 'experienced pundit' and shared the radio commentary with him which I thoroughly enjoyed. However, it was bitterly cold, completely the opposite to Pisa, and I spent most of the match stamping my feet. I was jealous to see that one of the Italian media men had brought an oil filled radiator with him which he plugged in the press box.

Boro lost 3-0 and then had to attend a function given afterwards in their honour by the Italians. I needed to file reports to the *Newcastle Journal* after the final whistle and by the time I got to the reception, all the food had been eaten. It's a tough job, this journalism lark.

Then it was back on the coach to make the return journey over the mountains to spend the night in a hotel in Rome. It was after nine o'clock when I finally got something to eat. After a quick trip to the bar, I ended up writing reports in my room until 1.30am.

Alastair had assured me that his watch alarm would go off at 7.30am. It went off OK, but at 8.30am. Vive the hour's time difference in Italy. The late start left me with no opportunity to eat any breakfast as I had to concentrate on sending over the *Gazette* reports - all five of them. By the time I dashed into the breakfast room at five past ten, the best they could offer was a cup of coffee.

Thankfully the club had organised an evening flight back to England which gave us the chance to see a bit of the Eternal City. I joined up with Ali, John Murray from TFM and Boro fan Graham Bunn and went to see the sights. The Coliseum took my breath away. Then we saw the Senate ruins and went to the Vatican and St Peter's Cathedral where I was threatened with ejection by a priest for shouting to Ali across the floor of the remarkably impressive building. Later we saw Trevi's Fountain and walked the Spanish Steps before tramping back to the hotel feeling absolutely shattered.

On the way back to our hotel we bumped into one of the Boro youngsters, who shall remain nameless, standing outside a McDonald's restaurant. He proceeded to tell us what a dreadful place Rome was and how he had spent the day in McDonald's eating so many Big Macs and so many other burgers because that was the only thing worth doing. Sad but true. As far as I was concerned, as far as away games go, this was one of the better ones, despite the lack of food.

The following day I received a phone call at home from Henry Moszkowicz who said that he expected to be accepted back on to the Boro board the following Monday. I printed the story in good faith as he was the leading shareholder but it caused some consternation at Ayresome Park and I received an angry call from Keith Lamb.

Monday came and went without Henry returning to the board, and on the Wednesday Lamb invited me to his office to explain the situation regarding the boardroom ups and downs. He also very kindly filled me in with the latest details on the move from Ayresome Park.

It was a busy day because Henry rang later with a broadside against the club, while I then received a call from Steve Gibson. I knew that a lot was happening behind the scenes but I suspected, probably for the first time, that Steve and Keith were comfortable in the belief that they would eventually sort out everything to their satisfaction. They did not like to see what they regarded as negative stories appearing in the *Gazette*, especially with negotiations taking place with regard to the new stadium, and I could understand their feelings. But Steve and Keith seemed to accept that I had a job to do and that Henry was entitled to voice his opinion as leading shareholder.

When Lennie made it clear in the *Gazette* that he was hoping to spend some money, I was not the only one who fully expected him to bring in another forward. Boro were desperately short of firepower. In the event, he went to Tranmere Rovers and paid £750,000 for their Bishop Auckland-born centre-back Steve Vickers.

So all the available money was spent on a defender and it was not a deal which inspired the fans at the time. Boro were struggling for goals and this signing did nothing to change the frustrations on the terraces.

In the long run, Vickers proved to be a great signing and was another superb legacy which Lawrence left the Boro. Vickers was a stalwart and regular in Bryan Robson's line-up and went on to play more than 250 league games for the club. He was a dependable, if unspectacular defender, and I found him a great guy and a good friend.

But Vickers' arrival on Teesside initially made no obvious difference to results and the fans were baying for Lennie's head before the halfway stage of the season. The crowd of 6,828 which had watched the home defeat by Bolton was the lowest since the first few weeks following liquidation in 1986. There was a danger that the bad old days were returning.

On December 4 I went to Bristol City with Gordon Cox, reporter Tony Webster and Coxy's friend Ian. We drove across the Severn Bridge to take Ian to Chepstow Races before turning around and going to Ashton Gate.

The match was a boring goalless draw but the day was brightened up considerably after the final whistle. Alastair Brownlee and Coxy were sitting in a very small, two-man enclosed glass box which was fitted up with radio facilities. They finished work on their radio programme just after 6pm. As they were starting to pack away their gear, they suddenly started banging, shouting and screaming in a state of utter panic and flailing their arms around.

I raced out of the newspapers' side of the press box to see a large bat which had apparently appeared virtually from nowhere, fluttering around inside the box and flapping wildly just above their heads.

I'm sure the bat was much more frightened than the two erstwhile radio men, but neither Ali, Coxy or the bat could get out of the box. They were both screaming in abject fear while the bat flapped around above them. The whole hilarious incident went on for around five minutes by which time I was in pain from laughing.

Eventually the bat found its way out and the two frightened reporters were able to breathe again. The incident became etched in history as the original Bat Out Of Hell 3, and Ali and Coxy were known as Batman and Robin for a while. Afterwards we returned to the Batmobile to pick up Ian from Chepstow. It was midnight when I got home.

Five days before Christmas I accompanied *Evening Gazette* sports editor Allan Boughey to the Teesside Development Corporation offices at Teesdale Park for a presentation about Boro's new ground, two days before the official stadium launch. We had gone there expecting a run of the mill briefing but were taken aback when our visit started with a rather nasty tirade against the *Gazette* by the club. Such was the strength of the attack that the TDC reacted by refusing to hand us details of the new stadium after all.

Eventually, after some negotiating and some valuable support from Keith Lamb, the TDC agreed to give us the documents the following afternoon. It meant we could still publish the story on the Wednesday which was the launch day but, overall, the whole Monday event took place in a very bad atmosphere. It may not have been something new to my ears, but Allan Boughey was particularly shocked by some of the things which had been said to us.

I met Colin Henderson in the street near the *Gazette* when I returned, and had a chat. Later I went up to Ayresome to interview John Hendrie for his column. I met Steve Gibson on the way out and he made clear his frustration over a story I had written the previous Saturday as, apparently, it had upset a lot of people at the club. While Steve had not attended the TDC briefing, this explained the bad atmosphere from earlier in the day.

It was not until 4.40pm on the Tuesday that the documents arrived from the TDC, by which time the *Gazette* office Christmas party was in full swing. So I had to depart the festivities in order to write up the story for the following day's paper. The atmosphere at Wednesday's press conference was a lot better and it appeared that any bad feeling had dissipated.

I enjoyed a rare Boxing Day off because it fell on a Sunday, but travelled to Nottingham Forest for the Boro's next game on the Monday. I set off early with Gordon Cox because Boro Junior Reds were due to meet their Forest counterparts in a friendly game at 10.30am. The kids got changed and were keen to get going, but when the ref arrived he refused to start the game because he claimed the pitch was frozen. It seemed OK to me, but without a ref there was no game.

Alastair Brownlee quickly organised a seven-a-side kickabout between the Boro lads and then we left to travel to the City Ground. Ali was livid to discover later that Torquay United's Junior Yellows were also in Nottingham that day and had played Forest Junior Reds on the same pitch immediately following the Boro lads' departure. It was more than a bit fishy.

When we got to the stadium I discovered that my press pass was not there and for a long time it seemed as though Forest were not going to let me in. The situation was finally sorted out shortly before the kick-off. Boro drew 1-1 with Alan Moore grabbing the goal.

Two days later, as a result of sickness, myself and Gordon Fairbairn were the only two staff at work on the Gazette sports desk. I was shattered when I got home and fell asleep after tea. I overslept and then faced a hectic race to get to Ayresome Park in time for the kick-off against Tranmere Rovers. I needn't have bothered as it was a tame goalless draw.

Boro were suffering from the same lack of energy. They had won just one of their last 12 games and were in a rut.

CHAPTER 16

BORO revived their ailing fortunes quite considerably in the second half of the 1993/94 season, but it came too late to save Lennie Lawrence. The fans had had enough of the manager and the writing was on the wall as he approached the end of his third year in charge.

When Lennie went, I was sorry to see him go. I always felt he had put his heart and soul into the club even though, like every manager under the sun, he had made mistakes. On the other hand I believe that virtually every manager has a shelf life at every club, and I knew that Lennie had reached his sell-by date with the Boro.

I always believed that Lennie was given his extra year's contract as a convenience measure, rather than in thanks for what he had achieved in the past or could realistically hope to achieve in the future.

He was perceived as a capable, competent manager who could guide the team through a difficult period while the boardroom battle was finally resolved for once and for all.

I believed Lennie felt that his third year at Ayresome Park was a marriage of convenience, too. However, when he walked out of the door, he left with a smile and with his head held high.

It should not be forgotten that Lennie was heavily involved and instrumental in bringing Bryan Robson to the club as his successor, which was not the action of a man suffering from sour grapes.

From the fans' point of view, the final two years of Lennie's reign will always be regarded as a bad period in the club's history. I hope the same fans will re-evaluate, study the facts and maybe start to understand that Lennie did a surprisingly good job under impossible circumstances in his final season at the helm. I'm sure there were other managers who could have done better, but there are many who would have done much, much worse.

While Lennie was striving to try to turn results around during the 1993/94, it was obvious that the club could not move forward until the boardroom battle was sorted. From my personal point of view, I was sick of writing stories for the *Evening Gazette* which projected the views of one boardroom faction or the other, and then having to stand up to the criticism which ensued from the 'opposition' once the stories had appeared in print.

While, as I have said, I always felt that I was the unfortunate pig in the middle, I knew that both factions from the boardroom appreciated that I had a job to do. It must have appeared to them that I was taking sides whenever I printed the views of one of the two camps. Once their anger had subsided I never got the impression that I was regarded with suspicion or as the demon from the fiery furnace.

Both parties desperately tried to keep me on their side. I was perhaps the most relieved man on Teesside when the long drawn-out boardroom saga finally reached a conclusion.

The stability in the boardroom came a little bit late to help save the season from mediocrity though, as I say Boro did stage something of a mini-revival in the second half of the campaign once their key players returned from injury.

Boro opened 1994 with a trip to the Manor Ground to play Oxford United on New Year's Day. It's not the best day of the year to face a long journey on the road but I wisely stayed clear of the evil drink the previous evening and was in fine fettle. However, I had to be very quiet as I tiptoed around the house in the early morning, trying to avoid the sleeping bodies which were strewn all over downstairs.

There was a heavy frost, and everywhere was white as I drove to Gordon Cox's house. There was very little traffic on the roads and we pulled up at the stadium at ten to twelve. We had over three hours to kill but fortunately we met up with Clive Hetherington from *The Northern Echo* and TFM Radio duo John Murray and David Mills who had stayed overnight in the area and had welcomed in the New Year locally, so we killed the time with a bit of light banter. Boro got a point from the game with a 1-1 draw thanks to a goal from Jamie Pollock. We made a quick getaway afterwards and I was at home by 9.45pm.

The following week we were on the road again, this time to travel to Cardiff City for the FA Cup third-round tie. There was another heavy frost and the roads were decidedly dodgy when we left Gordon Cox's house at 7.15am. We got there in good time and Coxy dropped me off in the City Centre so that I could go for a stroll and have a look at some of the architecture.

I got a taxi to Ninian Park at 2pm and found myself standing at the back of a long snaking queue to get my press ticket. Complimentaries and press passes were being handed out at the same window. For a while I wondered if I would make the kick-off. Fortunately I was in the stadium by 2.45pm and took my seat at the back of the tight, wooden press box.

The atmosphere in the stadium was quite oppressive, as it always seems to be at Ninian Park, but Boro dealt with it reasonably well and forced a replay with a 2-2 draw. The whole of the journey home was made in pouring rain and I was late rolling in.

On the Tuesday night I sat in the directors' box at Ayresome for the first and only time when I was a guest of Terry Lawton from Phoenix Racing who was sponsoring the youth team. Boro Juniors were playing Nottingham Forest and Terry laid on a sumptuous meal before the kick-off, with titbits at half-time and after the final whistle.

It was the only time I ever had a meal at Ayresome Park before a match. Alastair Brownlee and Gordon Cox were also there and we thoroughly enjoyed what was a very rare experience for pressmen.

The following day I realised that the battle for control of the Boro was reaching a climax. I received a call from Henry Moszkowicz asking me to go to London to see him. I would have loved to have done so, but I couldn't possibly spare the time. In the event Henry said that he would come to Teesside instead, and he did.

Henry duly arrived in Middlesbrough and phoned me from the Hospitality Inn and he asked me to go and see him there. He had arranged a press conference at the hotel but wanted to speak to me beforehand. I had no doubts that this was Henry's last major throw of the dice to try to get back on to the board. We chatted for a full hour and a half and got on well. It was the first time I had chatted face to face with Henry for a long time and at first I found him to be a little agitated, but he settled down and gave me plenty of quotes backing his claims for a directorship. As he was still the leading shareholder he had a very strong argument.

Afterwards, Henry welcomed the rest of the local media to the official press conference in one of the private rooms at the Hospitality Inn. It was relatively well attended and included both regional TV stations.

Henry made his points, but I don't think he was as convincing as he would have hoped to be. In fact, while I was happy to put Henry's views into print and reported them correctly, his visit to Teesside reinforced my recent belief that the tide was ebbing away from him and from Colin Henderson, who was supporting Henry's return to the boardroom.

Chairman Steve Gibson and the other directors were in apparent power at Ayresome Park and were pressing ahead with their ambitious plans for the future in the belief that they would eventually gain full control of the club. The proposed new stadium was about to become a reality, while new staff were being appointed to prepare the way for the future developments, including former Cleveland police chief Terry Tasker who had been appointed stadium operations manager.

However, while there were developments on high, things were less fruitful on the pitch. Boro lost their FA Cup third round replay at home to Cardiff City on the Wednesday evening, going down 2-1 after extra time. The fans were shell-shocked and the feeling at the final whistle was one of disbelief. It was impossible to interview any of the players afterwards, as they left the stadium with their chins on the ground.

Boro were hardly any better on the Saturday, being held to a 1-1 draw by Watford. Afterwards I was approached by Jamie Pollock who was annoyed by a piece I had written during the week criticising his disciplinary record. Jamie was a wholehearted player and I would never have wanted him to change his playing style because he was so crucial to the team. He was also a forthright and direct talker, which again is preferable to a player who maybe would complain to his team-mates but say nothing to me. Those were the days when you could guarantee that every player would read every word that was written about Boro in the *Gazette*, and I didn't expect them to agree with every opinion I expressed. After a chat, and listening to Jamie's views on the subject, I was happy to shake hands with him and ensure there were no grievances.

Boro's failure to beat Watford had done little to appease the increasingly frustrated fans, and Lennie Lawrence was coming under heavy pressure. He was well aware of the dire situation he was facing when I rang him early on the Monday morning but stressed his determination to see it through.

After lunch I went to Ayresome to see Lennie in his office in order to ghost-write his fortnightly column. That afternoon he gave me one of the frankest and most forthright interviews that I ever got from him. He went into great details about the current state of affairs, the effect of the injuries and what was needed to turn things around.

His arguments made sense to me but I knew it was impossible to turn things around overnight with such a small squad. The one thing Lennie didn't have was a miracle wand but I could see that he was as committed as ever to try to improve the club's fortunes.

Given time, he believed he would get there in the end given a bit of luck. But Boro's hopes of returning to the Premier League at the first attempt had all but disappeared and time was something I suspected Lennie did not have.

I went to see chairman Steve Gibson the following day and he spent two and a half hours giving me extensive details of his plans for the future. It was all off the record stuff, but it was great background information and I appreciated the opportunity to listen.

I was left in no doubts that Gibson was going to leave no stone unturned to take the Boro on to the next level, and keep them there. He still did not have control of the club, but I got the impression that he felt it was all a matter of time.

Boro entertained Millwall in early February amid a banner demonstration in the South Stand which was aimed at both Lennie and the board. It would have been a major news item if Boro had lost. However, they stepped up on recent performances and played well, winning 4-2 with Craig Hignett grabbing a couple of goals. It was Boro's best win since October and took the edge off the protest.

On the Wednesday Keith Lamb called me to Ayresome to give me advance notice of planned boardroom and shareholding changes. Colin Henderson had been voted off the board and was to be replaced as ICI representative by George Cooke.

The official story was announced the following day at a press conference which was hosted by Fiona Bell, a public relations expert who had been brought in as trouble-shooter during this time of change.

I met up with George Cooke in mid-afternoon and found him a very pleasant and personable man. I could see that he was keen to get on with the job and make a contribution in the boardroom.

Boro were starting to pick up as the injured players returned. They went to Derby County towards the end of February and won 1-0 with a goal from Steve Vickers - not that I saw much of the game. It was the coldest night I can ever remember at a football match and my eyes watered virtually throughout the whole game and gave the impression that I was crying buckets.

We had suffered from a reasonably heavy snowfall in Teesside and there was plenty of it lying around on the frozen ground when Gordon Cox and I set off for Derby.

There was no snow lying in Derby, even though we had to endure several strong flurries during the evening. Unfortunately the infernal under-soil heating at the Baseball Ground ensured that the match took place.

A friendly hack in the press box claimed before the kick-off that it was -9C. I can only imagine what the temperature was at the end of the game, but it was grossly unfair on the fans to have to sit in such conditions. I could not concentrate at all. I was wearing three pullovers and three pairs of socks, which is very unusual, but I could hardly stand it. Never has a final whistle been so welcome.

There might even have been a similar scenario at Leicester on the Saturday.

I had spent the previous evening working out how to put my boots on over four pairs of socks, but the match failed a Saturday morning inspection and Coxy and I did not even have to set off. Boro had travelled down on the Friday and so I rang Lennie Lawrence and Keith Lamb at their hotel for a few comments before enjoying a rare Saturday afternoon around the TV.

There was another cold match in early March, this time at Luton, but at least the temperatures had picked up somewhat and the snow had disappeared. Coxy's mate Lennie Shepherd had offered to give us a lift to Kenilworth Road, though I ended up in the back of the car cramped in between heavyweights Coxy and Alastair Brownlee. I could not move a muscle on the journey and could hardly stand up straight when we got to the stadium. I could not sleep a wink on the way back with elbows sticking in my ribs, but the banter was good which helped ease the pain.

Two days later came one of the most significant developments in the history of Middlesbrough Football Club.

I had received a call on the Wednesday from former chairman Colin Henderson who had asked to see me. I arranged to visit him at his home the following day. At that time I played five-a-side football every Thursday evening and planned to drive over to his home once I had showered and dressed.

However, shortly before setting off for five-a-side, I took a call from Keith Lamb who informed me that Steve Gibson had been to London during the day and secured an agreement to buy the full allocation of shares which were held by Henry Moszkowicz.

Effectively it meant that Steve now owned 68 per cent of the club's share and finally had full control. It gave him the opportunity to push through his ambitious plans for the future. ICI were the only other shareholder, holding the remaining 32 per cent.

There was an extraordinary general shareholders' meeting planned for the following day and one of the major items on the agenda would be the proposal that Colin Henderson would be officially voted off the board.

I was mightily relieved that the battle was over because I had been stuck in the middle on too many occasions. I felt a great deal of sympathy for Colin Henderson when I drove to his house because I knew that his heart was in the right place. He had fallen out with most of the other Boro directors, though only because of a difference of opinion on the right way forward for the club. During Colin's time as chairman, Boro had risen from the ashes of liquidation to enjoy new-found stability and success on the pitch.

Nothing stands still in football, however, and Gibson was now on the verge of taking the club to a whole new level.

Henderson greeted me as I arrived at his home and I did not beat about the bush. I told him of Keith Lamb's phone call and Colin knew immediately that the fight was lost.

He took the news very well and he was diplomatic in his comments towards the new regime. While we were talking, Colin received a phone call from his solicitor which confirmed the news. We enjoyed a cup of tea and parted on good company. I knew that it was the end of my dealings with Colin and also with Henry Moszkowicz. A new era was dawning at the Boro and these two men, who had done so much to ensure the survival of the club, were now confined to the past.

The following day I headed off for London to see Teesside boxer Cornelius Carr make his bid to win the British super-middleweight title. I had followed Carr's career since he was a 12-year-old boxing as an amateur in Grangetown and I found the prospect of seeing him fight for the British title exciting.

However, my first task of the day was to dash to Ayresome Park to attend the Boro shareholders' extraordinary general meeting. The meeting was fortunately relatively brief and, as expected, ended the directorship of Colin Henderson and officially replaced him with George Cooke.

Then I hurried back to the *Evening Gazette* to file my copy before ordering a taxi to take me to Eston where I joined Cornelius' boxing trainer and mentor Martin Turner and a coach full of fervent supporters for the trip to the fight venue at the York Hall in Bethnal Green.

I was sweating by the time I got on the coach but it turned out that I needn't have rushed. The coach was due to leave Eston at 10.45am but it was a full hour later before all the boxing fans had emerged from the local winery and taken their seats.

However, the journey was uneventful and I enjoyed the chat with the Grangetown lads. We arrived in London at 5pm and I caught a tube to the Bloomsbury Park Hotel at Russell Square, which was my base. Following a quick shower I was back on the tube to travel across London to reach the fight venue. The York Hall had long been one of the main centres of the British professional boxing game and I could not wait to see it for the first time. However, I was very, very disappointed. The hall was much smaller than I expected and very narrow. With only a few hundred people present, nor was there any atmosphere during the warm-up fights.

However, it all changed when Cornelius Carr stepped into the ring to tackle the champion, James Cook from Peckham. Carr's magnificent supporters took control and gave their man remarkable noisy backing throughout the whole of the 12 rounds.

The hall erupted when Carr sent Cook on to the seat of his pants in the fifth round and afterwards there was rarely any doubt that Carr would become the first Teessider for around 80 years to win a British boxing title.

Afterwards I interviewed the jubilant Cornelius in his dressing room before attending the press conference which was hosted by his manager Mickey Duff in a pokey little office on the first floor.

There were six or seven of us crammed in the office shoulder to shoulder and surrounding Duff. The guy pressing close to my right shoulder was none other than the rock singer Morrissey, who was a great fan of Cornelius at that time and had even used the boxer's photograph on the front cover of one of his CDs. I had spotted Morrissey earlier, watching the title fight from his seat in the front row and I could tell that he enjoyed every minute of it.

I'm not sure if I've ever told Bernie Slaven about this story, but as Bernie is Morrissey's greatest fan, it's bound to send him green with envy. I rubbed shoulders with Morrissey, Bernie!

The walk back to the tube station was a bit dodgy being late at night, with a lot of rough-looking customers hanging around but I encountered no problems from the locals and, after writing up my reports over a cup of tea in my hotel room, was in bed at 12.30am.

I was up early the next morning to phone the fight copy to the *Evening Gazette* and then headed off to Camden Town where I wanted to take in a record fair. Boro were at Leicester that afternoon so, following a quick squint through the racks, I dashed back to St Pancras Station where I caught the 11am train.

There were the usual problems on the line which seem to follow me around on trains, and it was not until 1pm that I arrived in Leicester. However, I had a little time to kill and decided to take a look around the City Centre before catching a cab to Filbert Street.

When I started searching for a cab I could not find a taxi rank, but I walked into a dingy taxi office at two o'clock to ask for a cab.

"A taxi will be here in five minutes," said the guy behind the glass counter.

I waited and waited and nothing happened.

"Five minutes mate," said the guy, five minutes later.

Repeatedly I asked the receptionist where the cab was and he maintained that it was on its way very shortly. By the time a taxi eventually turned up at 2.30pm, I was in a cold sweat.

I would have been at Filbert Street some time ago if I had set off to walk at the same time as I first began looking for a taxi, but the more time which ticked away in the taxi office, the more I was committed to waiting.

No sooner had the taxi set off than we hit a long bank of slow-moving traffic. The situation was hopeless. I would have missed the kick-off if I had stayed in the cab, so I paid up, got out and ran the remainder of the way to the stadium. It's a glamorous job, this journalism.

I quickly picked up my press pass, clambered up to the stadium's new press box and took my allotted seat at five to three, sweating profusely. One of the press lads had kindly phoned over the teams to the *Sports Gazette*, so I was able to move into gear as soon as the match kicked off. However, I wondered whether it had all been worthwhile. Boro were disappointing and lost 2-0. Afterwards I was given a lift back to Stockton by TFMs John Murray and caught a taxi home from there. It had been a hectic three days but I had enjoyed it.

On the Monday I was handed a message to ring Henry Moszkowicz. He just wanted to complete the formalities after selling his shareholding to Steve Gibson. I had a very amiable chat with him – which turned out to be for the last time. Henry said that, in some respects, he wished things might have turned out differently but, on the other hand, there was no ill feeling and he wished Steve Gibson and the Boro all the best for the future. I suspected that he was relieved to be out of it and was now happy to concentrate on his business interests while resuming his support of the team as a fan from afar.

The following day Boro entertained Southend United and former Boro boss Willie Maddren was a visitor to the press room. I had an enjoyable chat with him. Willie had recently sold his successful sports shops and was looking for a new venture within the game as a scout or something similar, or even in the media.

Boro beat Southend 1-0 and were beginning to move into gear again. They followed up with an impressive 3-0 win against West Brom, before preparing for the big test in a midweek match at Crystal Palace, who were top of the league.

I caught the train to London and made my way to the Queen's Hotel at Crystal Palace which was the usual overnight venue for the north-east media men. In fact I met up with Clive Hetherington from *The Northern Echo* and John Murray and we enjoyed a few rounds of sandwiches together for tea.

The Queen's Hotel was a well known hotel in that area and perfectly situated for scribes looking for overnight stays. However, it had changed hands and was not going through the best of times.

Clive's early impressions of the Queen's upon his arrival were not good. First of all he had been walking along a corridor when a whole wall panel fell on him. Then, when he unlocked the door to the room he had been given, there was a guy sitting on the bed in his underpants. Naturally Clive returned to reception in a state of incredulity and was handed the key to another room without comment.

Boro played really well throughout the game at Selhurst Park and won 1-0 with a goal from Craig Hignett. I got a taxi back to the hotel with Clive and John and then made the mistake of accepting their invitation to have a nightcap in the bar. By the time I returned to my room and wrote up reports, interviews and stories, it was very late indeed. When I received my 7.15am wake-up call I felt as if I hadn't been to sleep.

On the Saturday Boro were at Birmingham and I was grateful for a lift from Boro fan Lennie Downs who was one of my five-a-side colleagues. We had a decent trip down with plenty of convivial chat and stopped for a coffee at Trowell where I bumped into *Hartlepool Mail* duo Neil Watson and Tom Collins, who were on their way to London to report on the national schoolboys' boxing finals.

Lennie Lawrence handed me a ticket in order for Lennie Downs to watch the match from a prime position and then I struggled my way up to the tight little press box and managed to squeeze into a seat on the end of the row. Boro were unable to repeat their sparkling performance from Selhurst Park, going down 1-0 to a last-minute goal. It was one of the most depressing final whistles I can ever remember.

I interviewed Lennie Lawrence in the car park afterwards because there was no press room at St Andrews at that time. Lennie was absolutely fuming about the lack of concentration from his players in the closing seconds of the game. Afterwards I travelled home with Gordon Cox and Alastair Brownlee, though we said very little on the way back – unusual for Ali – because the defeat was so frustrating.

I was on holiday the following week so I started work on researching a book which I was planning to write with my pal John Wilson, tentatively entitled Ayresome Park Memories. With Ayresome now definitely due for closure in the summer of 1995, it seemed appropriate to bring out a book celebrating the 92 years of the stadium.

So on the Monday I spent five hours in the *Evening Gazette* vaults, lovingly known as the dungeon, working my way through the dusty, yellowing files, with only a few tuna and cucumber sandwiches and a flask of coffee for company.

I started writing the book the following day at home and the week of solid graft was broken only when I travelled to Sheffield Arena with Gordon Cox and his pals Ian and Ernie to see Meat Loaf in concert. I recall that I thoroughly enjoyed it, though my only vivid memory today is seeing Meat Loaf's heavy frame on the stage floor. He fell head over heels while attempting a tricky rock star-type swivel which was clearly a little too difficult for him.

On Easter Monday Boro were at Tranmere for an evening fixture and I set off early with Gordon Cox in order to take in Wetherby Races on the way. It was a bitterly cold day with a biting wind, but there was a big crowd at the racetrack. I started off well with a winner and followed it up with a handful of losers. But, hey, that's racing.

We had just missed a snowstorm when we arrived at Prenton Park and the weather was Baltic. Boro didn't relish the conditions as much as I didn't fancy the match and they were stuffed 4-0 - I've had better Easters. At least I could enjoy my four and a half hours sleep when I got home.

A 2-0 home defeat at the hands of Portsmouth in mid-April more or less ended Boro's faint hopes of reaching the play-offs and was the moment where I felt for certain that Lennie Lawrence would definitely not be given a new contract extension. He had done a relatively good job to turn things around since Christmas, despite the sniping from the terraces, but I could not see him surviving beyond this season.

After a heavy 4-1 defeat at Bolton the writing was definitely on the wall for Lennie. When I sat down with him in his office to interview him for his fortnightly *Gazette* column, he made it absolutely clear that he felt he was on the verge of being sacked. He talked me through many of the major events during the season and again packed a reasonable argument in insisting that the campaign had not been too bad considering all the problems. I felt at that time that Lennie wanted to stay on and have another crack at the job next season but, with the fans deserting the club in droves, I did not think it was likely.

The following day Boro showed their true colours when thumping Barnsley 5-0; but the performance didn't please everybody. On the way out after the final whistle, one of the regular season-ticket holders who sat in front of the press box said: "Having a season ticket here is worse than having Aids." Ah the Teesside humour. You can't beat it.

Boro's last home match was a Sunday televised game against Crystal Palace which they proceeded to lose 3-2. Comedians Bob Mortimer and Sean Hughes, who support Boro and Palace respectively, were special guests at the game. I had the chance to talk to both of them, though neither asked for my autograph. They were filmed on the pitch afterwards going through several different comedy sketches which brightened up an otherwise drab afternoon.

The following morning I received an early tip-off from Keith Lamb that Lennie Lawrence's tenure was coming to an end. It was no surprise and I wrote up the story in time for all editions of the *Gazette*. Then I drove to Ayresome to pick up the official statement after Keith had relayed the news to Lennie.

After rewriting my stories, I went back to Ayresome to look for Lennie but he wasn't there. Of all people to bump into, I met Bernie Slaven now strutting his stuff for Port Vale who was delighted to hear the news of Lennie's demise.

Next I set off for Lennie's house in Egglescliffe and sat outside in the car to wait for him. He arrived after around half an hour and greeted me with the comment: "I knew you'd be here."

Lennie invited me in and we had a long chat over a welcome cuppa. He didn't want to be quoted on the record, which disappointed me, but again he spoke at length about the way the season had gone and the contribution he had made.

He was very disappointed to have lost his job because he genuinely believed he could pick things up again the following season, given a bit of cash to spend.

Bearing in mind the ongoing boardroom squabbles at the start of the 1993/94 season, Lennie also intimated that he had been handed an extra year's contract as a convenience to do a job under difficult circumstances and that his name was never going to stay on the Boro manager's door long term. He was philosophical about the club's decision to end his spell at Ayresome and was confident that he would quickly find another managerial post. In the event he had several offers and eventually plumped for the job at Bradford City.

The comment that I remember most at our final meeting was Lennie saying: "I just hope with the passage of time, some of the fans who were not happy will look back and think that I didn't do too bad a job after all with the resources available. That's all I ask."

I don't think he was given a fair crack of the whip by either the club or the fans in his final year, even though I accept that the club's resources were very thin at the time. I felt Lennie made a lot of mistakes when Boro were relegated from the inaugural Premier League and could not have argued if he had been dismissed at that time. But I thought he got a lot of things right in his final season while operating with his hands tied behind his back.

While I was sorry to see him go, Lennie was not the right man to take Boro into the kind of future that Steve Gibson was planning. So the parting of the ways was inevitable at that stage, whatever had gone before.

Lennie's time had come, and he was too good a manager not to be able to continue in his chosen career elsewhere. I've met Lennie on several occasions since and he remains one of football's good guys. He's still as honest and accommodating as he's ever been and I'm delighted that he still works within the game in a major role at Bristol Rovers.

The following day I sat with DJ and PR consultant Paul Gough at the Hennessy Player of the Year Awards at Newcastle Civic Centre and had the chance to talk later with Steve Gibson and fellow director George Cooke about Boro's plans for the future.

Within 24 hours I was on my way to Birmingham for the ABA boxing championships at the National Indoor Arena. I travelled with *Gazette* photographer Colin Robertson to see Middlesbrough boxer Andy Green's bid to win the ABA lightweight title. I bumped into Neil Watson and Frank Reid from the Hartlepool Mail who were there to see Alan Temple, and also Dave Allard from the Ipswich newspaper who was following one of his local lads.

Andy was fifth on and fought Ian Smith from London. It was very close and I was relieved when Andy was handed the majority verdict. I interviewed him in the dressing rooms afterwards, watched the Temple fight and then was on the road home with Colin at 9.15pm.

John Pickering was caretaker manager of the Boro for their final game of the campaign at Charlton Athletic on the Sunday and led the team to a terrific 5-2 victory. I drove down with Gordon Cox and Alastair Brownlee in glorious sunshine.

Charlton were back at The Valley, though the stadium was still in the process of being rebuilt. The press box consisted of a combination of scaffolding and loose wooden planks. There was a sheer drop directly behind where I was sitting on an unsecured chair.

It was not good for my vertigo because I could not stop contemplating what might happen if I fell backwards. If the match had been played at Middlesbrough, there is no way the safety committee would have allowed such a potentially dangerous area to be used by working media. It didn't seem to matter at Charlton and, in any case, they had to accommodate us somewhere.

Anyway, the match was terrific, with John Hendrie scoring a dramatic hat-trick. John Pickering, a man who tended to be unhappy in the media limelight, sent out former Charlton midfielder Andy Peake to carry out the press interviews afterwards.

However, I was delighted for John that Boro had won so well because he was such a lovely man.

I was due to go on holiday to Cyprus shortly after the season finished but there was still time to pick up one almighty exclusive.

I was tipped off that Manchester United legend Bryan Robson, arguably the biggest name in the British game, was about to be appointed as the new Boro boss. Could it be possible? I printed the story anyway.

CHAPTER 17

I WAS on holiday when Bryan Robson was appointed so I missed all the razzamatazz and hullabaloo at Ayresome Park when he was officially unveiled simultaneously to both the public and the media.

I had long been aware that England's former Captain Fantastic had agreed to take his first steps into management with the Boro. It was quite a coup for the club.

This was the most important signing that Steve Gibson ever made because Robson was off the top shelf and the man who could catapult the Boro into the big time.

I had no doubts that Robson's arrival would grab the imagination of the Teesside public. It was an appointment which would bring those missing fans back to the club and hopefully create a whole new fan base for the planned move to the Riverside Stadium in 12 months.

However, I thought Robbo's public unveiling at Ayresome Park could have been stage-managed a little better. When I returned from holiday I checked through the *Evening Gazette*s and grimaced at the photographs of Robbo walking around the perimeter of the pitch signing autographs wearing a tweed-type jacket on top of football shorts. Quite why he could not have been found more appropriate gear for the dozens of waiting press cameras, I never could fathom. In any case, Robson was coming in to take over at the Boro as player-manager, so a team shirt – even one from the previous season – would not have looked out of place.

However, like the fans, I could not argue with the quality of the appointment. True, Robbo had no managerial experience, but that was a common trait shared by Boro managers before him such as Stan Anderson, Jack Charlton, Bobby Murdoch, Willie Maddren and Colin Todd. The Boro's ongoing policy of giving new talent the opportunity to cut their teeth as managers is part of the club's modern history which has continued to this day with the appointments of Steve McClaren and Gareth Southgate.

In any case, in 1994 Boro could hardly have gone for anybody bigger than Bryan Robson. The 37-year-old was straight out of Manchester United's best team for many years, a former England captain with 90 caps to his name and one of the best-known figures in world football. Robbo's ability to run a club was still to be proven, but it was unimaginable that he would fail to inspire the Boro players.

Interestingly, one of Lennie Lawrence's parting comments to Steve Gibson when he was sacked as Boro boss was that Robson would make an ideal successor. In fact Lennie even picked Robbo up at a hotel car park at Wetherby and drove him to the Cleveland Tontine for his initial meeting with Gibson.

By all accounts, Gibson and Robson hit it off immediately and Robbo accepted a three-year contract without any hassle. The duo went on to forge the foundations of a firm friendship which was to last throughout Robbo's reign at the Boro and beyond.

Gibson never failed to back Robbo to the hilt and always tried to give him everything he needed. Together they engineered the start of Boro's golden era.

It took me a few weeks to get to know Robbo well but once he trusted me he began to confide in me and give me stories. I always believed that I had a good working relationship with him.

Bryan was such a big name in the game that he could possibly have walked straight into a manager's job at a Premier League club. He had already had discussions with Boro's first division colleagues Wolves who had just finished the rebuilding of Molineux and had high hopes he would agree to go there.

However, Robbo was sold on Gibson's ambitious plans for the Boro which included the promise of big money to spend and the opportunity to take the club into the new stadium which was due to be erected on Teesside Development Corporation land in the Middlehaven area of Middlesbrough docks.

In many respects I felt this planned move to a new stadium placed extra pressure on the shoulders of Robson. The whole town would be hoping to see the midfield maestro start his second season in charge with Boro in the Premier League, to go hand in hand with the move to Middlehaven. Not that Robbo ever looked a man under pressure in his first few years on Teesside.

I hoped to meet him for the first time on June 1 when Boro issued a press release to announce that his first two signings were to be unveiled at Ayresome Park. When I drove to the stadium I discovered that Robbo wasn't there. So I met up with his assistant manager first.

This was Viv Anderson, Robbo's former England and Manchester United team-mate who was revealed as the first 'signing'. Viv had spent the last 12 months as manager of Barnsley but had jumped at the opportunity to move to Ayresome as Robbo's deputy.

The second signing was United's Welsh international Clayton Blackmore who arrived on a free transfer.

Anderson had found life difficult in the hot seat in his season at Barnsley where funding was thin and resources were restricted, so he had welcomed the chance to link up again with Robbo. The two were very close pals and Robbo clearly needed to have people around him he could trust. With this in mind I was delighted to see Robbo hang on to coach John Pickering who had been Lennie Lawrence's right-hand man and was well respected by all the players.

Blackmore was a useful signing because he could play virtually anywhere and offered Robson plenty of options as he worked out the strengths and weaknesses of the squad he had inherited.

The best signing Robson made that summer was Nigel Pearson. When I was informed that Boro were forking out £750,000 for the Sheffield Wednesday centre-half I was more than surprised. Pearson was recovering from a second broken leg and I doubted whether he would be capable of making the necessary impact on Teesside.

I could not have been more wrong - Nigel was a warrior. He was thoroughly committed and provided the physical power that Boro needed at the back. Nigel was also a strong character and a great captain on and off the field. He made a massive contribution towards maintaining morale in the dressing room.

There were one or two members of the media who found him difficult to deal with but Nigel was always great with me and we got on well. He never denied me an interview, even if he did keep me waiting longer than any other player outside the dressing room door at Ayresome Park. Many a time he promised me an interview and turned up to do it an hour later, but they all count.

It's just a pity that Nigel wasn't three or four years younger when he arrived, because when knee problems forced his eventual retirement it left a void which Boro struggled to fill.

I finally met Robson for the first time two weeks later. I was on a day off and was spending my time at Ayresome Park in the file room going through the club's minutes from the early 1900s. Keith Lamb had given me permission to scan the minutes as research for my forthcoming book Ayresome Park Memories.

I had been informed by Keith that Robbo was coming in that day and had arranged to meet him at 2pm for an informal chat but this meeting was scrapped in late morning when I was told that Robson would be arriving at Ayresome with a new signing who would be unveiled at a hastily arranged press conference.

The new signing turned out to be Neil Cox, Boro's very first £1m buy. It all came out of the blue. It was a story I had completely missed which, fortunately, is something that hasn't happened too often over the years.

I had plenty of time to interview Neil after the official unveiling and found him a pleasant guy displaying an immediate sense of humour. The fact that Boro were prepared to fork out such a big fee on a defender, albeit one from Premier League side Aston Villa, was an immediate indication of Gibson's ambition and the backing that Robbo would receive over the years.

However, the signing had scuppered my plans for an in-depth chat with Robson, and my first meeting with him, which took place following Cox's unveiling, was restricted to ten minutes. However, we got on reasonably well and I found him instantly likeable without any of the airs or graces which might normally accompany a man of his sporting stature. I felt lifted as a result of meeting Robbo and felt confident he would turn the club around. I was certain his arrival would have the same impact on the squad once they returned for the start of pre-season training.

By mid-July I was getting on very well with Bryan and ringing him on a daily basis for the latest updates. However, ongoing stories on the new stadium development were not as easy to come by. On two separate occasions I had to pull stories from the *Evening Gazette* at virtually the last minute because individuals at the club got cold feet over the particular revelations I was making. I was left in no doubt that Boro were encountering problems with their delicate negotiations behind the scenes and that not everybody in Middlesbrough was happy to see the stadium built on the Middlehaven site.

My first match watching Bryan's team in action that summer was a friendly on a hot night at Darlington, which Boro won 3-0. Robson fielded trialist Jaime Moreno in the game and the Bolivian produced a telling performance, grabbing two of the goals. I spoke to him afterwards outside the Boro dressing room door with the aid of an interpreter. Jaime made it clear he would jump at the chance to join the Boro. Three days later his wish came true as Boro held a press conference to announce his signing.

On the last Saturday in July I realised a personal ambition when I finally got to see my favourite Scottish side Raith Rovers. Boro had arranged a friendly at Starks Park and I drove there and back on the day. At first I thought that I might not make it on time because I was stuck in horrendous traffic on the

Edinburgh ring road, but I arrived in time to have a stroll around the stadium before the kick-off.

My first view of the inside of the ground gave me a culture shock. Starks Park was old and tatty and I could not get over the way in which part of the pitch fell away almost into a gully near one corner flag. So much for the romance of football. But I enjoyed the experience and lost none of my personal feelings for Raith, even if Boro did lose 1-0.

Three days later I was back up in Scotland for a second friendly, this time at Ayr United. I travelled with Gordon Cox and our first port of call was nearby Prestwick, where Coxy spent part of his formative years playing on the beach when on holiday at his uncle Sam's. It was an impressive area. From the beach we could see the isles of Kintyre, Arran and Bute.

It was hot on the beach and a pleasant sultry evening when we arrived at Somerset Park. I enjoyed looking around the stadium; it was attractive, if again, undeveloped. Boro also enjoyed the experience and won 2-1, with Robson – who did not play in the previous match at Ayr - scoring both of the goals. However, the long journey back to Teesside was tiresome and it was after 2.30 by the time I limped into bed.

The following Monday I went to Ayresome for the unveiling of another new signing, Alan Miller. The keeper had arrived from Arsenal, though he had played only a few games for the Gunners over six years. I found him a pleasant lad, but I felt a little disappointed for Steve Pears because clearly Alan had been brought in to play regularly in the first team.

Pearsy had been the last line of defence throughout my time reporting on the Boro's fortunes and I got on with him very well. He had been injured early in pre-season and, with no prospect of him being ready for the start of the first division fixtures, Robson needed Miller because otherwise he would have been short of experience between the sticks.

Even so, the arrival of Alan Miller and the end of Pears' run as No.1 more or less closed the book on the Boro's post-liquidation era. The same week I moved into a new era, too, when receiving my first mobile phone. It was even sponsored, having been bought and maintained by Teesside businessman and devout Boro fan John Davey.

The Robson era kicked off on the Saturday with the opening Division One game at home to Burnley. I'd not seen so many media men together at Ayresome Park for years. Dozens of strange faces packed the press room. Robbo mania was in evidence everywhere and the game was a near sell-out too. I was even called on to do a Radio Five Live interview before the game, talking about the effect that Robbo's arrival had had on Teesside.

Boro won 2-0, which was a relief because the media circus would otherwise have battered Robbo, which wouldn't have been the best of starts for morale and confidence. Robbo played the whole game in the hot sun wearing Boro's No.7 shirt and I found myself – probably like every other fan – concentrating on his every move.

It was remarkable just to be able to watch a football legend of Robbo's high stature playing for the Boro and he didn't disappoint, even if the legs were not as sprightly as they used to be.

John Hendrie stole most of the Sunday newspaper headlines, grabbing both of the goals, but my fellow hacks had long faces afterwards when Viv Anderson turned up for the post-match press conference.

There was no sign of Robbo who no doubt was appreciating the opportunity to wind down after a typically hectic opening game. In addition he must have been in strong demand in the guest lounges, so Robbo had his reasons for sending Viv out to face the media instead even if his non-appearance didn't go down well.

It made little difference to me because I could get what would now prove to be exclusive quotes from Robbo on Monday for that day's *Evening Gazette*. However, my media colleagues didn't let it lie, and Robbo was hammered in the Monday morning papers for failing to attend the press conference. When I went to see him on Monday afternoon he was absolutely fuming and hurt after reading some of the media. John Donoghue from the *Daily Express* was also at Ayresome that afternoon and explained to Robbo exactly why he had been expected to appear in front of the waiting press. Despite Robbo's anger, John seemed to win the day with his persuasive argument and, after that, more often than not it was Bryan and not Viv who appeared at the press conferences.

The following weekend I travelled to Southend with Gordon Cox and fellow journalist Tony Webster for Robbo's first away game. We arrived early and Coxy took us along the seafront to admire the view, though I much preferred Seaton Carew. We got to the ground just as the market was closing and I had a chat with regular Boro fan Frankie Bamford outside the stadium.

It was almost unbearable in the small press box in the intense August heat and at half-time I managed to find a seat outside among the home fans. Boro enjoyed the humidity, however, and won 2-0 at a canter with the effervescent Hendrie again scoring both goals.

Afterwards we gave a lift home to Terry Cochrane, who had just started working for TFM. The former Boro winger, a lovely fella, never stopped talking, as might be expected from an Irishman, and the journey home simply flew by.

When I went to see Robbo on the Monday he gave me a belter of a story when he revealed he was negotiating to try to bring his former England team-mate Gary Lineker to the club.

Lineker, now 33, was playing in Japan with Grampus Eight but his contract was due to end in December. I knew he would be a big, big signing and would increase Boro's new profile even higher.

Robbo was serious in his attempts to bring Lineker to Teesside and later had several conversations with the free-scoring striker. In the event Lineker eventually opted to go into the media instead, but it was a pointer to the fact that Robbo was not afraid to try to tempt big-name players to the Boro.

There was already a buzz within the Boro dressing room. Robson inspired his players to win their first four games. The new players were settling in very quickly and the whole squad had a spring in their step. There was a sense of belief which I had not felt for some time. The players were in awe of the manager, as well they might be, and simply being on the same pitch as Robbo must have made them feel ten feet tall. There was no doubt from the start that Boro would be among the first division promotion contenders.

However, as Boro began to lose their early-season adrenaline they were made to realise that simply having Bryan Robson in their line-up was not going to be enough to keep them in the promotion melting pot.

Boro drew 1-1 at Watford in early September, despite the home side having gone down to ten men after 22 minutes when goalkeeper Kevin Miller was dismissed for bringing down Robbo outside the box. The goal was the first that Boro had conceded since the campaign started.

Afterwards I could hardly pick out Robson in the smoke filled press room when he entered to carry out his interviews but, as usual, he kept his audience hanging on his every word.

Boro then faced national scrutiny in a televised derby game at home to Sunderland. They started badly and trailed 2-0 early in the second half. However, Boro rallied and sent the fans home happy when they came back from the dead in the closing minutes to force a 2-2 draw thanks to a spectacular goal from Alan Moore and Nigel Pearson's first for the club.

A last-minute penalty from Craig Hignett then brought a vital midweek win against West Brom. Boro had to win the points the hard way in this match, having lost their inspirational gaffer in the opening minutes when Robbo limped off with a foot injury.

Bryan was not to play again until December as he battled to recover, but remained an influential presence off the pitch.

CHAPTER 18

AFTER five weeks in charge at Ayresome Park, Bryan Robson had already achieved everything that could have been expected from him. Boro were top of Division One, unbeaten in seven games and had conceded just two goals.

The bad atmosphere which had prevailed at the club in the opening five months of 1994 had long since disappeared. Suddenly the Boro had a feel-good factor about them.

The players were buoyant and the next game could not come along quickly enough.

The fans were still monitoring developments and were a little slow in returning in huge numbers. A healthy 23,000-plus watched Robson's Boro debut in the opening day win against Burnley, but then attendances began to dip. In fact fewer than 15,000 turned up for the midweek win against West Brom.

I was more interested in the team, because I knew that success on the field would bring back the fans. My daily trips to Ayresome Park were now thoroughly enjoyable again, as the players were bubbly and full of light-hearted quips. There was a fresh feeling around the dressing room and interviews were easy to come by, which was important.

The positive start to the campaign had lifted everybody. Even so, Boro did not have the biggest of squads and the injuries were already beginning to take their toll. In fact Robson was one of several players missing when Boro went to Port Vale in mid-September to try to defend their unbeaten record. Unfortunately it wasn't to be and the Boro flag was finally lowered for the first time. They went down 2-1 and were knocked off the top spot to boot.

Any visit to Port Vale is always quaint, but a struggle at the same time. Every time I have been to Vale Park I had to climb the steps up the back of the main stand to the press box which was situated in two separate Portakabins resting on the roof. If you can't get a position at the front of whichever cabin you select then you can't see all of the game, particularly the near side of the pitch. While I managed to find a suitable seat on this occasion, Alastair Brownlee and Gordon Cox did their Radio Cleveland commentary outside on the roof. They were sitting on two wooden chairs and were open to the elements. I was praying for a shower or two during the game, but was out of luck.

I was off work the following week and spent most of the time doing research for Ayresome Park Memories. I spent four delightful hours in the company of George Hardwick on the Monday. The club kindly provided us with a plush room at Ayresome Park and we went through the details of George's remarkable life-story. He was a great guy to talk to and was always happy to stop for a chat whenever I bumped into him. There was not much that George Hardwick didn't experience in his action-packed life. His death was a big loss to everybody connected with the Boro.

I've always remembered the terrific job he did as manager of Sunderland in the 1964/65 season. He went to Roker Park on a short-term contract when they were struggling to stay in the first division, but lifted the whole club and staved off relegation. George was promised a full contract if he won the battle to avoid the drop, but the Sunderland directors showed him the door instead.

It was Hardwick who handed Brian Clough his first coaching role and eventually wanted to promote Cloughie to coach at Sunderland. Cloughie's days at Roker were also numbered once George was gone, and a potential top-notch partnership never happened.

I always wondered how Boro's history might have been different if the board of directors here had realised the potential of appointing the Hardwick-Clough dream team that summer. This was the start of the season which saw Boro end up in the third division for the first time. It would have been so, so different under Hardwick and Clough, and so would the whole Boro story since.

The following day after meeting George, Boro were at Scarborough in the Coca-Cola Cup. As I was on holiday, I drove down with John Wilson and paid to stand among the Boro fans in the open end. I thoroughly enjoyed 'slumming it', even if it did rain relentlessly throughout the game.

I was absolutely saturated at the final whistle, but as Boro won 4-1 it hardly mattered. Fish and chips in Pickering on the way home were also much enjoyed, while we bumped into Boro director George Cooke in the chippie and had a pleasant chat.

On the Wednesday I went to see Harold Shepherdson, arguably the club's greatest servant of all time. I already knew Harold very well, mainly from the media work he had done in recent years. Harold was at the forefront of the wave of modern thinking coaches who revolutionised the game in the

Fifties. He went all over the world with England and must have had opportunities to join bigger clubs at the time.

Yet he stayed loyal to the Boro. Harold's own playing career had been cut short by injury, but his wealth of Boro stories was invaluable. Again, the club suffered a big loss when he died.

On the Thursday it was off to Chesterfield to see John Hickton! John and his wife Rosemary are always very accommodating and friendly, and he had all his scrapbooks and cuttings ready when John and I arrived. Hickton has always loved the fact that Boro fans still want to see and read about him long after his playing career has ended. He's a down to earth guy who is almost embarrassed at the adulation he still receives. I enjoyed John's company, though on the way back we were stuck in horrendous traffic on the A1 and it ended up being a 13-hour day.

The following week I was back at work and accompanied Robbo to Middlesbrough Dock for his 'Walk in the Wilderness'. He had agreed to take part in a media-friendly trip around the site of the future stadium. It was my first visit to the area and I was amazed to find that it was virtually a wasteland, just a heap of mud and rubble. I could not imagine how Boro could possibly build a stadium, with all its infrastructure, in time for the start of the next season.

Boro suffered a hiccup in mid-October, after losing at home for the first time on a remarkably hot day to Tranmere Rovers. It was particularly frustrating because Boro had battered Rovers throughout the game but could not score.

With Robbie Mustoe injured, Robbo told me that he was trying to tie up a deal to bring Liverpool's gritty midfielder Steve McMahon to Teesside. Robbo wanted McMahon on loan, but Liverpool preferred a permanent deal and in the end the move failed to materialise.

Boro could have done with McMahon the following weekend when they went to Luton Town and were blitzed 5-1.

It was not a good day all round. I travelled with Gordon Cox, former player Gary Gill, who was working for BBC Radio Cleveland, and Ray Robertson, formerly with *The Northern Echo*, and we found ourselves stuck in an horrendous queue of traffic on the A1 near Wetherby. To make matters worse it was another red-hot day. We discovered eventually that a lorry had jack-knifed and read later than the driver had died. We just made it to Kenilworth Road on time and then had to sit through Boro being walloped.

On the Monday I set off for north-east Italy with the Boro squad for the Anglo Italian Cup tie against Udinese. I was joined by Mick Lowes and Terry

Cochrane from TFM, who were the only other journalists attending from this country.

We had no problems on the flight from Teesside to Heathrow but when we alighted at the London airport, Clayton Blackmore revealed that he had forgotten to bring his passport. It created a massive headache for our tour guide Alba Siletti though, after some hard work, Clayton was eventually issued with a visitor's passport and we caught the flight to Venice as planned.

When we arrived at Venice, Alan Miller's bag was missing which was a bit of a worry because it contained all his specialist goalkeeping gear. Fortunately it was found after a long spell of sitting around in the baggage reclaim area, and we were at last free to make the 90-minute coach journey to Udine.

After the evening meal I caught a taxi into town with Mick and Terry. We found the centre near deserted, but we came across a friendly bar and the radio lads poured a few drinks down my throat.

The following morning I woke up with the hangover from hell which may have had something to do with the amount of alcohol I had consumed the previous evening. Rule No.1; don't accept an invitation to go drinking with journalists. Rule No.2, if considering accepting an invitation to go drinking with journalists, see Rule No.1.

Mick failed to surface for breakfast so, with buzzing head, I caught a cab into town with Terry, Keith Lamb and Jack Ord from the club. We bumped into Mick Lowes as we walked around. I found the town typical Italian which made it attractive, if devoid of special character. I spent much of the day walking with Keith and Jack and enjoying the odd coffee before catching a cab back to the hotel.

The early evening tea was cold toast and warm coffee which I can hardly imagine put the players in the right frame of mind for the game. Where was all the pasta? There was none to be seen. So cold toast it was.

When we arrived at the Stadio Friuli, I found it was most impressive. Udinese had the feel of a big club, despite a temporary stint in Serie B. The press box was huge, with more than 100 individual desks. I had ordered a phone which was there on my allotted desk and a relief to see, because I was able to do my job.

Unfortunately it was bitterly, bitterly cold and completely the opposite from the humid conditions we had experienced in Pisa 12 months earlier. To make matters worse there were only 300 people in the stadium and the game ended 0-0. I had not packed my trusty long johns and could hardly feel my legs at the final whistle.

The following day I had arranged a 6am wake-up call, but it didn't come and I had a mad panic when copy typist Carole woke me with a call from the *Evening Gazette* at 6.45am. Fortunately Carole is top class and I managed to phone all my reports and match facts over to the *Gazette* in double-quick time, before racing down to catch the departing coach at 7.15am. There was no chance of any breakfast, though I picked up a packet of cold toast on the way out.

The flights back were eventless, other than the fact that I sat next to young defender Andy Todd on the flight home from Heathrow and he was airsick. I was to discover how he felt because it was to happen to me on a flight home from Italy a few years later.

On the Sunday there was another long trip, this time to play a televised match at Portsmouth. I was up with the larks at 6.20am and drove through to Middlesbrough to meet up with my five-a-side colleague Lennie Downs, who had offered me a lift because Gordon Cox had travelled down on the Saturday to stay overnight with friends.

Save for the usual traffic jam in Newbury, we made good time and were in Portsmouth just after one o'clock. Boro drew 0-0 but controlled the game throughout and should have won by four goals. I always love my trips to Fratton Park, because the ground has so much atmosphere - but the result was a disappointment.

I was staying up with my sister Daphne in nearby Denmead, so brother-in-law Phil picked me up after the game. I enjoyed a typical Sunday lunch at their home and then went out with Phil for a couple of drinks. It was the most civilised finale I've ever had to a Boro away game.

Coxy was supposed to pick me up at nine the following morning and I rushed to send over my reports to the *Gazette* in good time. He phoned later to say that he was in Portsmouth's dockland and was intending to visit HMS Victory. Then he phoned again to say he was looking around the Mary Rose as well. When in Portsmouth do as the sailors do. It was a quarter to one when Coxy finally turned up at Denmead, but I was still very grateful for the lift home.

It was a hectic time of the season because we were off to Aston Villa on the Wednesday for a Coca-Cola Cup tie, which Boro lost 1-0. Before the game I watched the Boro Junior Reds playing their local counterparts in the impressive indoor cricket centre which has been erected next to Villa Park.

Afterwards, a couple of jobsworth stewards refused me access to the Boro players, so I was grateful to Boro physio Tommy Johnson for taking me through the barrier so that I could wrap up chats with Steve Vickers, Alan Miller and John Hendrie.

Bryan Robson took a week's holiday in early November which fitted in well with the football, or rather lack of it, because Boro's game at Reading was postponed. I kept in close contact with Robbo's assistant manager Viv Anderson all week and he provided me with plenty of stories to keep the ball rolling.

Naturally Viv's comments did not carry the same weight as Robbo's because of the perceived differing status of the two former England internationals. In fact the groans from my fellow media pals reverberated around the room every time Viv appeared at a press conference instead of Robbo but I always found Viv available and forthcoming and he kept the nitty-gritty stories flowing for the *Gazette*.

I did have a problem getting hold of Viv on the Sunday before flying out to Ancona for the Anglo Italian Cup tie on Monday November 14 but he saved my skin when he phoned me late in the afternoon and I was able to write up the advance stories.

The Boro team coach left Ayresome Park at 7.30am and, when I boarded, I was not surprised to see a complete squad of players and young lads. Viv had warned me that the club was not sending any regulars to Italy.

In addition to the reserves, there were eleven Boro fans on the coach. They had been offered the opportunity to travel with the team to help fill up the charter flight from Manchester. Boro had to sell their full allocation of one-third of the seats on the 110-seater plane. Sheffield United, who were at Cesena, and Swindon, at Ascoli, were also on the same flight in what was effectively a cost- cutting exercise.

Unfortunately there was one Boro player missing when we left the stadium, Jaime Moreno. So we had to drive to his hotel in Norton to pick him up which involved waking him.

Then we got stuck in horrendous traffic on the M62, as you might expect early on a Monday morning. It was bumper-to-bumper stuff and it quickly became obvious that we would not arrive at the airport in sufficient time to catch the flight.

In the event the plane was delayed for an hour by our late arrival, no doubt much to the annoyance of the other two teams.

However, we enjoyed a pleasant flight and I was soon settling in with the fans in the City Hotel, in the centre of Ancona. The team was billeted in the Hotel Jolly, on the top of a hill outside of the city.

There wasn't enough room to swing a cat in my room but it was adequate. I hastily wrote up a couple of interviews and sent them over to the *Gazette* before joining radio duo Mick Lowes and Terry Cochrane, and the fans, at a restaurant 200 yards from our hotel which was providing our meals. Once filled to the brim with delicious hot pasta, and having developed a healthy rapport with the fans, we all headed off into town and spent a pleasant evening tasting the local wine at the Rosa café, before struggling back to our hotel.

I had no hangover the following morning, which was a miracle. I spent an hour or so filing copy and then had the rest of the day free before the evening kick-off. I walked around the city with the fans in the morning and then had lunch in a pizzeria with Mick and Terry before taking a look at the dominating dockland area of Ancona.

Later the three of us took a taxi up to the cathedral which overlooked the city.

After an ice cream for tea, we boarded the coach and picked up the team for the short journey to the Trattoria Victoria. It was a modern, but three-sided stadium without much character. Fortunately my ordered phone was waiting for me on the appointed press desk, so I was happy. I was able to file a report to our sister paper, *the Journal* in Newcastle, after the game. Boro's young lads did their best on the night but this was a game they were never going to win and they went down 3-1. To make matters worse, defender Andy Todd was sent off in the closing minutes.

Unfortunately there was to be no pleasant second evening in a hotel bed. We headed straight back to Ancona airport after the game and set off for Manchester at half-past one in the morning. The flight took just over three hours. We had a relatively quick transfer to the awaiting coach at Manchester and arrived back at Ayresome Park at 6.30am.

I drove straight to the *Evening Gazette* in Borough Road, with matchsticks propping up my eyelids, and started knocking out my reports. I managed to stay awake thanks to the help of several strong coffees. In addition to writing up the reports for the *Gazette*, I also had to write advance stories for the coming Saturday's *Sports Gazette*.

So it was 10.30 by the time I was free to set off for home.

I enjoyed an hour's kip on the sofa before ringing around the senior players for advance interviews. Derek Whyte gave me a particularly good piece and

I wrote it up and phoned it over to the *Gazette* before the end of the afternoon.

The jet lag didn't hit me until the following day, though Boro-wise it was pretty quiet. My only commitment was in driving to Ayresome Park to interview Boro physio Mark Nile for his weekly column in the *Sports Gazette*. I returned home shattered at 4pm and fell fast asleep in a chair in front of the fire. It was my five-a-side night and I ended up oversleeping and missing the start of the game. I think we were three or four goals down when I finally arrived at the gym at Norton School, much to the chagrin of my four team-mates.

The following day was hectic. I followed up Robbo's press conference by picking up interviews with Neil Cox and Paul Wilkinson. I wanted to rush back to the *Gazette* to write everything up but discovered that my car was blocked in by Jamie Pollock's vehicle. As Jamie was training it created a brief dilemma. Eventually Boro coach David Geddis saved the day when he got Jamie's keys and let me out.

Once everything was written up I headed home for a much-needed week's holiday.

CHAPTER 19

BRYAN Robson's first season in charge at the Boro was an adrenaline-packed rollercoaster. Everybody wanted a slice of the action.

It was a hectic experience for players and fans alike but, especially for the media. Every football journalist in the country seemed to want a piece of Robbo, and I needed my portion every single day.

Having enjoyed a virtual free rein in picking up exclusives for the *Evening Gazette* in recent years, I now found myself competing for stories against the biggest national media interest in the club that I had ever known. Boro were suddenly very, very high profile. They were receiving the kind of high-intensity media treatment normally only reserved for the big clubs in the Premier League.

It was something which was completely new to me. National journalists who I had never met before, particularly the big guns from the Sunday papers, were turning up regularly at Ayresome Park. Most of these guys had known Robbo for years because of his regular contact with them through both Manchester United and England.

It was a good learning process for me and I was starting to have to fight to keep my head above water. This situation would become the norm in the future, as Boro moved into the region of Juninho and Ravanelli and eventually beyond.

The increased media interest signalled above everything else that the big time had returned to Teesside. With Robson in charge, Boro were being treated again as a big club. It was something which really hadn't happened since Boro were in the old first division during that eight-year run which was supervised by first Jack Charlton and then John Neal.

Boro's games were being reported in newspapers which normally rarely touched the rebranded first division. It didn't matter what happened in the game, Robbo's name was prominent in both the headline and the first paragraph of the story.

While I was surprised at the way in which everybody wanted a slice of Robson, I was fortunate that he appreciated the value of the local newspaper. Bryan never failed to give me an interview on any day that he was on duty at

Ayresome Park or later at the training headquarters at Rockliffe Park. So my task of getting the Boro day-to-day news across to the fans was not restricted, even though some of the bigger stories were now appearing first in national newspaper by-lines courtesy of players' agents.

In Robbo's first season, when he was based only at Ayresome, I usually arrived at the ground around 9.30am and waited patiently for him to find the time for a chat.

Sometimes I was waiting until a minute or two before training started. But Robbo always spotted me standing in the corner of the training room which was situated outside the home dressing room, and he found the time to stride across and answer my questions in time to get the story in that evening's *Gazette*.

Our relationship was just how I wanted it to be and – while the gradual emergence of agents meant that many stories were now breaking at national level - I felt that I was able to get answers to the local questions that mattered.

The battle to get exclusive stories in Robson's first season kept me on my toes as a journalist, at a time when my personal workload was already significantly increased. I was spending much of my spare time working on my book Ayresome Park Memories and rarely had a single evening free during the whole week.

It had been a hectic start to the new campaign, although Robbo had already fitted in a week's holiday. So I was relieved to be able to get away for a week as well, even if I did spend most of it working on Ayresome Park Memories.

After watching Boro regain top spot by beating Wolves on the Sunday, thanks to John Hendrie's ninth goal of the season, the following day I met up with Boro legend Brian Clough. The man himself was signing copies of his autobiography at Waterstones in Middlesbrough and I had offered to give up the day's holiday by reporting the story of the signing for the *Gazette*. I could hardly not make such an offer, because it gave me the opportunity to get an interview with Cloughie for Ayresome Park Memories.

I had met Cloughie on a few occasions over the years and he was always prepared to give me the time of day. He could be abrupt with some people who wanted his time, but he was good to me and I respected him for that.

I arrived at Waterstones at 11.30am, in the hope of tying up an interview with Cloughie before the signing session started in an hour. In the event he arrived with only a few minutes to spare before the official session started. He wanted to start signing books immediately, especially as there was a long queue of people waiting patiently, so when I asked for a chat he suggested I returned at two o'clock.

The session had been due to end at two but the queue of fans still snaked right around the bookstore, so Cloughie risked the threat of writer's cramp by continuing to sign books until 3.15pm. Finally he retired for a cup of tea to a store room at the back of the shop, where he started to sign stock copies of the autobiography while answering my questions at the same time.

However, it was difficult to conduct a full interview mainly because of regular interruptions and Cloughie suggested that I wrote to him at his home in Derby to arrange a convenient time for an official interview, which was brilliant.

The following day co-author John Wilson and I met up with Cloughie's old striking partner Alan Peacock in the Ayresome Business Lounge for the book. Alan is always good for a few quotes and loves recalling all the anecdotes from his time at Ayresome.

He never fails to have a broad smile on his face and, as a modern-day ambassador at the Riverside and a founder of the Boro Former Players Association, is as heavily involved in the game as ever.

After leaving Alan, John and I headed off to see Bernie Slaven at his home. Bernie is always good for a few strong quotes and he was delighted to see us and pick up all the latest gossip from Ayresome. We chatted in his conservatory, where Bernie showed me all the cuttings that he had meticulously cut out of the *Gazette* and filed in scrapbooks. They included all the stories I had written about him over the years.

Bernie's good pal Curtis Fleming also popped in for a chat while we were there.

On the way home John and I headed down to Middlehaven to check the progress on the new stadium. It just looked like a typical building site to me, more like a mud heap on the Moon than the foundations of a future football stadium. In no way did it appear as if the stadium could possibly be erected and completed in time for the new season.

To make matters worse, Boro had changed building contractors in mid-stream. The company which was original contracted to build the stadium, Tilbury Douglas, had been replaced by Taylor Woodrow. It meant bringing a new workforce on to the site at a time when every day was precious.

The site was being patrolled for security purposes and a friendly policeman was happy to chat. He gave the impression he was the official copper for the construction site and was fully informed on all the latest developments. He detailed everything that was going on and gave me some insight into how the work was progressing, despite there being little to see with the naked eye.

The following day it was the turn of David Mills and Micky Fenton to be interviewed for Ayresome Park Memories in the Ayresome Business Lounge. David is a very forthright talker and a deep thinker and came up with some great stories from his two stints with the club. In fact he was still rattling away when Micky turned up at 2pm for his appointment. There wasn't much that Micky hadn't seen or done in more than 30 years at the club and he also provided some terrific material. At the age of 81 he retained all his faculties and his memory was spot on.

Alan Peacock popped in briefly to see Micky and reminded him of the time he arrived at Ayresome in a brand new car in the mid Sixties. Micky left his proud new possession in Warwick Street while he supervised the training session on the pitch. When he returned to the vehicle after training he discovered it was covered from top to bottom in whitewash. Thirty years on Micky could finally see the funny side.

In early December Steve Pears hosted a lunchtime photo session at Pyrgi's Restaurant on Linthorpe Road as part of the launch for his testimonial. Photographer Doug Moody accompanied me from the *Gazette* and we met up with John Hendrie, Paul Wilkinson and Alan Moore, who were supporting Steve on the day. I picked up some tasty interviews but didn't have time to stay for the lunch which was on offer, and left just as Doug and the lads were tucking into a very impressive spread.

The following midweek, Boro were at Reading in a rearranged match and I travelled down to Berkshire by train. I had booked into the Rainbow Corner Hotel and decided to walk from the station, using the directions given to me by Clive Baskerville from the *Reading Evening Post*. In the event I made a hash of reading his instructions and walked for a mile and a half or more in the wrong direction. By the time I got back to the station I was absolutely knackered.

I had tea in a Burger King and came out to discover it was raining cats and dogs. A copy of the *Evening Post* provided me with a semi-useful brolly, though it was soon saturated and I ended up looking like a drowned rat. Finally I hailed a taxi, shook off half a gallon of water on the back seat and enjoyed a much-needed shower when I got to the hotel.

The rain had stopped when I arrived at Elm Park but it was cold and windy. Boro played well and led through a penalty from Paul Wilkinson only to concede a late goal and had to settle for a 1-1 draw. When I finally came out of the stadium, the place was almost deserted. There was no sign of life in the street outside and the chances of hailing a taxi were slim to nil.

Fortunately I was saved by two friends of Robbie Mustoe, who had travelled over from Oxford to watch him play. Unfortunately they didn't see too much of him in action because Robbie collected the first red card of his career during the game.

Robbie's pals emerged from Elm Park, spotted me, and offered me a lift back to the hotel. It was a terrific gesture that was much appreciated. As a result I had everything written up and was in bed for 12.30am.

Boro held on to top spot despite a 2-1 home defeat at the hands of Southend United but eight days later were given a shot in the arm when Robbo made his long awaited comeback from injury at Burnley. Boro won 3-0 at a canter at Turf Moor with John Hendrie scoring all three goals for his first hat-trick of the campaign. The win took Boro six points clear at the top of the first division.

I travelled across to Burnley with Gordon Cox and Gary Gill and, on the way, we turned off towards at a pleasant village called Langho to drop in on Stuart Ripley. Gilly had arranged to interview Rippers for a Christmas programme on BBC Radio Cleveland.

As might be expected the house was very impressive, being in the style of a mock Tudor mansion and set among well established trees. Rippers was as laid back as ever but was delighted to see us. The visit developed into a longer stay than we had anticipated and eventually Coxy and I had to leave to set off for Turf Moor, leaving Rippers to drive Gilly over later. Gilly eventually arrived at the ground two minutes before kick-off.

My own player interviews for Ayresome Park Memories were coming thick and fast. The following week I met up with Willie Maddren, Wilf Mannion and Billy Horner on consecutive days.

Willie in particular was great. His memory was spot on and he told me a lot of horror stories from the pre-liquidation era which I had never heard before. We talked for hours and I made a note at the time that it was one of the best interviews I had ever done.

The following day I set off to meet Wilf. It was the first time I had met the maestro face to face and I was pleased to see he retained all his faculties, and could tell a good story or two. Wilf was one of Boro's all-time greats; the best of all, according to those who were fortunate enough to see him play. While Boro would always be close to Wilf's heart, he made it clear he still retained some bitterness towards the club. The fact that they refused to sell him after the War, and give him the chance to earn a bit of cash to complement his special talents, still rankled.

The next day I set off to see Billy Horner. I have known Billy for many years, so no introduction was needed. I met up with him at the Victoria Ground where I met Hartlepool boss David McCreery and had the opportunity for a chat.

On Boxing Day, Boro were at Sheffield United. I've never enjoyed Boxing Day football as a reporter, especially as Boro are invariably away from home, and this was no different. The day started badly when I put my flask of coffee into the car and it promptly fell over and smashed. I bought two cans of Coke at a newsagent's as a replacement and then left them behind when I transferred my gear to Gordon Cox's car for the journey to Sheffield.

We picked up Gary Gill on the way and fortunately reached Sheffield without further mishap. The match kicked off at 12.30pm and was memorable for being one of the most physical games I have ever seen - it was amazing there were no serious injuries. Boro kept their nerve and drew 1-1 with Craig Hignett grabbing the goal. It was pouring down when we left Bramall Lane and we were all soaked by the time we reached Coxy's car. Boxing Day football. You can keep it for me.

Two days later the heavy rain returned for Boro's home game against Notts County.

Robbo's men won 2-1 but suffered a blow when Neil Cox left the field with a broken collarbone. I was accompanied at the game by Peter Spence, a Los Angeles-based engineer from Middlesbrough who edited a successful football magazine in California. It was a rare visit home for Peter and he clearly enjoyed every minute of the game, despite the appalling weather conditions.

On the last day of the year, I travelled with Alastair Brownlee, Coxy and Gilly for a match at Stoke City. We drove through thick slush over the M62 and when we arrived at Stoke it was perishing. To make matters worse the press room was locked and the officials did not find the key until 15 minutes before kick-off, when it was too late to take advantage of the facilities. I was absolutely chilled to the bone long before the kick-off. I shivered my way through the whole game, which Boro drew 1-1 with Steve Vickers on the scoresheet. The saving grace was that the M62 was not blocked on the journey home, despite further snowfalls, and I was back in the house for 9.45pm.

Happy New Year!

1995 started on a negative note for the Boro fans when the home game against Barnsley was abandoned at half-time. I could not understand why referee Paul Harrison had given the game the go ahead in the first place. The ground was rock hard and the temperature was below freezing, so there was no chance of an improvement.

The 45 minutes of 'action' served up was a bit of a joke as both sides struggled to keep their feet on the treacherous surface. There were a lot more changes of footwear than there were passes to feet. We still saw three goals, with Boro leading 2-1 when the ref blew for half-time.

I was not the slightest bit surprised when the game was called off at the interval because the whole thing had been a farce. There was a large holiday crowd in the stadium and initially it appeared the fans seemed to have accepted the decision as they trudged home.

However, the following day the *Gazette* sports desk phone lines were hot. Every time you put the phone down it rang again with another angry caller. We were completely inundated with calls from complaining supporters and could not get any work done. Later in the week we also received a hefty mailbag which helped fill a couple of pages of letters.

It transpired that there had been a public announcement immediately after the Barnsley game which gave the fans the impression they would be receiving a full refund. Whatever was actually announced was contradicted by the official statement by the club which came later. Boro stressed in their press release that ticket holders would be admitted for half-price when the game was rearranged. This infuriated many fans, who felt that the club had backtracked on its original promise.

The following Saturday I made my first and only, so far, trip to Swansea. Boro were drawn there in the third round of the FA Cup. Gordon Cox drove us down to south Wales and we arrived in plenty of time to have a good look around. I was very disappointed upon seeing the Vetch Field. I like old stadia with character but this one had none. It was as bad a stadium as I had seen, backing sombrely on to a prison. There was even a row of houses whose back yards were situated within the ground.

To make matters worse the pitch was diabolical. It was very heavy and virtually waterlogged and of no particular use to either side.

The press box was even worse. It was a Portakabin, suspended from the roof of the main stand. What few windows it had were filthy.

It was even worse for Coxy. He had to climb up to a radio box which resembled an open bath tub suspended from the roof of the stand opposite. To make life even more difficult, Coxy had to scramble up a precarious rope ladder to reach it.

There's no way I could have done it. But watching Coxy and the other radio lads taking their lives in their hands at least gave me something to laugh about on an otherwise miserable day.

I couldn't possibly have reported the game for the *Gazette* from the press box, so I sat outside in the middle of a group of Boro fans which helped create a bit of atmosphere. I had my notepad on my knee, my phone in one hand, my stop-watch in the other and my pen in my mouth. Every time the fans around me jumped up I had to sit still in case I lost all my possessions, but somehow I managed.

It was not much of a Cup tie, as might be imagined on the boggy pitch, but both sides worked hard in the mud and a 1-1 draw was a fitting result. The Swans led 1-0 at the interval and, after Alan Moore had finally netted the equaliser, Boro had enough chances to go on and win it. The journey home was long, boring and uneventful, and I walked into the house as the clock struck midnight.

The following week we faced another long trip when travelling to Swindon Town for a league game. Teesside was hit by a carpet of heavy frost and it took me some time to gain entry into my car through the frozen locks. I eventually made it, and linked up with Gordon Cox.

The journey was considerably brightened by Gary Gill who managed to get hold of Coxy's three large vegetable samosas when Gordon was otherwise occupied. Coxy had been looking forward to enjoying a delicious meal at lunchtime, only to discover upon opening the paper bag that each of the samosas had a large bite taken out of every one. It was even funnier because Coxy at first seemed to believe that he must have bought them in that condition. However, when he eventually noticed that there was a piece of used chewing gum in one of the samosas, the penny finally dropped.

On the Tuesday, Boro entertained Swansea in the Cup replay and it was to be one of my most disappointing nights as a Boro fan. It was a lousy evening with a howling gale and constant blustery showers, and Boro proceeded to lose 2-1 to their lower-league opponents.

I was even more frustrated when Bryan Robson came into the press room afterwards and was almost blasé in his comments.

Outside I managed to grab hold of John Hendrie for an interview and my disgruntlement boiled over in a series of negative questions which clearly upset him. John's response was to take a deep breath and then give me a talking-to about the difficulties players faced trying to win every game, living up to expectations and then staying focused after bad defeats in order to make sure they performed to their maximum next time.

It was virtually a lecture, something I'd never previously experienced from a player, and I found it a complete eye-opener. I couldn't argue with a single word John said. His heavy emphasis on the fact that all players were human and could not always win, even when trying their hardest, was to stick with me. In fact I've never forgotten John's words. I've introduced his thinking into mine and I've always believed that I am a better journalist for the experience.

Funnily enough I rang Nigel Pearson the following day for his version of events and I found myself asking questions based more on Hendrie's comments than on my own feelings after the final whistle of the Cup tie.

The following Saturday news broke that Boro were about to sign a German striker called Uwe Fuchs from Kaiserslautern. The player had been recommended to Robson by former Nottingham Forest and Arsenal striker Tony Woodcock who had finished his playing career in Germany but stayed on to work as a coach and talent spotter. Woodcock has since returned to England and jointly runs a sport media business with Viv Anderson.

I knew nothing about Fuchs when I was given the information of his impending arrival but it was a big story at the time and I sent over what details I could pick up to the *Sports Gazette*. Foreign signings at that time were still few and far between at any English club and so it was a different type of transfer signing to write about.

I suspect most Boro fans were delighted to see that Robson was bringing in a striker, whether foreign or not. Boro were struggling for goals to maintain their promotion push while there were worries about Paul Wilkinson who was sidelined with a knee injury. So the move made sense, especially as I was told that Fuchs was a big, powerful centre-forward.

Boro could have done with him that afternoon because they were held to a 1-1 draw by Grimsby Town in another howling rain-swept gale. Craig Hignett had a penalty saved but Robbie Mustoe salvaged a late point.

In early February Boro legend George Hardwick celebrated his 75th birthday at Ayresome Park and most of his pals from the world of football arrived as guests, including Brian Clough, Micky Fenton and Wilf Mannion. George was a regular visitor to Ayresome as a matchday host and it was the perfect venue for his birthday get-together, ahead of Boro's game against Reading.

I had the chance of a brief chat with all the major guests and also interviewed George, Micky and Wilf in front of a camera for a forthcoming DVD release.

Unfortunately Boro could not complete George's birthday celebrations in style because they went down 1-0 to Reading that day. This shock defeat knocked Boro out of an automatic promotion spot for the first time since October, and all the players were gutted afterwards. They had not won a game since December, something we have witnessed on many occasions at this particular time of year.

On the Monday I carried out interviews with Nigel Pearson, Derek Whyte, Alan Miller, Neil Cox and Uwe Fuchs. None of them were particularly outgoing. I'd not recorded such a sense of depression and frustration within the dressing room for a long time.

Hopes of Boro bouncing back the following weekend were foiled by heavy rain, though not before I had almost arrived at Boundary Park for the game at Oldham Athletic.

I set off with Alastair Brownlee, Gordon Cox and Gary Gill and it was raining cats and dogs. In fact eight hours of continuous rain had been forecast for the north. The closer we got to Oldham the worse it got.

At one stage, while trying to drive up a steep stretch of road on the M62, Coxy was faced by a frothing torrent of water flowing towards us and underneath the car which must have been six to eight inches deep.

We heard on the radio at 11.15am that Oldham did not feel an inspection was necessary, so we had to keep plodding on. It later transpired that as soon as the ref walked on to the pitch he called off the game immediately. We heard the news of the postponement at 12.30pm on the radio and turned around, having just reached the Oldham turn-off on the M62.

Ali, Coxy and Gilly were immediately re-routed to Darlington by BBC Radio Cleveland but I had the benefit of a free afternoon, save for writing stories for the *Sports Gazette* and also for our sister paper the *Sunday Sun*.

Boro were heading off to Spain for a few days warm-weather training on the Monday, so I spent part of Sunday ringing around the players for interviews. When they came back to Teesside on the Friday I made the mistake of making quips to a couple of them about their tans, and they jumped down my throat. It was clear they were still touchy about the lack of recent results and did not want to see this trip to Spain recorded as a holiday jaunt.

In the event the trip did them the world of good because they beat Charlton Athletic at Ayresome Park the following day, with Uwe Fuchs grabbing the crucial goal on his first start for the club. Robbo was also back that day after a second spell on the sidelines through injury, and again he was inspirational.

I was more pleased for Uwe. It was not just the winning goal, it was the whole manner of his outstanding physical performance. I suspected this game was Uwe's launching pad, especially as he received terrific support from the fans. He was also besieged by the media in the Ayresome Park tunnel after the final whistle and quickly developed into a cult figure on Teesside.

CHAPTER 20

BORO'S promotion show was firmly back on the road in the middle of February when they recorded a scintillating win away to fellow Premier League hopefuls Wolves at Molineux.

This game was Boro's biggest test of 1995 so far but they were up to the task and played some superb football, winning 2-0. Steve Vickers and Uwe Fuchs grabbed the goals, while it would have been three had not Chris Morris had a late penalty saved.

It was a particularly impressive win under the circumstances, because Molineux's overhaul was now complete and the home fans were up for the game. There was a capacity crowd and a terrific atmosphere. However, Boro gradually took the sting out of the home supporters' ardour and they were drifting away long before the final whistle.

Gordon Cox and I were very late in leaving Molineux, once all the interviews had been picked up and filed. Then we stopped for fish and chips on the way home. After drop offs in Middlesbrough, it was five to three when I climbed into bed.

The following Sunday we headed off to Millwall for a televised game at the New Den. Any hopes of a third consecutive Boro win were denied by a battling Lions side, and the game ended goalless. That was despite the performance of player-boss Bryan Robson who was outstanding.

In Robbo's efforts to grab a late winning goal for the team he threw himself in vain at a corner and collided heavily with a post - it was a sickening collision. Robbo had to leave the field to have a dozen stitches inserted in a nasty gash just above his left eye. In his immediate games after Millwall, Bryan played with a huge bandage protecting the wound.

The scar has remained with him to this day and, whenever I see Robbo on TV, the first thing I notice is the mark above his eye which came from his committed display at Millwall in 1995.

On February 28, Boro officially opened their visitors' centre for their new stadium on the Middlehaven site. It seemed a mild, pleasant morning when I left the *Evening Gazette* offices in Borough Road, but it was freezing down at Middlesbrough Dock. I suspected that this apparent step into the Arctic

Circle might be a sign of things to come and was determined to ensure I was well stocked up with long johns when reporting games at the stadium.

The visitors' centre turned out to be two Portakabins joined together, providing a good view of the work which was being done on the stadium's foundations. A great deal of progress had been made on erecting the West and East stands since I last visited the site. At last I could get an impression of what the finished product would look like, but with only six months to go before the start of the next campaign, time was clearly of the essence.

I picked up interviews with Keith Lamb and director George Cooke as well as players Robbie Mustoe and Chris Morris. Everybody was thoroughly upbeat about the new venture. The one point on which they all agreed was that Boro really needed to be playing their first season in their new stadium in the Premier League.

The following weekend Uwe Fuchs confirmed his cult status when scoring all three goals in a 3-0 home win against Bristol City. The big German striker left no doubts that he was really enjoying life in the first division and had adapted well to English football. The win strengthened Boro's position in the top two, though there was only one automatic promotion place up for grabs that season and the team needed to maintain its current run of form.

Uwe was again surrounded by media men in the Ayresome tunnel after the match and was virtually pinned up against the brick wall outside the dressing room, but Uwe handled the questions well and showed good knowledge of the English language. He came across very well in his answers and gave the impression he had developed strong feelings for the club.

Jaime Moreno's knowledge of English was not as good, but he had been working hard on learning the language. I managed to conduct an interview with him for the first time without the aid of an interpreter on the Monday. The talented Bolivian emphasised his wish to try to hold down a regular place in the side.

However, the team was virtually picking itself at that time. Uwe Fuchs was now scoring in almost every game and looking a huge threat in the opposition penalty area. However, his scoring contribution in a home match against Derby County was not enough, allied to a second goal from Jamie Pollock, as Boro went down to a shock 4-2 defeat. If nothing else, it showed that Boro still needed to dig deep if they were to win the promotion struggle.

The Derby defeat knocked Boro into third position in the division and further away from the automatic promotion place. It left Robbo with ten games left to mastermind a revival, if he was to take Boro into the Premier League to coincide with the move to the new stadium.

At this time he had not adopted the sweeper system which was to become a feature of the team's pattern of play in the Premier League. Steve Vickers was a virtual ever-present in 1993/94, though Nigel Pearson did miss a chunk of the early part of the campaign. Derek Whyte took Pearson's place in his absence, but Derek reverted to left-back for most of the remainder of the campaign.

Jamie Pollock, Clayton Blackmore and Alan Moore were all regulars in the middle of the park, while Robbie Mustoe tended to come in for regular games because of injuries to other players, particularly Robson. Even without Robbo, Boro were as competitive as anybody else in the division in the midfield area and this was arguably the crucial unit in the line-up.

John Hendrie's conversion from winger to striker proved very effective because he ended the campaign as top scorer, though Paul Wilkinson was not as prolific as he had been in recent years, which led to Uwe Fuchs coming in and commanding a place up front.

I was on a week's holiday following the Derby defeat but I accompanied my fellow Ayresome Park Memories author John Wilson to Sunderland on the Tuesday. We had tickets for the game and stood in the midst of the Boro fans on the Roker End. The atmosphere in the crowd was terrific, which was just as well because the match was poor.

However, it hardly mattered because Boro came up trumps on the night with a 1-0 win. Victory was secured thanks to Jamie Pollock's tremendous solo goal, which sent Boro back to the top of the table and lifted the whole dressing room. It came at a price, as a fractured cheekbone during the early stages of the match ended Robbie Mustoe's season.

The following Sunday Boro beat Port Vale 3-0 at Ayresome, with the help of a memorable first goal for the club from the gaffer. Robbo was forced to play in new boots because his favourite pair had split during the win at Sunderland, but they obviously brought immediate good luck. The win sent Boro four points clear at the top.

I was tipped off the following day that Boro were about to bring in another striker by signing the Norwegian international Jan Aage Fjortoft from Swindon Town, so that was the main story in the *Gazette* that night.

Fjortoft was a beanpole striker who had been a prolific scorer for the Robins and had already notched 25 goals in the current campaign. He was a top-class signing, especially as he would surely produce the goods the following season if Boro reached the Premier League.

When I first met Fjortoft, I was very impressed. He was articulate and intelligent, spoke English better than most of the current squad, and used phrases and words which even had me scrambling for the dictionary.

However what mattered most was that Jan was a good player and, even though he needed three or four games to settle in at Boro, he scored some vital goals in the promotion run-in.

Fjortoft made his debut at West Brom on All Fools' Day when Boro had plenty of strikers available but few defenders. Boro were so short at the back that 38-year-old assistant boss Viv Anderson was pressed into service for the first time since joining the club. Robson had wisely registered Anderson as a player and, although there had been no real plans to name Viv in a starting line-up, this was an emergency.

In the event, Viv had an absolute stormer and Boro won 3-1, mainly as a result of some inspirational forward play from Alan Moore.

Viv was rather nonchalant about his performance when I spoke to him afterwards, but his contribution had been huge. Although Viv didn't admit to it, he must have been playing through the pain barrier. It was a gruelling game and his muscles must have been stretched to the limit.

Boro had signed a new defender on transfer deadline day when bringing in Phil Whelan from Ipswich Town. Unfortunately there was a cock-up over his registration forms which, the Football Association claimed, did not arrive with them until after the 5pm registration deadline. Even so, the FA announced that Phil was officially a Boro player, but they wouldn't allow him to kick a ball for the club until the following season.

Robbo was spitting blood when I first interviewed him after discovering that he had signed a player he couldn't select. But the gaffer's decision to bring Viv out of mothballs was a masterstroke and the promotion push was unaffected.

Boro did lose their next game, a rearranged midweek trip to Oldham, but it was to be their only defeat during the remainder of the campaign. It was a typical Oldham night, with squally showers, and I got soaked in the car park afterwards waiting for interviews.

I had taken sandwiches to eat and still had a couple left over for supper but Alastair Brownlee and Gordon Cox were not so fortunate. After driving around but failing to find a chippie in Oldham we raced across the Pennines to the Wetherby Whaler and walked in just as they were closing the doors at 11.30pm. In the event Ali and Coxy had to settle for warmed-up pies and no chips which more or less summed up the day.

Easter was a bit of a damp squib. A late Uwe Fuchs goal gave Boro the equaliser at Notts County, while Boro were held by the same scoreline at home to Sheffield United on the Monday.

It was another incredibly physical game against the Blades and Fuchs over-reacted to the violence and got himself sent off. At least I had plenty to write about afterwards when Robson called Scarborough referee Bill Burns a cheat. When Robbo's comment was put to United boss Dave Bassett, he called Uwe and Boro goalscorer Jan Fjortoft cheats. It made for great copy even if it was the kind of stuff that FA inquiries are made of.

The battle to win the sole automatic promotion spot put all the leading sides under heavy pressure. All of them, including Boro, were struggling to win their games in the run-in. Boro missed the chance to virtually clinch it when being held to a third consecutive 1-1 draw, this time at Barnsley. Viv Anderson was again pressed into service against his former club while Fjortoft scored a remarkable solo goal.

It was a horrendous day as the rain poured down relentlessly and it was difficult for both sides. There was water all over the pitch. Only the non-stop spiking of the turf by the ground staff for more than an hour before the kick-off had allowed the game to start.

Gordon Cox and I got soaked just walking from the car to the stadium, while the rain blew constantly into the press box throughout the match. However, it was worse for Boro's 2,800 travelling fans. They were housed in the open end of the ground which had no protection from the elements. In the event they were able to snap up plastic coats from Barnsley's well oiled commercial machine at £1 a time. So the away end was transformed into a sea of see-through plastic sheeting.

All that was left now for Boro was the final league game at Ayresome Park against Luton Town, followed by a trip to Tranmere Rovers.

The club did themselves proud for the Luton game, making sure that it was a day of celebration to commemorate the end of competitive football at the 92-year-old stadium. The players also made their contribution, winning 2-1 thanks to a brace from John Hendrie.

It was a perfect day, in fact the best of the year so far with warm sunshine throughout. The celebration events on the pitch started at 1pm, though I was more interested in what was going on behind the scenes. I made my way to the special reception area in a marquee inside the gym, which was attended by dozens of former Boro players. It gave me the opportunity to talk to a few former players that I hardly knew, like Willie Whigham, Ronnie Dicks and David Hodgson, while I also had an enjoyable chat with Tony Mowbray.

The only downside was that former Boro half-back Harry Bell grabbed hold of me and asked me why I had not returned his photos which he had kindly loaned me for Ayresome Park Memories. I didn't want to tell Harry that I had posted them back to him a few weeks earlier, and so I told a little white lie and said I would sort them out immediately. I could only hope that the parcel was stuck in the sorting office at Newcastle, where there had been a strike for several weeks. I was upset that Harry had not yet got his photos because I knew how priceless the pictures would be to him.

In the event Harry never ever came back to me so I assumed he must have received them once the postal strike ended.

The match turned out to be nerve-racking, especially as Boro missed clear-cut chance after chance. The packed stadium was desperately willing the team on, which only served to increase the pressure.

But Boro got the points in the end even if the ensuing lap of honour was a little premature. Boro were still not definitely promoted and needed a result eight days later at Tranmere to make sure – unless other games in midweek went their way.

On the Wednesday, Tony Mowbray phoned me for his interview piece for Ayresome Park Memories. It was great to talk to him in a quiet situation and we chatted for half the night.

After finishing our chat I was left with just enough time to catch the end of BBC Radio Cleveland's live broadcast of the Stoke City-Bolton Wanderers game. Bolton had to win the game to stay in promotion contention but they were held to a draw which effectively ensured Boro of their place in Premier League. I can still remember Alastair Brownlee's excited radio commentary as every Boro fan became a Stoke supporter for the evening.

When the Boro players reported for training the following day they were greeted with bottles of champagne rather than footballs. The legendary photos of Bryan Robson being showered with champagne by the players appeared in the *Evening Gazette* that night and remain one of the memorable moments of the promotion campaign.

It meant that the final game at Tranmere was rather meaningless, even though Boro received remarkable backing from 3,500 travelling fans. The uneventful encounter ended 1-1 but at least the visiting supporters seemed to enjoy the day and were in full voice.

After the game I grabbed Uwe Fuchs for a chat and he told me that he didn't think he would be kept on for the following season. I was shocked, especially as Robbo had previously told me that Kaiserslautern were looking only for £500,000 to make the move permanent.

Uwe had made a massive contribution towards the club winning promotion, scoring nine valuable goals in 13 appearances. Even though I knew full well that there was no sentiment in football, I could hardly see the sense of not offering Uwe at least a one-year contract. Even if he was not directly in

Robbo's plans, he was big and strong and potentially a great squad player.

However, I also knew that Robbo was after bigger fish because he had confided to me that, if the team won promotion, he had put together a list of major targets which had already been sanctioned by Steve Gibson and which would amaze and delight the fans.

In fact I had carried an exclusive as long ago as January that Robbo had made an ambitious bid to try to prise away England striker Nick Barmby from Spurs. Robbo was perfectly happy to have the story made public. Barmby, one of the English game's brightest young talents, was known to be unsettled at White Hart Lane. However, Spurs were not prepared to sell at that time.

I still felt for Uwe. I could tell he was bitterly disappointed to be leaving because he had fitted into the dressing room very well and wanted to stay. In hindsight the decision not to keep him proved a huge mistake the following year when Boro suffered from horrendous injuries to their strikers and needed a man like Uwe to get them through.

We stopped off at the Wetherby Whaler on the way home from Tranmere and that's when the promotion party really hit home. There were Boro fans everywhere, many in fancy dress, milling all around us. Gordon Cox and I joined in the party atmosphere as we chatted with the fans and enjoyed our fish and chips.

I was delighted for Robbo and the players that such a gruelling campaign had ended with success. Robbo had done very well in his first season in management. Most of his signings had been spot on and most had been signed with the Premier League in mind.

The gaffer's motivational talents were beyond question and he had consistently got the best out of his players. For most of the season Paul Wilkinson was the only experienced and orthodox striker on the club's books, even though John Hendrie had taken to his centre-forward duties in terrific fashion and finished top scorer with 15 league goals.

The arrival of Uwe Fuchs had given the promotion push added impetus once he had settled in, while the ensuing swoop for Jan Fjortoft was done mainly with the Premier League in mind.

Having played throughout his career at the highest level, there were no fears that Robson would have any problems leading the team into the Premier League. It was something that everybody was eagerly awaiting that summer, especially with the prospect of playing in a brand new stadium.

Boro's success was celebrated at the north-east Football Writers' annual dinner at the Three Tuns in Durham the following Sunday, though my main memory is of an inebriated Sunderland fan who grabbed the microphone during the proceedings. The fan was virtually in tears as he made an elongated impassioned plea for the people who ran his club to buck up their ideas. It was an embarrassing moment for the FWA officials but it gave me something to smile about on an evening where I was driving, and therefore not drinking.

The following day I met up with Steve Gibson and Keith Lamb at Ayresome Park for a personal briefing on the new stadium. It was the first time I had been privy to the plans for the infrastructure of the stadium and I was gobsmacked. It was much more impressive than I had anticipated and it was clear that Gibson had no intentions of cutting any corners.

That night I rang Steve Pears, who had returned slightly early from the players' short break in Portugal in order to complete plans for his testimonial, which was to be the last official game at Ayresome Park. It was also to be Steve's last game for the Boro, because he had been handed a free transfer.

The rest of the Boro players were due to return from Portugal the following day, along with Viv Anderson, who had provided the team with some hilarity when mislaying his false front teeth and therefore walking around with a huge gap in his mouth.

I was delighted that Steve attracted such a huge turn-out at Ayresome because he had been a terrific servant to the club. A crowd of 19,000 turned up to see a relatively entertaining game against a Select XI.

Boro's players received their medals and the Division One Championship trophy before the kick-off, but the biggest cheer was reserved for the closing minutes when Steve scored the final goal from the penalty spot. It's a goal of which Steve remains very proud, because quite rightly he points out that it was the very last one scored at Ayresome Park. Afterwards there was a poignant moment at his celebratory party afterwards when I had a chat with Uwe Fuchs for the final time.

So, several chapters to the history book of the Boro were closed that night. The biggest, naturally, was the departure from Ayresome to play in a spanking new stadium down by Middlesbrough Dock.

The move was to create a whole new mindset on Teesside, and a new generation of fans, with the beginning of the switch towards a more family-orientated support.

For some fans the switch of grounds also closed a door. Their love of the 92-year-old Ayresome Park was never replaced by the same feelings for the new stadium, even though the quality of football arguably reached heights never previously witnessed.

On the other hand, as one door closed, another opened. The remarkable events of Boro's next ten years completely outshone what had been previously achieved since the dark days of liquidation - but that's all material for volume two.

Up the Boro!